PRAIRIE STATE COLLEGE

3 2783 00131 4411

The Psychology of Personhood

Philosophical, Historical, Social-Developmental, and Narrative Perspectives

What is a person? Surprisingly little attention is given to this question in psychology. For much of the past century, psychology has tended to focus on the systematic study of processes rather than on the persons who enact and embody them. In contrast to the reductionist picture of much mainstream theorizing, which construes persons as their mental lives, behaviors, or neurophysiological particulars, *The Psychology of Personhood* presents persons as irreducibly embodied and socially situated beings. Placing the study of persons at the center of psychology, this book presents novel insights on the typical, everyday actions and experiences of persons in relation to each other and to the broader society and culture. Leading scholars from diverse academic disciplines paint an integrative portrait of the psychological person within evolutionary, historical, cultural, developmental, and everyday contexts.

JACK MARTIN is Burnaby Mountain Professor in Psychology at Simon Fraser University, Burnaby, British Columbia, Canada. He is an associate editor of *New Ideas in Psychology* and is on the editorial boards of the *Journal of Theoretical and Philosophical Psychology* and *Theory and Psychology*.

MARK H. BICKHARD is Henry R. Luce Professor in Cognitive Robotics and the Philosophy of Knowledge at Lehigh University, Bethlehem, Pennsylvania, US. He is Editor of *New Ideas in Psychology*.

D1496253

The Psychology of Personhood

Philosophical, Historical, Social-Developmental, and Narrative Perspectives

Edited by

Jack Martin and Mark H. Bickhard

PRAIRIE STATE COLLEGE
LIBRARY

CAMBRIDGE
UNIVERSITY PRESS

CAMBRIDGE
UNIVERSITY PRESS

University Printing House, Cambridge CB2 8BS, United Kingdom

Cambridge University Press is part of the University of Cambridge.

It furthers the University's mission by disseminating knowledge in the pursuit of education, learning and research at the highest international levels of excellence.

www.cambridge.org
Information on this title: www.cambridge.org/9781107477759

© Cambridge University Press 2013

This publication is in copyright. Subject to statutory exception
and to the provisions of relevant collective licensing agreements,
no reproduction of any part may take place without the written
permission of Cambridge University Press.

First published 2013
First paperback edition 2014

A catalogue record for this publication is available from the British Library

Library of Congress Cataloguing in Publication data
The psychology of personhood : philosophical, historical, social-developmental
and narrative perspectives / edited by Jack Martin and Mark H. Bickhard.
    p.   cm.
Includes bibliographical references and index.
ISBN 978-1-107-01808-2 (hardback)
1. Self.   2. Self – Social aspects.   3. Identity (Psychology)   4. Personalism.
5. Psychology – Social aspects.   I. Martin, Jack, 1950–   II. Bickhard, Mark H.
BF697.P769   2012
155.2 – dc23   2012023183

ISBN 978-1-107-01808-2 Hardback
ISBN 978-1-107-47775-9 Paperback

Cambridge University Press has no responsibility for the persistence or accuracy of
URLs for external or third-party internet websites referred to in this publication,
and does not guarantee that any content on such websites is, or will remain, accurate
or appropriate.

Contents

Part IV Narrative perspectives

Contributors

JOHN BARRESI Department of Psychology, Dalhousie University, Halifax, Nova Scotia, Canada

MARK H. BICKHARD Departments of Philosophy and Psychology, Lehigh University, Bethlehem, Pennsylvania, US

KURT DANZIGER Department of Psychology, York University, Toronto, Ontario, Canada

MARK FREEMAN Department of Psychology, College of the Holy Cross, Worcester, Massachusetts, US

ALEX GILLESPIE Department of Psychology, University of Stirling, UK

CHARLES GUIGNON Department of Philosophy, University of South Florida, Tampa, Florida, US

RUTHELLEN JOSSELSON School of Psychology, The Fielding Graduate University, Santa Barbara, California, US

JAMES T. LAMIELL Department of Psychology, Georgetown University, Washington, DC, US

AMIA LIEBLICH Department of Psychology, The Hebrew University, Jerusalem, Israel

JACK MARTIN Department of Psychology, Simon Fraser University, Burnaby, British Columbia, Canada

RAYMOND MARTIN Department of Philosophy, Union College, Schenectady, New York, US

CHRIS MOORE Department of Psychology, Dalhousie University, Halifax, Nova Scotia, Canada

ANNA STETSENKO Program in Developmental Psychology, Graduate Center, The City University, New York, US

JEFF SUGARMAN Faculty of Education, Simon Fraser University, Burnaby, British Columbia, Canada

MICHAEL A. TISSAW Psychology Department, State University of New York, Potsdam, New York, US

1 Introducing persons and the psychology of personhood

Jack Martin and Mark H. Bickhard

This book is about persons. Given what most of us think about when we hear the word "psychology," it is surprising that so much disciplinary psychology over the past 100 to 150 years has had relatively little to say about persons and their lives. Fortunately, this state of affairs has begun to change very rapidly. The purpose of this book is to introduce the seemingly new, yet in some ways long-standing, study of persons in psychology. At this time, the psychology of personhood is being resurrected and transformed through the philosophical, historical, social-developmental, and narrative inquiries of a number of psychologists. What unites these recent developments is their commitment to a psychology of personhood that emphasizes the holistic interactivity of persons within the biophysical and socio-cultural world. The focus of contemporary psychology of personhood is holistic, in the sense that it eschews attempts to reduce persons to their mental lives, behaviors, and/or neurophysiological, biological particulars and parts. It also focuses on the everyday experiences and lives of ordinary people, rather than on exceptional individuals or those afflicted by various pathologies. This book is a collective product of the ideas and contributions of a number of contemporary psychologists who have established reputations for conducting philosophical, historical, social-developmental, and narrative inquiries into what it is to be a person in the usual sense of that term, a sense that is implicit in our ordinary language.

The concept of a person

Although an understanding of personhood is implicit in our everyday linguistic and relational practices, a more explicitly conceptual consideration of personhood is necessary for our purposes. The concept of a person is applicable to human beings understood as social beings who are members of a moral community. Persons are biological in so far as they are embodied, but their embodiment is enacted within a world that is simultaneously both biophysical and socio-cultural. It is the interactivity of persons within the biophysical and socio-cultural world that is responsible, both evolutionarily and developmentally, for their possession of a distinctive range of powers. These powers constitute a suite of social, psychological capabilities, including the use of language, the creation of culture, self-consciousness, and self-understanding, an agency that includes intentionality and two-way volitional control (to act or refrain from acting), a reasoning intelligence, a moral concern, the ability to take and integrate different perspectives, and the experience of psychological time in which past experiences interact with current circumstances and anticipated futures to afford alternative possibilities for thinking and acting. Persons also may be described in terms of their personalities (unique combinations of temperament and action tendencies), identities (anchored by physical characteristics, social positioning and circumstances, and autobiographical recollections, reflections, and projects), and character (as judged by their conduct and circumstances, using relevant moral and rational criteria of their community). Because of their abilities to internalize norms of conduct, take the perspectives of particular others and social groups, and reason, persons are answerable for their deeds. Thus, the concept of a person has historically been salient in religious, political, legal, and educational contexts, practices, and institutions.

Unlike the members of other animal species, persons are not understood only in terms of their corporeal and adaptive attributes and capacities, but also in terms of their own self interpretations and ascriptions. Because various aspects of persons include or refer to biophysical characteristics, socio-cultural positionings, norms, and self-interpretations, the concept of a person applies across the physical sciences, social sciences, and humanities. Personhood is a necessarily interdisciplinary subject. Moreover, the concept of the person is an irreducibly holistic one. An adequate psychology of personhood cannot focus on cognitive, biological, social, or cultural aspects of persons in isolation, but must capture all of these dimensions as they have interacted, evolved, and developed over historical, social, and biographical time, and as they continue to interact in the present. To understand persons as the unique biological-cultural hybrids that they are, characterized by the suite of social, psychological, rational, and moral capabilities and concerns described above, requires a focus on their holistic interactivity within the biophysical and socio-cultural world. Perhaps it is the daunting nature of this challenge that explains what only can be regarded as the peculiar history of personhood within the discipline of psychology.[1]

Personhood and psychology

At different stages in its history as a distinctive discipline, psychology has been defined as the study of mind, the study of behavior, or the study of cognitive processes and structures. Although not often stated explicitly, and despite protracted excursions into comparative psychological experimentation with other animals and attempts to create artificial, machine intelligence, psychology clearly aims to understand human beings as persons. This aspiration is most obviously evident in the professional arm of disciplinary psychology, where educational, consulting, business, health care, and clinical applications of psychology have consistently targeted individuals understood as persons. Consequently, it is perplexing that relatively little attention within the history of disciplinary psychology has been devoted explicitly to conceptualizing persons and considering the proper manner of their study. The scant and infrequent attention given to such seemingly pivotal matters by most psychologists is even more surprising in recognition of the considerable interest in personhood evident during the first two decades following psychology's emergence as a distinctive discipline.

During the last two decades of the nineteenth century and early part of the twentieth century, several well-known psychologists endorsed the study of persons within their worldly contexts. William James, James Mark Baldwin, John Dewey, George Herbert Mead, Mary Whiton Calkins, William Stern, Pierre Janet, Lev Vygotsky, Heinz Werner, and Wilhelm Wundt (especially in his later years) all were concerned with the holistic activity and functioning of persons as uniquely capable psychological beings within their social contexts.[2] However, it was not long before the more speculative, philosophical, moral, and socio-cultural aspects of the work of these giants of the new discipline were expunged or simply overlooked, as the rapidly developing discipline and its adherents

---

[1] Given that the study of the person is of necessity an interdisciplinary project, the fact that most of the contributors to this volume are psychologists might seem inconsistent with this required interdisciplinarity. However, the focus of this book is "the psychology of personhood," and the contributing authors have been selected because they are distinguished psychologists or philosophers who have expertise in the disciplines of philosophy, history, and/or social, developmental, and narrative studies.

[2] J. Valsiner and R. van der Veer, *The Social Mind: Construction of the Idea* (Cambridge University Press, 2000).

moved quickly to establish the scientific standing of psychology in ways that would clearly distinguish it from other academic disciplines such as mental philosophy, and from a host of dubious practices such as phrenology, physiognomy, mesmerism, spiritualism, and mental healing.[3] As a science and scientifically based profession, psychology quickly adopted and adapted standards and practices of objectivity, together with techniques of measurement and experimentation, that it borrowed from more established sciences like physics, chemistry, biology, and physiology, frequently without any particularly clear understanding of desired linkages between the subject matters and methods of inquiry of these other sciences.[4] In consequence, the first psychological laboratories tended to focus their resources and energies on the study of components of the mental lives of persons in isolation from the contexts in which persons lived.

Thus, the first wave of scientific psychology was typified by attempts to isolate and study what were considered to be the basic components or elements of consciousness, such as sensations and feelings, with some carefully circumscribed theorizing about how these psychic elements might be organized, analyzed, and/or altered by the mind to yield experiences, emotions, and ideas. Methods such as reaction times and "just noticeable differences" were borrowed from psychophysics with the aim of mathematizing experimental results in ways intended to parallel the objectivity and precision of more established, successful sciences. How exactly such methods and results were to support the applications of the first professional psychologists was mostly ignored, it being deemed sufficient to parade such interventions under the general banner of scientific knowledge and progress. Consequently, it was not long until most psychologists were engaged in activities that could be pursued in the almost complete absence of conceptions of personhood. In fact, setting aside such conceptions and considerations avoided perceptions of the vast gap between early scientific psychology and any credible understanding of the functioning of persons in their everyday lives – a strategy, intended or not, that has continued to manifest in different guises throughout the entire history of psychological science and practice.[5]

The struggles of disciplinary, scientific, and professional psychology to come to grips with its subject matter soon became acutely evident, as experimentation to discern the basic elements of consciousness and

[3] L. T. Benjamin, Jr., *A Brief History of Modern Psychology* (Oxford: Blackwell, 2007).
[4] C. D. Green, M. Shore, and T. Teo, *The Transformation of Psychology: Influences of 19th-century Philosophy, Technology, and Natural Science* (Washington, DC: APA Books, 2004).
[5] K. Danziger, *Naming the Mind: How Psychology Found its Language* (London: Sage, 1997).

processes that could be merged into higher-order thoughts and feelings began to flounder methodologically, theoretically, and practically. Methods of introspection only could be applied to the most basic of sensations without introducing levels of inference that proved to be methodologically intractable in terms of producing comparable and consistent results across different laboratories. Different theories of the compounding of these basic elements into the cognitive and affective experiences of everyday life proliferated without any means of adjudication and applications of psychology far out-stripped any credible empirical basis in the psychological science of the day.

In response, psychology and psychologists shifted focus, away from the basic structures of consciousness to the study of the behaviors of humans and other animals in carefully controlled laboratory contexts. This shift in subject matter from structures of consciousness to functions of behavior often is described as the first revolution in the modern science of psychology. However, it also was a necessary shift in subject matter in response to the lack of progress being achieved by an earlier generation of mentalistic psychologists. And, once again, in a rush to establish the scientific viability of this new science of behavior, standards of objectivity and methodological procedures borrowed from more mature sciences helped to ensure that the latest version of psychological science would steer mostly clear of the everyday experiences and actions of persons in those social, cultural contexts in which they lived and worked.

However, behaviorism did represent certain advances in establishing the possible relevance of psychology to personhood. Despite ignoring most of the obvious differences between human beings and cats, dogs, or rats, the behaviorists did study the holistic activity of animals in carefully controlled environments, and were concerned with how the activity of the animals in these contexts resulted in the learning (or, at least, the habituation) of those various patterns of behavior that were conditioned and reinforced by the experimenters. Additionally, these results did have a direct relevance to the applications of professional behavioral psychologists who began to employ techniques of behavior modification in schools, workplaces, and other social institutions, including prisons and hospitals. Of course, in order to conduct their studies in ways that yielded replicable results, the behaviorists had to greatly restrict the environments within which their research subjects (human and non-human) acted. Consequently, not only was the activity of research subjects restricted to simple behaviors that could be studied and counted objectively, but the contexts within which such behaviors were produced were purposefully sterile, being stripped of any objects other than those used to manipulate the particular behaviors of interest to the experimenters.

Behavioral studies in social psychology that examined the responses
of human subjects were no exception.[6] The environments studied were
social only in the sense that they included a small number of carefully
scripted interactions between research participants and a total stranger
or small number of strangers (the experimenter and confederates of
the experimenter). Thus, such contexts were minimally, proximately,
and simplistically social. They included almost nothing of the broader
social, historical, or cultural dimensions, processes, artifacts, practices,
or institutions that populate and influence the lives of persons as they
do their banking, entertain guests, or struggle with complex family and
work situations and dilemmas. Nonetheless, despite its failure to come
to grips with the social, cultural embeddedness of persons, and despite
almost a complete absence of conceptual focus on persons and their
circumstances, behaviorism, as a framework for psychological inquiry,
succeeded in achieving a paradigmatic, near consensus among most psychologists by the early 1950s, before the early stirrings of contemporary
cognitive psychology, and its subsequent ascendancy during the second
half of the twentieth century.

Before considering cognitive psychology's treatment of persons and
personhood, it is important not to neglect the development of psychometric methods and personality psychology from the 1920s to the 1950s
and beyond. Despite being on the periphery of mainstream behaviorism,
the combination of personality theorizing and psychometric methodologies served to replace the earlier focus of psychologists like James,
Stern, and Janet on the interactivity of persons in historical, social, cultural, and developmental contexts, with an understanding of persons
as bearers or possessors of certain inner personality traits that could
be measured by various psychological instruments (mostly paper-and-
pencil questionnaires on which subjects self-reported). Although her-
alded, and still practiced, as the scientific psychology of personality, such
an approach effectively reduces personality understood as a combination
of the character and action tendencies of persons to personality as ascertained from aggregates of subjects' self-reported ratings on psychologists'
carefully prepared questionnaires – ratings that typically are made at a
considerable physical, social, and psychological remove from the interactive lives of the persons who make the ratings.[7] Of equal, if not greater,

---

[6] K. Danziger, Making social psychology experimental: A conceptual history, 1920–1970. *Journal of the History of the Behavioral Sciences* **34** (2000) 329–347.
[7] See, for example, Danziger, *Naming the Mind*, S. Greer, Is there a "self" in self research? Or, how measuring the self made it disappear. *Social Practice/Psychological Theorizing* **1** (2007) 51–68, and I. A. M. Nicholson, *Inventing Personality: Gordon Allport*

conceptual significance with respect to personhood is the highly debatable understanding that such personality assessments actually measure personality as an inner possession (set of personality traits) of individuals. This understanding assumes that most of the determining sources of one's personhood reside in deeply interior psychological structures and processes within individuals that nonetheless can be unproblematically accessed, "observed," and reported by the individuals themselves, using methods and item formats that psychometricians and personality psychologists borrowed initially from public opinion polls in the US. To complicate matters even further, applications of psychometric, personality psychology came to trade more and more on the logically dubious idea that it was possible to extract knowledge of the personalities of individuals from studies of differences between groups of individuals on traits such as extroversion, neuroticism, agreeableness, conscientiousness, and openness.

With the dawn of cognitive psychology, it seemed possible that psychology's return to the study of mental or cognitive structures and processes – albeit with newly minted computational models and neurophysiological theories – might afford an opening for the study of important aspects of personhood such as reasoned and intentional action, moral concern, self-consciousness, self-understanding, and first-person experience, even if the integrated study of the embodied, situated interactivity of persons in full historical, socio-cultural context was not immediately in the cards. After more than fifty years into psychology's so-called second revolution (the first being the shift from mentalism to behaviorism), the cognitivist reign certainly differs from the behaviorism that preceded it, with respect to a proliferation of research and applications in areas related to personhood such as self-esteem, self-concept, self-efficacy, and self-regulation, all rendered in the language of inner cognitive processes and structures. However, a closer look at psychological theory and research in these areas reveals little conceptual sophistication concerning what the self is and how exactly it relates to conceptions of persons as much more than their psychological interiors.[8] Moreover, cognitive psychology has tended to adopt conceptions of human beings as information processing machines or neural networks that have largely reduced persons to the inner workings of metaphorical processes of computation (e.g., encoding, storage, retrieval, and application) or patterns of cerebral activity (e.g., activation, excitation, and inhibition in the cortex and elsewhere,

and the Science of Selfhood (Washington, DC: American Psychological Association Books, 2003).

[8] R. Harré, *Cognitive Science: A Philosophical Introduction* (London: Sage, 2002).

discernible through functional magnetic resonance imaging (fMRIs) and other imaging and recording techniques). It now is not unusual to read and listen to a new generation of cognitive neuroscientists attributing the thoughts, experiences, and actions of persons to different areas of their brains, and forgetting that it is persons interactive within the biophysical and socio-cultural world who make decisions, exercise self-control, or feel good about themselves.[9] Obviously, bodies are required for the worldly activity of persons. However, so too are interactivity within social, cultural practices and experiential biographical histories, neither of which is reducible to the inner workings of our brains and/or cognitive, computational systems (whatever the ontological status of the latter might be).

In sum, the history of disciplinary psychology is a history of successive attempts to reduce persons – first, to basic operations and structures of their minds understood in mentalistic, componential terms, then to their behaviors as studied mostly in highly restricted micro-environments, and finally to internal cognitive, computational, and neurophysiological structures, processes, and patterns of activation. In addition, since the early years of the twentieth century, various attempts have been made to construct a psychological science of personality that makes extensive use of psychometric measures and statistical techniques that utilize self-report ratings of individuals concerning their understandings and evaluations of themselves in ways that lend themselves to interpreting such ratings as scientifically valid data about personality traits such as extroversion and neuroticism, and social-psychological attributes such as self-concept, self-regulation, and personal identity. One of the things that all of these reductive strategies share is an attempt to grossly simplify the complex lives of persons understood as embodied, rational, and moral agents interactive within evolutionary and developmental trajectories that include histories of constantly unfolding socio-cultural and biographical traditions, practices, artifacts, and identifications. Recognizing the constancy of this basic reductionism across shifts in the focus and methods of psychological science and professional practice over time does not mean that disciplinary psychology as practiced thus far is entirely irrelevant with respect to understanding persons, nor does it mean that personhood has been entirely ignored by all psychologists. However, it certainly does imply that most mainstream psychological theory, research, and practice are not optimally targeted at informing our understanding of ourselves as persons.

---

[9] M. R. Bennett and P. M. S. Hacker, *Philosophical Foundations of Neuroscience* (Oxford: Blackwell, 2003).

Nonetheless, the historical record is not all bad news for a credible psychology of personhood. As already mentioned, there was an impressive first wave of what might be considered a promising psychology of personhood during the founding years of disciplinary psychology in the late nineteenth and early twentieth centuries. Additionally, despite the subsequent succession of highly popular, but mostly reductive systems of psychological science – from mentalism to behaviorism to cognitivism – small pockets of psychologists, who pursued less reductive approaches to psychological inquiry and practice, continued to understand and study persons in more holistic, contextualized, and integrative ways. Indeed, the ideas of the first generation of psychologists of personhood (i.e., James, Dewey, the later Wundt, Janet, Mead, Vygotsky, Stern, and others) continued to garner small numbers of supporters and advocates throughout the twentieth century and into the twenty-first.[10] Within American psychology, examples included Gestalt psychology (as imported from Germany before and during the second world war), post-war humanistic psychology (including phenomenological, existential, and hermeneutic approaches to the study of persons), more social forms of psychoanalytically informed psychology (especially as developed by Adler, Sullivan, and their colleagues), and a growing wave of social, historical, and cultural psychology that belatedly hit the US and Canada in the late 1960s, stimulated by the works of Lev Vygotsky and other Russian psychologists.

In addition, several prominent personality psychologists who had become enamored of more robustly holistic conceptions of persons and who had begun to adopt biographical and narrative methods for understanding persons and their lives began to meet together on a regular basis under the banner of "personology," a term linked to the ideas of earlier personality theorists (like Henry Murray and Gordon Allport, and to an even longer-standing, interdisciplinary commitment to the understanding of persons) who envisioned a personality psychology that went well beyond personality assessments alone.[11] Moreover, in some of psychology's most popular subdivisions like developmental psychology (influenced by the activity and interactivity foci of Baldwin, Werner, Piaget, and others) concern for the holistic activity of persons in social, developmental context always had resisted the more excessive forms of behaviorism and cognitivism that achieved such wide-spread popularity at different times in the history of mainstream psychology.

[10] Valsiner and van der Veer, *The Social Mind*.
[11] I. E. Alexander, *Personology: Method and Content in Personality Assessment and Psychobiography* (Durham, NC: Duke University Press, 1990).

Consequently, with the development of more theoretically informed discourses (e.g., social constructionism, discursive psychology, neoconstructivism) in psychology during the last two decades of the twentieth century and into the first decades of the twenty-first century, the stage was set for a revival, or second wave of the psychology of personhood, one which attempts to use theoretical and historical frameworks, and methods of qualitative, narrative inquiry, and social-developmental theorizing to conceptualize and study persons in holistic, contextualized ways as interactive, communal agents. However, although this new wave of psychological focus and inquiry has now been underway for at least twenty years, it is only recently that a growing number of psychologists who have participated in this second wave of the psychology of personhood have begun to identify themselves explicitly as psychologists of personhood, and to write directly about personhood and the challenges and opportunities it poses for disciplinary psychology. Consequently, the time is right for a volume that explores and examines the psychology of personhood, with an emphasis on philosophical, historical, social-developmental, and narrative dimensions of this important, and increasingly, if somewhat belatedly, recognized area of psychological scholarship.

The psychology of personhood: contents and themes

This book is organized into four parts to reflect the salience of philosophical, historical, social-developmental, and narrative thinking and inquiry in the contemporary psychology of personhood. This organization reflects the major dimensions of recent work in the psychology of personhood as described above. In addition, the ordering of these four parts introduces conceptual and broader philosophical concerns with respect to personhood, before persons are considered in historical and social-developmental contexts within which they are constituted as the unique beings that they are. Ending with narrative perspectives in the psychology of personhood provides more concrete illustrations of the ways in which a psychology of personhood can enhance our general understanding of the nature of persons and their lives, and enrich our particular understanding of specific persons, their circumstances, and their accomplishments.

All of our authors strongly reject the notion of persons as encapsulated individuals that has dominated disciplinary psychology from its beginnings. Their positive proposals exploring this relatively new theoretical space, however, are at times divergent. Consequently, this volume by no means offers a unified understanding of the person that is devoid of disagreements and uncertainties concerning the limits and nature of our understanding of ourselves and others. Nonetheless, despite such differences and challenges, all those who have contributed to this volume consistently advocate the importance of the person as a concept that is necessarily central to the development and maintenance of any viable psychology.

Part I of our book contains two chapters that discuss important philosophical perspectives on persons and how they might be understood. The first task of any sensible approach to personhood, in psychology or any other subject, is to become as clear as possible about what concepts such as person, personhood, and personality entail. In the first of these chapters, Chapter 2, Michael Tissaw examines the concepts of person and personality, and considers the ontology of persons from the perspective of Ludwig Wittgenstein's philosophical, grammatical analysis, especially as practiced currently by Peter Hacker, and applied within the discursive psychology of Rom Harré. Tissaw's dual foci are on what we mean when we use words like person and personality, and what a psychology of personhood, informed by an appropriate grammatical investigation into these terms and their uses, might look like. Tissaw's philosophical, grammatical analysis reveals several common confusions in the ways in which psychologists and others talk about and understand persons, highlights ways in which both persons and talk about persons are embedded in moral discourses and ways of living, and challenges the idea that persons are composed of psychological parts that cause thinking, behavior, and social interactivity.

The second chapter, by Charles Guignon (Chapter 3), also is concerned with philosophical matters in the psychology of personhood, but employs understandings of hermeneutic phenomenology, as elaborated in the works of Martin Heidegger, to describe persons as they appear in ordinary, everyday life. From this perspective, persons live in a world of meanings within which they imbue their existence with significance and concern. Eschewing a substance ontology of personhood, Guignon understands personhood as a narrative self-interpretation that unfolds between birth and death. A person, on this account, is an individual who constantly assesses, implicitly and explicitly, their primary desires in terms of higher-order desires and significations. Guignon, like Tissaw, but from a different philosophical perspective, emphasizes the person as a socially and culturally situated moral agent. For Guignon, such an agent is indebted to the historical traditions of a community, within and through which the agent's self-interpreted life narrative makes possible a kind of freedom that enables meaningful choice.

Part II of our book consists of three chapters that approach personhood in psychology from different historical perspectives. In the first of these,

Chapter 4, historian of psychology Kurt Danziger provides a history of the person that reveals our contemporary psychological conceptions of the person to be of relatively recent historical origin. Danziger argues and demonstrates that understandings of the person that are specifically psychological have been superimposed on rich layers of alternative and historically earlier meanings of the concept. Among the most salient and influential of these are legal and moral conceptions of the person that arose in ancient Greece and Rome and carried over to Medieval Europe. Other early uses of the "person" concept were grammatical and theological. Only very gradually, during the Renaissance, Enlightenment, and Romantic periods, did more individualistic conceptions of personhood emerge, and eventually become associated with ideas concerning private personal experience and uniqueness. It was not until the end of the nineteenth century that conceptions of the person as possibly abnormal and requiring medical intervention emerged. All of these various conceptions paved the way for early psychologists to conceptualize the person in terms of ego, self, and personality. Danziger provides an informative chronology of these conceptions, replete with illustrations and elaborations of their most significant aspects.

In the second historical chapter, Chapter 5, Jeff Sugarman describes and elaborates "historical ontology," as it has been developed and applied by Ian Hacking and Nikolas Rose, both of whom have drawn inspiration from the historical theories and studies of Michel Foucault. Historical ontology is an approach to historical inquiry in psychology that examines the ways in which the language, research, interventions, and institutionalized practices of disciplinary psychology contribute to the "making up of persons," who act under the various descriptions, and in accordance with the theoretical and institutional frameworks, advanced by psychologists and others. Sugarman, following Hacking and Rose, demonstrates that the scientific and professional practices of psychologists have created possibilities for acting out features and ways of being persons that are notable for their subjective, internal emphases, foci that fit especially well with liberal democratic values and modes of governance. He is especially interested in the ways in which psychology has theorized human agency. With Foucault, he concludes that "we have the capacity not only to adopt and wield psychological descriptions, but also, to react to them, to revise them and to transform them." In this way, he links what can be learned from historical ontology to our ongoing quest for freedom. However, he makes it clear that this is a freedom that must recognize the inescapable historical and socio-cultural roots of our personhood.

In the third and final historical chapter, Chapter 6, James Lamiell revisits and reinvigorates the "critical personalism" of German psychologist and philosopher, William Stern. Stern's distinction between persons and things emphasized that persons, in direct opposition to things, are unitary, self-activated, and goal-oriented beings. The person as *unitas multiplex*, as a goal-directed entity, acts within the world in ways that are afforded and supplemented by the world itself. For Stern, dispositions of a person are not fixed causal forces, but mere potentialities that unfold within a worldly context that supports particular actions. Rather than being fully determinate of a person's actions, dispositions always must be supplemented by the world, especially within interactivity with others. On these and related theoretical ideas, Stern proposed a differential psychology that distinguished clearly between knowledge of aggregate variables and knowledge of individuals, making it clear that the former in no way supplies or applies the latter. Lamiell's project in re-discovering and interpreting Stern in the context of contemporary personality psychology is to point clearly to the misunderstandings so prevalent in personality psychology that stem from a wide-spread failure to understand and abide by Stern's critical distinction. Yet, despite the fact that knowledge of individual differences carries absolutely no implications whatsoever for knowledge of individuals, personality psychology continues to trade on exactly such logically impossible connections, veiled by a plethora of statistical methods and conceptual elisions. Lamiell provides specific historical details about how Stern's work and ideas have been ignored and misunderstood, and in doing so, creates a powerful case study of some of the ways in which psychology has tended to reduce and erode personhood.

Part III of our book contains four chapters that explore social-developmental and evolutionary perspectives on persons and personhood. The first, Chapter 7, by John Barresi, Chris Moore, and Raymond Martin, provides a rich and nuanced consideration of developmental and evolutionary theory and research that fits nicely within their own approach to the psychology of personhood. Adopting aspects of Peter Strawson's non-dualistic account of persons, Barresi, Moore, and Martin's "intentional relations theory (IRT)" offers a conceptually coherent and empirically supported account of how, both ontogenetically and phylogenetically, it is possible for human beings to accomplish one of the most central and defining capabilities of personhood – understanding and integrating the intentional activities of themselves and others. Their core idea is that humans are uniquely able to do this because they recognize matches between their own and others' actions in the context of shared interactions with others and objects. In both evolution and development, the result of such joint engagements, especially when accompanied by communicative and linguistic exchanges, is an understanding of self and other as persons, embodied agents capable of engaging in intentional relations that are object or goal directed. Using their four-level framework for the social understanding of intentional relations, Barresi *et al.* distinguish the intentional relations engaged by persons from those engaged by other animals. They argue that it is only human persons who are capable of representing mental phenomena of self and other in a common format that enables complex forms of reciprocal altruism among unrelated members of a group.

The next social-developmental chapter, Chapter 8, is by Jack Martin and Alex Gillespie, who outline their "position exchange theory (PET)." This perspective on the development of self and other understanding and perspective taking in many ways complements the perspective taken by Barresi *et al.* However, Martin and Gillespie want to emphasize that direct participation with others in historically evolved and socio-culturally embedded and sanctioned practices of interactivity is a necessary precursors to more abstracted, psychological ways of understanding persons and taking their perspectives. In particular, they focus on how we occupy different social positions within routine sequences of everyday interactivity, such as giving and receiving objects, and childhood games such as peek-a-boo and hide-and-seek. Such exchanges gradually enable developing persons to understand and integrate the perspectives associated with different positions within these conventional sequences of interactivity. When children are able to physically and socially occupy a position such as that of "giver" or "seeker," and simultaneously recall, anticipate, and understand the perspectives associated with both the position occupied and its complementary, related position, they achieve a basic, physically and socially supported form of perspective taking. With the acquisition of enhanced communicative capabilities, more advanced forms of perspective taking enable older children to distance themselves from their immediate surroundings and take more abstracted perspectives that afford them a greater range of possibilities for acting in ways that are, at least in part, self-determined. Martin and Gillespie supply several examples, drawn from both social-psychological experimentation and everyday observations, of the ways in which position exchange enables greater self–other understanding and higher levels of perspective taking and problem solving.

Mark Bickhard follows with Chapter 9, offering a succinct summary of the interactivist approach to the development of persons, a social-developmental perspective he has developed and defended over the past two decades. Central to Bickhard's account is the ontological and normative emergence of persons as agents. This emergence occurs as individuals develop as social beings in co-constitutive interaction with the social and cultural realities within which their development occurs. As complex agents, persons interact with each other in myriad social situations that pose what Bickhard refers to as coordination problems that require joint activity with others – others that individuals recognize as complex agents like themselves. The upshot is a uniquely human form of co-constitution in which "socio-cultural processes create, via development, the persons who constitute the emergence base for those socio-cultural processes." In this model, language is a particularly important socio-cultural tool system for constructing, maintaining, and changing situation conventions. Social development intrinsically involves the development of initially implicit, and increasingly explicit, understandings of others' views of one's self, views that become embedded in one's being, and being accepted as, a social agent. In this way, the social ontology of persons is intrinsically normative. Persons have an existential and ethical stake in being the social-ontological person that they have become. In sum, "a person's existence as a social being presupposes their general legitimacy and acceptance as a socio-cultural agent. A refusal on the part of others to accept that legitimacy can constitute a challenge to their being as a person."

The final chapter (Chapter 10) in the social-developmental section of our book is by Anna Stetsenko. Stetsenko takes what she refers to as a "transformative activist stance (TAS)" toward persons and their development. TAS is a historical, socio-cultural approach that is grounded in Stetsenko's interpretation of the works and goals of Lev Vygotsky. TAS takes a deeply relational view of humans as interactive agents who constantly create their lives and nature as they simultaneously transform their world. This collaborative, transformative interactivity is the ontological foundation of human development, one that incorporates and supersedes both adaptation and relationality. By taking a forward-looking stance on their lives that involves social, collective commitments, persons exist as transformative agents. "Persons are agents not only for whom things matter but *who themselves matter in history, culture, and society* and, moreover, who come into Being as unique individuals exactly through and to the extent that they matter in these processes by making a contribution to them."

The final part of *The Psychology of Personhood*, Part IV, contains two chapters that describe narrative perspectives. The first, by Amia Lieblich and Ruthellen Josselson, Chapter 11, explores the concepts of "narrative" and "identity" as they apply to persons. In so doing, Lieblich and

Josselson provide a history of work that has linked these concepts, a history that culminates in a description of the contemporary narrative psychology of personhood. This is a psychology that demonstrates how "personal narratives are woven by the threads of identity that constitute personhood." Testimony to the success of narrative psychology includes the facts that few contemporary psychologists would deny the importance of life narratives in the study of personhood, and that most current conceptions of persons make reference to life narrative and/or autobiography.

The second chapter that takes a narrative perspective, and which also concludes our volume, Chapter 12, is by Mark Freeman. In it, Freeman integrates what he regards as "fundamental ingredients of narrative identity" into "a comprehensive image." Freeman begins by explaining why the idea of identity requires narrative. He then elaborates the centrality of "temporality" and "otherness" to narratives of personhood and self-understanding. In so doing, Freeman also demonstrates how the spheres of temporality and otherness can be put together to provide a model of narrative identity and its formation. In the closing sections of his chapter, Freeman illustrates some of the interpretive richness of his approach by drawing from his personal life and relationships to demonstrate how "the idea of narrative identity and the idea of personhood are intimately related to one another."

The essays that make up this book provide both an introduction to the psychology of personhood, and an invitation to participate in it. As a possible first step, we encourage readers to engage with the chapters that follow, with a view to exploring and developing further their own thinking about persons and how they might be understood and studied within a more holistic, integrative, and methodologically open psychology. Although this book has been organized to encourage readers to work through its various chapters in the order in which they are presented, some readers may find it more congenial to their interests and backgrounds to determine their own paths through the subsequent chapters, perhaps choosing to begin with material that most intrigues them or with which they are already somewhat familiar. But, however it is navigated, we hope that our volume will occasion critical reflection on the fragmentation and narrow specialization that typify so much contemporary psychology, and offer an alternative way of thinking about what we believe is the necessarily central subject matter of psychology – the person as embodied and interactively embedded within the constantly evolving biophysical and socio-cultural world.

Part I

Philosophical, conceptual perspectives

2   The person concept and the ontology of persons

Michael A. Tissaw

This chapter is concerned with two questions. First, what can grammatical investigation tell us about the meanings of words that are fundamental to conceptually sound theorizing and research in the psychology of personhood? (In particular, what do we mean by "person" and "personality"?) Second, what would a psychology of personhood, informed by grammatical investigation, look like?

In the first of three sections to follow, I discuss some fundamental terms and ideas relevant to understanding the purposes of grammatical investigation. These will include the distinction between surface and depth grammar and their connections with sense and nonsense. Other terms and some methodological issues pertaining to grammatical investigation are addressed in the second section, where we turn to Peter Hacker's analysis of the "person" concept via his "philosophical anthropology," which investigates the network of concepts we use to study ourselves, in part by accounting for potential sources of confusion in our uses of those concepts.[1] In the final section, I consider points at which grammatical investigation and its results meet empirical theorizing and research, specifically in discursive psychology's account of the development of personhood. The point is to suggest ways in which the philosophical investigation of categories and psychological concepts can inform empirical theories of personhood. One way that philosophical anthropology and discursive psychology concur is in the distinction between "human being" and "person," primarily on the basis of potentialities to acquire a range of abilities characteristic of persons. Thus, I conclude with some remarks on the moral positioning of human beings prior to their becoming persons and grammatical investigation as a value-laden enterprise.

I need to make one qualification. Obviously, the foregoing suggests a contrast between empirical perspectives on personhood informed by grammatical investigation and past or extant perspectives not so

---

[1] P. M. S. Hacker, *Human Nature: The Categorial Framework* (Oxford: Blackwell, 2007).

informed. I am very restrictive in referencing the latter because I want to focus on the philosophical foundations of sound theory and research in the psychology of personhood. In any case, I believe that we will see enough in our brief encounter with unsound theory to apply and expand on the lessons learned elsewhere.

Some fundamentals of grammatical investigation

Grammatical investigation refers to the methods of descriptive analysis of rules of word use in the tradition of analytical philosophy typically associated with Ludwig Wittgenstein. Its general purpose is to illuminate the meanings of words by describing their varieties of use and for the most part it is motivated by the ways our everyday, customary uses of words *influence our thinking* as theorists and researchers in the humanities, social, and behavioral sciences and natural sciences. Thus, there is a sense in which grammatical investigation is *psychological* investigation.

There are many ways to conduct grammatical investigation and the extent to which we need to do it can vary considerably. It depends on the word or words of interest and the extent to which we are unclear about their meanings. In Wittgenstein's philosophy, assembling a sufficient number of uses of a word (or words) amounts to an explanation of meaning. But we do not assemble uses just to explain meaning. We do so in order to understand why we have become confused by our uses of words. This means we must be of a temperament to acknowledge our confusion.

Wittgenstein's distinction between surface and depth grammar is the most straightforward and general way to explain how our uses of words in everyday contexts result in our being conceptually confused in other more specialized contexts.[2] Surface grammar includes the obvious superficial appearance of a sentence or its constituents, including its syntax and word composition. Depth grammar pertains to possible and impossible uses of a word or sentence, how they can be combined with other words or sentences and consequences of their uses in varieties of context. For example, there is no obvious difference in surface grammar of "to mean" and "to say." So, are we to assume that both are action-verbs? No. For I cannot decide to mean, be ordered to mean, agree or refuse to mean, remember or forget to mean, mean quickly or slowly, elegantly or gladly

---

[2] L. Wittgenstein, *Philosophical Investigations* (Oxford: Blackwell, 1953) §664.

and so on.[3] In other words, the rules of use of "to mean" do not follow those of an action verb like "to say." Their depth grammars are different.

Here is another example. We describe our own and other persons' personalities in many ways. The appearance of "has" in "She has a really outgoing personality" may imply that the person in question actually *possesses* an outgoing personality. The surface grammar of the sentence is just like "She has a really flashy car." In our everyday lives, expressions of this sort typically pose no problems. But in psychology, they may lead us to think of "personality" as having the function of a noun. Actually, the potential problem lies not just in our speaking of persons as "having" personalities, but in the very idea that we *describe* our own and other persons' personalities, as if there were some *thing* there to describe behind the behavior that fits "outgoing," "introverted," etc.

It may seem pretty trivial to suggest that "personality" does not function as a noun; that it is not a thing possessed in some sense by persons. Who thinks that way anyway? There is a difference between speaking and writing on personality in ways that indicate we *might* think personality is a thing and actually believing personality is a thing! Unfortunately, the history of psychology suggests otherwise. For example, Danziger observes that "psychological knowledge claims in the Galtonian [style of research in psychology] generally derived their significance from their reference to *inherent properties* [emphasis added] that were built into each individual . . . " and that "the structure of such claims remained unaltered where the original geneticist basis was dropped and replaced by a noncommittal reference to 'traits'."[4] We can get more specific. Consider McAdams and Pals' claim that "dispositional traits are those broad, non-conditional, decontextualized, generally linear and bipolar, and implicitly comparative dimensions of human individuality that go by such names as *extraversion, dominance, friendliness, dutifulness, depressiveness, the tendency to feel vulnerable*, and so on."[5] Well persons, not traits, are extroverted or introverted, dominant or submissive, friendly or unfriendly, dutiful or derelict in their duties, depressed or feeling quite well. Persons, not traits, may be characterized as "non-conditional" (for example when a

---

[3] These examples and my distinction between surface and depth grammar are owed to P. M. S. Hacker's exegesis of *Philosophical Investigations* §664 in *Wittgenstein: Mind and Will*, Vol. 4 of an *Analytical Commentary on the Philosophical Investigations* (Oxford: Blackwell, 1996) 708–709.

[4] K. Danziger, *Constructing the Subject: Historical Origins of Psychological Research* (Cambridge University Press, 1990) 112.

[5] D. P. McAdams and J. L. Pals, A new big five: Fundamental principles for an integrative science of personality. *American Psychologist* **61** (2006) 207.

person stubbornly remains committed to an opinion in the face of obvious contrary evidence). And what could it mean to suggest that traits are "decontextualized"? If McAdams and Pals are referring to *persons'* traits, are they suggesting that traits and persons are decontextualized, or just the former and not the latter? I don't know about traits, but I know that persons are not decontextualized! Further along, they add: "If the momentary constellation of any person's thoughts, feelings, and behaviors make up his or her current *state*, then traits may be seen as the most common kinds of states that a person experiences across situations and over time." McAdams and Pals seem to suggest that traits are states. Grammatically, thoughts, feelings, and behaviors have what Wittgenstein called "genuine duration."[6] In other words – and among other things – they can be clocked. (They can be said to have a beginning and an end.) It is not clear that traits, as defined above, can be clocked. Also, in what sense can persons be said to *experience* traits? It seems to me that McAdams and Pals are in a muddle.

These are just a few problems that thoroughgoing investigation of depth grammar can bring out. The sense that our uses of words have put us in a muddle is the most common motivation for grammatical investigation. This sense signals the possibility of our being in the midst of a *philosophical* problem because "we do not command a clear view of the use of our words."[7] One way to achieve a clearer view is to examine depth grammar to the point where we reveal the source(s) of our confusion. But, this means that we must be aware of the potential for surface grammar to lull us to sleep and thus have no impetus to investigate depth grammar. Definitions of key concepts in the social and behavioral sciences are notorious for leading to this sense of being in a muddle. Why? One reason is that in order to define a single word (or a few words) we have to use at least one sentence whose depth grammar may differ in significant ways from its surface grammar. It should be apparent why difficulties can multiply if the definition consists of more than one sentence.

Sense and nonsense

I have questioned the sense in which persons can be said to experience traits. This brings us to one more bit of terminology that is characteristic of grammatical analysis: sense and nonsense. A good way to explain these

---

[6] L. Wittgenstein, *Remarks on the Philosophy of Psychology, Vol. 2*, C. G. Luckhardt and M. A. E. Aue (trans.) (Oxford: Blackwell, 1980) §63.
[7] See for example Wittgenstein, *Philosophical Investigations*, §§122–3.

terms is by contrast to the centrality of truth and falsity in science, as do Bennett and Hacker:

What truth and falsity is to science, sense and nonsense is to philosophy. Observational and theoretical error result in falsehood; conceptual error results in lack of sense... Nonsense is often generated when an expression is used contrary to the rules for its use... Nonsense is also commonly generated when an existing expression is given a new, perhaps technical or quasi-technical use, and the new use is inadvertently crossed with the old... It is the task of the conceptual critic to identify such transgressions of the bounds of sense.[8]

The purpose of Bennett and Hacker's grammatical investigations of the uses of psychological concepts in everyday life and in neuroscience is to show that when neuroscientists ascribe psychological attributes to the brain or other parts of persons (e.g., "to perceive," "to remember") they are uttering nonsense, or a "form of words that says nothing."[9] The likely culprit is comfort with surface grammar and inattention to depth grammar. Persons who use computers often ascribe psychological attributes to their machines. We speak of "smart phones." We know the extent to which advances in computing have influenced psychological theory and research.

So, there is a tight connection between sense and nonsense on one hand and surface and depth grammar on the other hand. In an important methodological remark, Wittgenstein encourages us to "establish an order in our knowledge of the use of language" by "constantly giving prominence to distinctions which our ordinary forms of language easily make us overlook." He adds that "the confusions which occupy us arise when language is like an engine idling, not when it is doing work."[10] Whenever possible, we must be open to the unease that nonsense produces in us – when we are not getting real work done with our uses of language. I have called this "having a nose for nonsense."[11]

Not that nonsense always is generated by inattention to our non-technical "ordinary forms of language." In the social and behavioral sciences, nonsense can result from our efforts to define and make use of specialized "constructs" (e.g., "trait" in the psychology of personhood). Investigating these specialized terms involves first establishing whether or not they are intended to be used in a customary or non-customary sense. Then, the grammatical investigator "must show that the scientist

---

[8] M. R. Bennett and P. M. S. Hacker, *Philosophical Foundations of Neuroscience* (Oxford: Blackwell, 2003) 6.

[9] Bennett and Hacker, *Philosophical Foundations of Neuroscience*, 74.

[10] Wittgenstein, *Philosophical Investigations*, §132.

[11] M. A. Tissaw, Making sense of neonatal imitation. *Theory and Psychology* **17** (2007) 223.

intends to use it in a new sense but has inadvertently crossed the new sense with the old. The wayward scientist should, whenever possible, be condemned out of his own mouth."[12]

It is unfortunate that Hacker's investigations of the "person" concept – to which we now turn – do little to condemn wayward psychologists of personhood out of their own mouths. At points, he mentions psychological perspectives, but he is not specific with respect to past and extant empirically based theories of personhood. The psychology of personhood could use a good dose of grammatical investigations that are specific to current theorizing in the discipline. I will say a bit more on this below.

"Person" as category and concept

In *Individuals*, Peter Strawson suggests "it is easier to understand how we can see each other, and ourselves, as persons, if we think first of the fact that we act, and act on each other, and act in accordance with a common human nature."[13] The recommendation seems to be that certain difficulties can be avoided if we keep in mind the fundamental conceptual connection between "person" and words pertaining to our actions and our common human nature. By "actions," Strawson means movements that "we interpret... in terms of intention." Now "to interpret" can mean a lot of things. In Strawson's case, what it does not mean is that we interpret movements as intentional via reference to anything "inner." When we interpret movements as intentional, our bases for doing so include the convergence of overt behavior, contexts in which movements occur, and grammatical rules of application of "to intend" and its cognates. It is true that we interpret the movements of many animals as intentional. But this is irrelevant to Strawson's suggestion that when it comes to understanding how we see ourselves and each other *as persons*, we must not sever our interpretations from *human nature*.

There is some obvious thematic continuity in Strawson's linking "person" to actions and human nature and the subject of this section: Peter Hacker's *Human Nature: The Categorial Framework*; specifically its final chapter, entitled "The Person." It may be the most important book on topics relevant to the psychology of personhood that analytical philosophy has on offer. My aim is to do some justice to the book as a whole on the way to discussing Hacker's grammatical investigation of "person," which includes some extension of Strawson's ideas.

---

[12] Bennett and Hacker, *Philosophical Foundations of Neuroscience*, 6.
[13] P. F. Strawson, *Individuals: An Essay in Descriptive Metaphysics* (London: Methuen, 1959) 109.

Philosophical anthropology

Human Nature is a work of "philosophical anthropology," or "investigation into *the conceptual scheme* in terms of which we describe ourselves and our complex moral and social relationships, give expression to our inner life, explain, justify or excuse the thoughts, feelings and actions of human beings."[14] Philosophical anthropology aims not to produce a theory of human nature, but to identify and illuminate philosophical problems toward setting the study of human beings on conceptually sound footing. Importantly, this includes historical analysis of sources of conceptual confusion in the study of human beings. With respect to discussion of the "person" concept, the sources of confusion have been various. (Religious doctrine for example.) We would be right to suspect a specific source has been inattention to depth grammar. However, the primary *general* source of confusion Hacker terms the "Cartesian-empiricist tradition," which for centuries has provided a "radically defective" conceptual framework that lives on in the humanities and social sciences.[15] Again, we would gain much from detailed expositions on the extent to which the defective framework informs current theorizing in the psychology of personhood. A more thorough reading of McAdam and Pals' theorizing on personality traits illustrates one case. There are many more.

The substantive chapters of Hacker's book can be seen as arranged in groups of three, according to categories of increasing specificity; beginning with substance, causation, and power, then to agency, explanation in terms of teleology, and reasons for human action, then to the mind, the self and body, and finally the person.[16] These fundamental categories structure the conceptual scheme we use to investigate ourselves and their progression suggests why Hacker reserves "The Person" for final analysis. Step-wise through the categories, we use language to speak and think about ourselves and others of our kind as substances of a particular type, as being both subject to material causes and of having volitional powers, as being able to engage in purposeful behavior, as being able to give reasons for our actions, as having distinctive qualities of intellect (including rational thought), as having unique identities, and of having a body.[17] There is much, much more. But what more there is presumably will fall under the basic categories.

Before turning to some specific sources of confusion about the "person" concept, I want to mention a few things about the relationship

---

[14] Hacker, *Human Nature*, 10–11.   [15] Hacker, *Human Nature*, 310.
[16] See S. Mulhall, Hacker on human nature. *The Philosophical Quarterly* **60** (2009) 407.
[17] See Hacker, *Human Nature*, 311.

between what analytical philosophy can tell us about the concept and empirical research on personhood. Hacker argues that "the study of the nature of things" belongs not just to the empirical sciences, but to philosophy.[18] Empirical research surely has and can contribute to our knowledge of human nature and persons. But, among other things, it cannot tell us *why* we think of ourselves and other human beings *as persons*. It is not trivial that grammatical investigation can do this. Perhaps more salient is the possibility that the results of grammatical investigation will contradict theories of personhood informed by empirical research. McAdams and Pals' theoretical perspective is just one of many that implicitly portray persons as being composed of parts (traits). What if grammatical investigation shows that "person" is not a substance concept? This would be a problem; for only substances can be composed of parts.

Sources of confusion

In light of Hacker's work, I want to address two general sources of confusion that have framed debates on the "person" concept. The first may be characterized as varieties of use. "Person" can be used in many ways and it has many cognates and fungibles. We use "person" in connection with our own and others' personality, as in "I'm a better person for it" and "She's a different person after the car accident." (As we have seen, "personality" has its own potential sources of confusion in varieties of use. We should not overlook either that many pet owners attribute personality to their animals.) We use "person" in connection with physical features and sometimes substitute it with "body," as in "That's a really tall person!" and "A body never had it so good." "A person," "any person," "all persons," and "no persons" have respective potential equivalents in "somebody," "anybody," "everybody," and "nobody" (or "someone," etc.). Also, we can use "mind" to stand in for "person," as in "I saw the best minds of my generation..." Sometimes we speak as if to conflate "mind" with personal intention, as in "He's of a mind to go over there and settle it" and as if we *possess* our mind and body and/or that our mind and body somehow are separate, yet communicative: "My mind says yes, but my body says no." Potential confusions multiply in our uses of, for example, "I," "self," "identity," "soul," and ways in which we connect talk of persons to moral responsibility, memory, and experience.[19]

---

[18] Hacker, *Human Nature*, 7.
[19] Hacker gives a more thorough set of examples in *Human Nature*, 288. Most of my examples are alternatives to his.

Actually, two types of "verbs of experience," as Wittgenstein called them, lie at the root of the second potential source of confusion. He observed that what characterizes them is "the fact that the third person of the present is to be identified by observation [of behavior], the first person not. Sentences in the third person of the present: information. In the first person present, expression."[20] As Hacker puts it, "third-person ascription of psychological predicates rests on behavioral criteria," while "first-person utterances do not." The danger lies in our being "prone to confuse the absence of 'outer,' behavioral criteria with the presence of 'inner,' mental criteria, to which the subject . . . has privileged access."[21] For example, compare the third-person "She's very happy" with the first-person "I'm very happy." The third-person utterance is *descriptive*; it is not part of the person's happiness and it may be true or false. Our saying "She's very happy" is based on behavioral criteria that we count as indicative of happiness. We say it on the basis of our having learned how to apply the concept of happiness to certain kinds of behavior-in-context (e.g., a beaming smile at the presentation of a diploma). By contrast, the first-person utterance is *expressive*; it is part of what it is for the person uttering it to be happy – we could say it is part of the performance of happiness – and usually there is no question as to its veracity. It is true that we may say "I'm very happy" insincerely, as a joke, and so on. But, when we say it sincerely, we do not say it based on observing our own performance of happiness. Thus, we may think that because third-person descriptions of happiness are based on behavioral criteria and first-person are not, then the criteria of our own happiness must lie somewhere else – likely inside of us. Then, we may think that we alone have access to our own non-behavioral criteria of our own happiness. But, there are no such criteria. For introspection provides no single criterion or set of criteria that would give us confirmation of our happiness. We are just happy and say so. We express – and do not describe – our happiness. Thus, whatever is going on inside of us is irrelevant to others understanding the meaning of what we say.

This so-called "asymmetry principle" has deep implications for theorizing and research in the social and behavioral sciences.[22] In the psychology of personhood, for example, it may account for the tendency to assume that a person's first-person use of "I" *refers* in some sense to their identity, self or the like. Grammatically, the "I" in the first-person

---

[20] Wittgenstein, *Remarks on the Philosophy of Psychology, Vol. 2*, §63.
[21] Hacker, *Human Nature*, 288–289.
[22] See R. Harré and M. A. Tissaw, *Wittgenstein and Psychology: A Practical Guide* (Aldershot: Ashgate, 2005) ch. 9.

utterance "I am concerned about the economy" does not serve a referential function. It serves an *expressive* function. The ability to use "I" does not necessarily equate to the ability to refer to oneself, to one's identity. Rather, the exercise of the ability *is part of what it is to have a sense of personal identity.*[23]

"Animal," "human being," and the "person" concept

What does "person" mean? What is a person? What are we investigating when we study persons? It seems we cannot avoid invoking "human being" when attempting to answer questions of this sort. When we speak of a person, we speak of a human being. We might say, with Hacker: "Our concept of a person evolved above all as a concept applicable to human beings . . ."[24] Another way to put it is that "person" is conceptually parasitic on "human being." Knowing that "person" is not applicable to non-human animals enables us to evaluate as confused and inadequate definitions of "person" that apply also to non-human animals, however inadvertently.[25] The close association between "person" and "human being" *is* a source of confusion. But Hacker identifies a deeper source: "human being" is a *substance concept* (or "substance noun") and "person" is not.[26]

Hacker's strategy in arriving at this conclusion is characteristically Wittgensteinian. He begins by reminding us of "some commonplaces"; not in order to arrive at a single, essential difference between human beings and other living organisms – or between the concepts "human being" and "person" – but to clarify *what we are doing* when making such distinctions. What, then, are we doing when thinking and speaking of ourselves and others as persons? Hacker's general answer is that we are *qualifying* "a substance concept of an animal of such-and-such kind, earmarking the individual of the relevant kind possessing (or as being of such a nature as normally possessing) a distinctive range of powers, a personality, and the status of a moral being."[27] We do not use "person" to identify a certain kind of animal as a human being, so much as we use it to attribute to that animal certain kinds of *abilities.* "To be a person," says Hacker, "is not to be a certain kind of animal, but rather to be an animal of one kind or another with certain kinds of abilities."[28]

[23] See Harré and Tissaw, *Wittgenstein and Psychology,* 202–203.
[24] Hacker, *Human Nature,* 310.
[25] See M. A. Tissaw, A critical look at critical (neo)personalism: *Unitas multiplex* and the "person" concept. *New Ideas in Psychology* **28** (2010) 164.
[26] Hacker, *Human Nature,* 312–313.   [27] Hacker, *Human Nature,* 313.
[28] Hacker, *Human Nature,* 313.

It may be of interest that the conceptual bonding of "person" to certain kinds of abilities provides two reasons why "human person" is not redundant. First, not all human beings have the abilities Hacker has in mind. In other words, *not all human beings exhibit abilities criterial of personhood.* Second, Hacker does not exclude the possibility that the categorial term "person" might be applied at some point in the future to entities other than human beings. Right now, the only persons we know of are human beings. This could change.

Abilities are exercised materially, as practices. But this does not make "ability" a substance concept. One can have the ability to do something and never do it. So then where is the ability? It would be a mistake to assume that we can, so to speak, step back into the central nervous system to locate the materiality of an ability; for our uses of the word "ability" are not based on identification of "inner" material states that we may or may not count as criterial for possession of an ability.[29] This is one reason why "person," as a concept so wedded to abilities, is not a substance concept.

There is no single, essential ability that sets the category and concept "person" apart from "human being" or "animal." The abilities that are unique to persons form a family of concepts and we can get clear on much of what is to be included in this family by investigating whether persons alone meet criteria indicating their possession *as a set of abilities.* Again, while empirical investigation can assist us in making such determinations, our approach is grammatical – to investigate what it does and does not make sense to say about persons, as opposed to some human beings and all non-human animals. Here are some examples. Persons alone can provide criteria for the ability to give reasons for their actions, for choosing this or that based on reasons, or believing one thing and not believing another. As a matter of science, the question as to whether non-human animals can "reason" is controversial. But, there is no doubt that *giving reasons* is not possible without the ability to use some kind of rule-governed communicative symbol system, namely language. Also, persons alone can provide criteria for the ability to act purposively in accordance with a moral code, implying willingness to abide by cultural standards, the wish to avoid punishment, and so on. The question as to whether some animals are able to engage in rudimentary cultural practices is controversial as well. Even if we grant this ability to some species of animal, persons alone can provide criteria that they know their behaviors express their culture. We can add to these examples Strawson's observation that "person" is "the concept of a type of entity that *both* predicates ascribing

---

[29] See Harré and Tissaw, *Wittgenstein and Psychology*, 83–89.

states of consciousness *and* predicates ascribing corporeal characteristics . . . are equally applicable to a single individual of that single type."[30] I want to expand on this because it brings out two additional grammatical distinctions between "person" and "human being."

That Strawson distinguished between states of consciousness (P-predicates) and corporeal characteristics (M-predicates) on the way to concluding that "person" is a "primitive concept" is well known. The distinction is due to our being "tempted to think of a person as a sort of compound of two kinds of subjects: a subject of experiences . . . and a subject of corporeal attributes." But, he argued, "person" is not a compound at all. It is a *primitive concept* in that "the concept of a person is logically prior to that of an individual consciousness . . . [and] is not to be analyzed as that of an animated body or of an embodied anima."[31] Hacker endorses Strawson's primitive concept thesis, with qualifications. "Person" is a primitive concept if it cannot be analyzed as a Cartesian subject; as a combination of a mind-subject of P-predicates and a body-subject of M-predicates. But, he rightly observes that P-predicates also can be ascribed to many non-human animals. For example, we say that dogs are conscious, happy, frustrated, and so on. So, the possibility of ascribing P- and M-predicates to persons is not enough to set "person" off from "animal." Hacker does this by observing that only persons "are also *self*-ascribers of P-predicates (and M-predicates)."[32] Persons alone have the ability to say of themselves "I'm happy," "I'm frustrated," etc. and they alone can say *why* they are happy or frustrated. So here we have another way to distinguish "person" not only from "animal," but from "human being"; for self-ascription of predicates of states of consciousness is among many abilities that not all human beings possess.

What is required for such self-ascription? Obviously, the ability to use language and just about all that goes along with that ability, including perhaps foremost, the ability to engage in rational thought. The significance of rational thought leads Hacker to say that in addition to self-ascription of P- and M-predicates, as a way of getting clear on the "person" concept "it is perhaps more illuminating to say with Aristotle that we are unique possessors of a *rational psuchē* . . . ," which includes the abilities to reason and act for reasons and to deliberate and engage in genuine decision-making.[33] The ability to engage in full-fledged rational thought sets persons apart because it entails a considerable range of abilities and potential abilities – all exercised to varying degrees of skill – that cannot

---

[30] Strawson, *Individuals*, 97–98.
[31] Strawson, *Individuals*, 98–99.   [32] Hacker, *Human Nature*, 312.
[33] Hacker, *Human Nature*, 313; see 254–255 for Hacker's account of Aristotle's psuchē.

be matched by any other of the living entities. This is why "person" at the same time *qualifies* the substance concept "human being," yet *does not qualify* as a substance concept.

Taking stock: from "person" to "personality"

We have learned that varieties of use have the potential to confuse us with respect to the role of "person" and its cognates as we use them, which in actuality is to qualify the substance concept "human being" in terms of a unique range of abilities that are language-based, including perhaps foremost the ability of rational thought and the ability to act – or refuse to act – in accordance with cultural standards. "Person" is not a substance concept and any psychology of personhood that portrays the person as a thing composed of psychological parts is conceptually incoherent.

We have learned that lack of vigilance as to the asymmetry principle has the potential to lead us to think that words such as "I," "me," "myself," etc. serve a referential function – perhaps to something inner, such as an "I" or "self." Instead, they serve an *expressive* function. Their use is part of what it means to be a person with a sense of personal identity. Being ignorant of the asymmetry principle and depth grammar, many psychologists have expended much time and effort on "the I" and development of "the self."

What we have not considered is the conceptual relationship between "person" and "personality." As the former qualifies "human being," the latter may be seen as qualifying "person." However both are *developmental concepts*. As "human being" is a classification of biological status that includes the *potential* to acquire and exercise certain social, cognitive, and physical abilities, "person" is a classification that incorporates these with the *developmental acquisition and exercise* of the abilities beyond the means of non-human animals and young human infants. "Personality" adds to "person" the *characteristic* exercise of the abilities of persons.[34] In other words, as we use "person" with respect to the "what" of abilities possessed, we use "personality" with respect to the "how" of those abilities. Both are constituents of personhood. "Person" and "personality" both are achievement/ability concepts.

We are in a good position now to shift from grammatical investigation of "person" as a category and concept to the question how human beings become persons; more broadly from the tasks of philosophy to the psychology of personhood as human developmental science.

---

[34] Tissaw, A critical look at critical (neo)personalism, 165.

Where grammatical investigation meets the empirical: how we become persons

Discursive psychology's account of persons and their early psychological development is in lock-step with Wittgenstein's grammatical investigations of abilities-and-skills concepts and rule-following. To bring this out, I will present some proposals made by Rom Harré that have implications for conceptually sound theorizing on the transformation of infant human beings into persons. Throughout, we will see many similarities between Harré's views on personhood and conclusions drawn about the "person" concept in the previous section. There will be some repetition of topics.

The relationship of a person to [the world of signs and symbols] is to be understood through the idea of skillful action. A human being can live in the world of symbols and intentional normative activity only through the skills they have acquired, and *thereby become and continue to be a person* [emphasis added].[35]

This statement ought to remind us of Hacker's distinction between "human being" and "person" based on abilities unique to persons and Strawson's emphasis on actions. Again, human beings do not come into the world as persons. They *become* persons and maintain their personhood via acquisition and exercise of a range of abilities (exercised to different degrees of skill) that mark the grammatical domain of the concepts "person" and "personhood."

Wittgenstein's many remarks on abilities-and-skills concepts make it quite clear that the grammar of such concepts entails (1) teaching practices and standards of correctness, (2) active (intentional) engagement on the part of persons when exercising abilities to degrees of skill, and (3) that explanations for the exercise of abilities are stated as means to ends, not causes to effects.[36] In order to have the ability to do something skillfully, a person must be shown how to do it by another person who possesses the ability. What amounts to teaching and learning here can be achieved via explicit or implicit means. In explicit teaching contexts, the teacher clearly *intends* to assist the learner's acquisition of the ability. In implicit teaching, teachers exercise the ability *to get something done*, with or without awareness that they are playing a role in the acquisition of that ability by another person. In these contexts, the learner may pick up the ability to some degree of skill with little or no awareness. There are all sorts of possibilities. But, whether the teaching is explicit or implicit, the

---

[35] R. Harré and G. Gillett, *The Discursive Mind* (Thousand Oaks, CA: Sage Publications, 1994), 99.

[36] See Harré and Tissaw, *Wittgenstein and Psychology*, 88–90.

learner is not *caused* to acquire the ability or to exercise the ability after it is acquired. This is because persons *explain the learning and exercise of abilities in terms of reasons for acting.* Citing causes for acting is part of the grammar of excuses; but even to cite a cause as an excuse for acting (or not acting) is to give a reason.[37]

Discursive psychology's debt to Wittgenstein does not end at abilities and skills because there is an internal relationship between that grammar and the grammar of words pertaining to rules.[38] This relationship illuminates further the extent to which the "person" concept is infused with agency.

Following rules and acting in accordance with rules

Discursive psychology maintains that "the essence of psychological activity is rule-following" and Wittgenstein's distinction between following a rule and acting in accordance with a rule is central to how it conceives personhood and proposes to investigate it.[39] There are internal, grammatical connections between what our uses of abilities-and-skills concepts entail and the distinction between types of rules.

In Wittgenstein's sense, "rule" is a metaphor "intended to cover everything that people do in a more or less orderly fashion . . . wherever the distinctions between doing something correctly or incorrectly, carefully or carelessly and so on can be applied."[40] *Following a rule* is to carry out an activity on some form of explicit instruction (e.g., the swearing-in of an elected government leader). *Acting in accordance with a rule* is to act in a more or less orderly way while carrying out some activity (e.g., waiting in line at a movie theatre). Our actions in carrying out explicit and implicit rules *express* those rules. Basically, the grammatical distinction is between following explicit rules and acting in accordance with implicit norms. As with abilities, both types of rule-behavior are *normative* in at least two ways: they require explicit or implicit instruction in the form of teaching practices and the practices that express the rules are subject to standards of correctness. Obviously, in our day-to-day lives we act in accordance with rules far more often than we follow rules.

---

[37] J. L. Austin, A plea for excuses. *Proceedings of the Aristotelian Society* 57 (1957) 1–30.

[38] Harré doubtless has Wittgenstein in mind when he says "There seems to be a remarkable similarity between the techniques and results of analytical philosophy and those of discursive psychology." See R. Harré, Discursive psychology and the bounds of sense. *Organization Studies* 25 (2004) 1,435–1,453.

[39] Harré and Gillett, *The Discursive Mind*, p. 120. Wittgenstein's extended discussion of rules and rule-following occurs in *Philosophical Investigations*, §§143–242.

[40] Harré and Tissaw, *Wittgenstein and Psychology*, 123.

The idea of rule-expression is extremely important. It means that people need not (and do not) check anything "inner" in order to determine whether or not they or other persons are able to carry out practices competently, in accordance with explicit rules or implicit norms. The criteria for following rules and acting in accordance with rules are "outward." We do not consult brain states and/or processes in order to assess whether or not a child knows the alphabet. This is not to deny that the brains of children change in some way as they learn the alphabet. As observed previously, it is to say that brain states and/or processes are *irrelevant* to our assessment of whether the child has or has not learned the skill – is able to express the rules of recitation of the alphabet. The expression of a rule is in the practice itself. Grammatically, there is no "gap" – interpretive or otherwise – between a rule and the practice that realizes it, as the practice realizes the rule and the rule is realized in the practice.[41]

It is tempting to think that there is an *empirical* connection between carrying out some practice according to explicit rules or implicit norms, teaching practices, and standards of correctness. In keeping with our example, this likely is due to our knowing that a teacher's assessment of whether or not a child can recite the alphabet is a procedure. The *procedure* occurs and in that sense we may think of it as empirical; but the connection between rules, teaching practices, and standards of correctness is grammatical. We can see these internal grammatical connections by exploring the boundaries of sense. Saying "She can recite the alphabet!" presupposes that she has been taught to do so and failure (or partial success) at previous attempts to follow explicit rules. That a youngster can recite the alphabet without training, without having tried and failed, makes no sense.

We have yet to see the connection between all of the above and the claim that our use of abilities-and-skills concepts is to be explained in terms of means-to-ends, or active (intentional) engagement in normative practices. Wittgenstein does this in many ways, often obliquely. Harré does so directly by linking the training of rule-following to *dispositions*, which in turn brings us again to reasons for acting.

The idea is that when a person is being trained to follow a rule they are "being equipped with a disposition to respond to certain conditions in certain ways . . . not causally compelled to do so."[42] The purpose of a parent repeatedly telling their young child to "Stay close to me" is to equip the child with a disposition not to wander off on their own. They are being taught an explicit rule that will evolve gradually as the

---

[41] Harré and Tissaw, *Wittgenstein and Psychology*, 127.
[42] Harré and Gillett, *The Discursive Mind*, 121.

child matures, perhaps to an explicit instruction to be home each day or evening by a certain time. A standard cause–effect explanation for the effects of the explicit rule can gain traction only if we overlook the fact that the parent and child can (and do) explain the rule in terms of *reasons for acting*. For example, to a friend's query as to why they have to go home, a 12-year-old can say "Our family has dinner at six." This is to give a reason for an intended action (walking home) – not to state a *cause* for one's behavior. In other words, a rule gives a person

the tools to formulate certain reasons for action. It does so by giving them an adaptive and discursive reason to organize their activity in certain ways. The reason is the advantage attached to the use of a technique that has an established signifying role in the structure of social adaptation by their linguistic group. The evaluations and relationships within that discursive context give an actor a reason to incorporate a given range of... meaningful responses in their manifest behavior in certain conditions but neither the rule, nor the context, nor any set of conditions compels a person to behave thus and so in a mechanical or crudely deterministic way.[43]

The immediately foregoing should not be taken as crediting persons with "implausible freedoms." Human beings develop into persons in contexts not of their own choice and those contexts include historically and culturally situated practices and physical limitations that influence – even constrain – what they can become as persons. But discursive psychology insists that with respect to the domain of "the psychological," persons have some choice in organizing their day-to-day interactions with other persons and thereby organizing their lives.

This brings us to Harré's contributions to "positioning theory" as it pertains to personality development.[44] The courses and outcomes of interactions between and among persons are based, in part, on the ways in which they distribute rights and duties in discursive practices. Parents who prevent their 18-month-old from touching a hot cup of coffee assume and express an authoritative moral position within the discursive exchange. It is the sort of position that we do not expect infants to assume. We may expect an older sibling to assume and express a similar – but not quite the same – position with respect to a younger sibling who reaches for a container of hot liquid. The *ways in which* positions within discourses are expressed, maintained, and so on is a subject worthy of empirical research. But *that* there are positions to be assumed and

[43] Harré and Gillett, *The Discursive Mind*, 120–121.
[44] R. Harré and L. Van Langenhove, Varieties of positioning. *Journal for the Theory of Social Behavior* **21** (1991) 393–407. See also R. Harré and L. Van Langenhove (eds.) *Positioning Theory: Moral Contexts of Intentional Actions* (Oxford: Blackwell, 1999).

expressed is shown in the rules of word use (or grammar) pertaining to relationships of persons exercising discursive practices. The meanings of "teacher" and "learner" are relatable in part by the differing positions teachers and learners assume and express in their discursive practices with each other and other persons.

It is easy to see that the same sort of connection must hold between positions people express and what we mean by "personality," in virtue of the words persons use to speak of themselves and in the words other people use to speak of them. To be a person is, among other things, to assume and express positions in many discursive practices requiring social abilities and skills. To say that a person commits to certain positions within discourses they adopt is to say something about their personality, in particular the skillfulness with which they exercise their abilities to engage in rule-governed discursive practices. How did they come to be able to adopt positions in the first place? We might propose that they are given an "unskilled position" when they are born – perhaps even prior to that.

"Psychological symbiosis"

Well before formulating his discursive psychology, Harré appropriated the metaphor of "psychological symbiosis" to explain how personhood is acquired by very young human beings. It is intended to capture "the processes by which merely animate beings become self-conscious agents" in the "social episodes in which certain kinds of language games are played, engendering talk with appropriate cognitive properties, for instance self-expression of feelings and intentions."[45] This is where grammar meets the empirical. The grammars of abilities-and-skills concepts (including everything associated with teaching practices and standards of correctness, active engagement, and means–ends explanations in terms of reasons), rules, dispositions, and ostensibly positions all come into play in the minute-by-minute interactions within the symbiotic dyad of care-giver and infant.

Of course, the developmental research literature is replete with examples of interactions between care-givers and infants that could be described in terms of the symbiosis metaphor.[46] My concern here is not to discuss the character of these interactions even in very general

---

[45] R. Harré, *Personal Being: A Theory of Individual Psychology* (Cambridge, MA: Harvard University Press, 1984) 105.

[46] See for example my account of the concept's origins and uses by a number of developmentalists in M. Tissaw, Psychological symbiosis: Personalistic and constructionist considerations. *Theory and Psychology* **10** (2000) 847–876.

terms, but to emphasize the teaching relationship of a person already equipped with the abilities characteristic of persons and a human being not so equipped who is working towards the status of personhood.

We might say the processes of psychological symbiosis resemble what occurs in Vygotsky's zone of proximal development.[47] The difference is that one member of the dyad at first has no abilities, whereas in the zone of proximal development everyone has abilities.[48] How does the care-giver get the infant moving towards personhood? The answer is *supplementation of behavior with psychological abilities*. According to Harré, the care-giver begins by interacting with the infant *as if the infant has some of the abilities of a person*; as if the infant is a person to at least some extent. Symbiosis is not marked by the care-giver talking about the infant's needs, emotional displays, and so on. It is marked by the care-giver supplying the infant with some of what it is to be a person psychologically by supplementing the natural behaviors of the infant human being. That the overall goal is personhood is clear: "Psychological symbiosis is a supplementation by one person of another person's public display in order to satisfy the criteria of personhood with respect to psychological competencies and attributes in day-to-day use in a particular society in this or that specific social milieu."[49] Harré's second use of "person" in this above quote is not a mistake. What may count as psychologically symbiotic exchanges can and do occur after the achievement of personhood. Thus, Christina Erneling uses the symbiosis metaphor to explicate and defend her "domestication model of language acquisition."[50] This brings us to some important differences between early and later contexts of psychologically symbiotic exchanges. In early exchanges especially, care-givers must exploit the instinctive, natural behaviors of their infants. This is a brute fact of nature which may or may not be as relevant to later exchanges that involve implicit teaching and learning of language and other behaviors that express rules. However, grammatical investigation shows that the initial learning of language is based on trust, prior to the learning of doubt. It makes no sense to say that an infant has mastered the ability to doubt prior to learning to use words. As Wittgenstein puts it, "the child learns by believing the adult. Doubt comes after belief."[51]

---

[47] L. Vygotsky, *Thought and Language*, M. i Rech' (trans.) and A. Kozulin (ed.) (Cambridge, MA: The MIT Press, 1986).

[48] An infant's reflexes are not to be counted as abilities because it makes no sense to say that one is skilled at a reflex.

[49] Harré, *Personal Being*, 105.

[50] C. E. Erneling, *Understanding Language Acquisition: The Framework of Learning* (Albany, NY: State University of New York Press, 1993).

[51] L. Wittgenstein, *On Certainty*, G. E. M. Anscombe and G. H. Von Wright (eds.), D. Paul and G. E. M. Anscombe (trans.) (New York: Harper and Row, 1972) §160.

It is an easy step from here to Holiday's argument that societies *preserve the norm of truthfulness by sustaining sincerity and trust.*[52] In learning to use language, infants and young children naturally gain fundamental "moral powers."

It really makes no difference whether or not the psychology of personhood includes psychological symbiosis as part of its standard fare in explaining the development of persons. However, as a contributor to developmental science, at the very least the discipline must abide by the conceptual distinction between human beings and persons and should emphasize the processes of psychological supplementation that make personhood possible and contribute to each human person's individuality.

So, at what point does a human being become a person? The question may be inspired by a hankering for preciseness. I do not think there can be a clear answer to it. To the question of whether a "blurred concept [is] a concept at all," Wittgenstein asks: "Is an indistinct photograph a picture of a person at all? Is it even always an advantage to replace an indistinct picture by a sharp one? Isn't the indistinct one often exactly what we need?"[53] The words "person" and "personhood" are exactly what we need. They are useful, we know what they mean because we know the possibilities of their use and we have a good idea of how and why we can go wrong with their use.

Conclusion: on the moral positioning of human beings and persons

At several points we have seen that grammatical investigation indicates that "person" does not apply to all human beings. To address the possibility that this may be unsettling to some readers, the results of grammatical investigation need not predicate how members of any culture regard the status and treatment of human fetuses, neonates, and the mentally challenged. These are matters of value (not fact) and Wittgenstein is to be credited with distinguishing between grammars of fact and grammars of "form of life." Our uses of words – and investigation of them – *always* have to do with our values. (Even "grammars of fact" are value-laden.) In this way, investigation into "animal," "human being," and "person" is not merely grammatical investigation. In three ways it is *expression of values.* First, investigating our language to expose sources of confusion is one of many ways to try to make our world a better place. Second, at every turn

---

[52] A. Holiday, *Moral Powers: Normative Necessity in Language and History* (London: Routledge, 1988).

[53] Wittgenstein, *Philosophical Investigations*, §71.

grammatical investigation includes investigation into the moral codes by which we live. For the ways we use words are not fixed necessarily to the world of facts. They are connected to our training as members of a culture and there is no such thing as a culture without values. Part of what it means to be a human person is to be a member of a culture and we cannot separate "culture" from activities and artifacts that express values. Third, grammatical investigation affords accurate and responsible *empirical* explanation of the psychology of human beings and persons, as captured in the metaphor of psychological symbiosis. It results in a portrayal of human beings and persons as *agentive potentialities; not as things* composed of psychological parts that cause thinking, behavior, social interactions, and so on. In this way, especially, the goals of grammatical investigation share much with other perspectives on personhood.

3 Achieving personhood: the perspective of hermeneutic phenomenology

Charles Guignon

Becoming a person from the standpoint of hermeneutic phenomenology

Hermeneutic phenomenology is a movement in philosophy that can be traced back to Martin Heidegger (1889–1976) and, above all, to his seminal work, *Being and Time*.[1] Though this early Heideggerian work undertakes to reflect on the question "What is it to be in general?", only two of the projected six divisions were ever published, and those two (making up about 500 pages) focus on the narrower question, "What is it to be a human being?" It would be a mistake to think that, in asking this question, Heidegger is concerned with identifying the necessary features of human beings as such. Instead, he asks about what he calls *Dasein*, a German word meaning "existence," but used by Heidegger as a technical term to designate human beings insofar as they have an understanding of being. It should be clear, then, that the term "Dasein" denotes a subset of human beings and does not include infants, the comatose, or those suffering from extreme dementia.

Heidegger obviously has a great deal to say about what makes an entity an instance of Dasein in his special sense. But, in the second division of this work, he sets his sights even higher and tries to capture what he calls an "authentic" way of being Dasein. Following hints in works that follow *Being and Time*, I will suggest that this characterization is an attempt to capture what it is to be a *person*.[2] My concern in what follows will be to clarify Heidegger's conception of an authentic individual in order

---

[1] M. Heidegger, *Being and Time*, J. Macquarrie and E. Robinson (trans.) (New York: Harper and Row, 1962, orig. 1927).

[2] See, for instance, Heidegger's use of the word "person" and related terms in *The Essence of Human Freedom: An Introduction to Philosophy*, Ted Sadler (trans.) (London: Continuum, 2005), e.g., section 26a, The Essence of Man (Humanity) as Person (Personality), Personality and Self-Responsibility, 182–183. Heidegger carefully avoided any reference to "persons" in *Being and Time* because he thought the word had become so faddish that it carried too much potentially misleading conceptual luggage. See page 73 for an example of his rejection of the word.

to show how he understands the most fulfilled and realized form of personhood.

In order to initially demarcate what I am trying to get at in attributing this goal to Heidegger, it will be sufficient at the outset to draw on the characterization of the being of a person found in a contemporary author who was strongly influenced by hermeneutic phenomenology, namely, Charles Taylor. In his essay, "The concept of a person," Taylor suggests that a person is a human being who can be understood as an agent with certain capabilities: "A person is a being who has a sense of self, has a notion of the future and past, can hold values, make choices, who in short can adopt life-plans." To have these capacities, Taylor continues, a person must be "a being with its own point of view on things. The life-plan, the choices, the sense of self must be attributable to him as in some sense their point of origin. A person is a being who can be addressed and who can reply," and so may be called a "respondent." As a respondent, a person is *responsible* and can be held morally responsible for what he or she does. On my reading of this concept, a person is a human being who is able to be a *moral agent* in a very robust sense of that word.

Heidegger holds that human beings neither start out as persons nor do they automatically develop into persons. Instead, he sees becoming a person as an *achievement*. Heidegger would certainly grant that we are all capable of becoming persons – he holds that the "potentiality-for-being" a person is an "essential structure" of Dasein.[3] But, as will become apparent, he thinks that such an achievement requires a transformation that perhaps only a few will actually accomplish. At the same time, however, personhood is said to be the condition for fully realizing our identity as humans. The English word "authenticity" is a translation of the German word *eigentlich*, which means, among other things, "really" or "genuinely"). A condition for being human in the fullest sense, then, is that one achieve authenticity.

Before turning to Heidegger's account of authentic personhood, it will be helpful to say a bit about the method of hermeneutic phenomenology. One component of this method is, of course, *phenomenology*, a method first introduced by Heidegger's teacher Edmund Husserl (1859–1938). As Husserl conceives it, phenomenology has no interest in providing explanations in the way the sciences do, nor does it produce metaphysical speculations about what must obtain for the world to be as it is. In contrast to traditional methods, phenomenology is solely concerned with *description*, that is, with trying to characterize what things are like as

[3] What is meant by such terms as "potentiality-for-being" and "essential structure" will become clearer as we proceed.

they show up for us in our prereflective, pre-theoretical experience. For Husserl, this means initially "bracketing" or "holding in abeyance" the uncritical assumptions that make up the seemingly self-evident beliefs of "common sense" and the sciences. Phenomenology claims that the sciences, as well as so-called common sense, always operate with presuppositions about what things are. If we are to describe things as they present themselves in pre-theoretical experience, then, we need to set aside or put out of play these assumptions and strive to produce a presuppositionless, unbiased characterization of the subject matter that concerns us. On Heidegger's interpretation of phenomenological method, we must avoid making any reference to the mental, the physical, or to various kinds of causal connections. Our sole goal is to describe and clarify what initially appears on the scene as it appears – that is, the "phenomena."

Heidegger moved beyond Husserl's views by claiming that phenomenology, if it is to be a successful philosophical method, must also employ the method of hermeneutics, the "theory of interpretation."[4] Hermeneutics starts from the recognition that human phenomena are always essentially meaning-laden, so that any attempt to understand these phenomena must grasp the meanings shaping what humans do. Hermeneutics also holds that the meaning of human actions and creations is accessible to us because we ourselves are meaning-endowing beings who are part of a shared, intelligible lifeworld. Hermeneutic inquiry therefore always has a circular structure: it starts out from our often tacit sense of what things are all about, uses that background of understanding in order to interpret particular phenomena, and on the basis of these concrete interpretations revises its initial general sense of meanings making up the lifeworld. Hermeneutic phenomenology claims that in understanding the human, we are always trapped in a "hermeneutic circle," though this circularity should be seen not as something negative, but rather as something positive: it is the enabling condition that first gives us access to the human in general.

It is worthwhile saying a few words about hermeneutic phenomenology because, although the components of its name are recognizable, it is certainly the road less taken in psychology and philosophy. The dominant approach in both fields for nearly two centuries has been the movement or collection of movements known as naturalism. Though "naturalism" can be defined in different ways, its main claim is that the methods and ontological presuppositions of the natural sciences are sufficient

---

[4] See What Is Hermeneutics? In F. C. Richardson, B. J. Fowers, and C. B. Guignon, *Re-envisioning Psychology: Moral Dimensions of Theory and Practice* (San Francisco: Jossey-Bass, 1999) 199–236.

for understanding any phenomena whatsoever, including human phenomena. This means, among other things, that qualified researchers can objectively specify facts about components of the world, can formulate testable generalizations explaining the behavior of those entities in causal terms, and can produce intersubjective agreement concerning these facts and generalizations through replicable observation and experimentation. The "default setting" of contemporary naturalism is a thoroughgoing physicalism, the view that all that exists in the universe is physical substance in the sorts of causal relations countenanced by the best natural science of the day (or, alternatively, by the ideal natural science toward which all current research approximates).

The most common view of hermeneutic phenomenologists concerning naturalism is that its ideal may be appropriate to large areas of natural phenomena, but that it is completely inappropriate for understanding human beings and their creations. Naturalism presupposes what we might call an "objectifying ontology." It assumes that everything that exists can be objectively specified and understood in terms of univocal generalizations concerning initial states and outcomes. The ideal of objective specification presupposes an ability to abstract out meanings and values from the phenomenon as it appears (what Wilfrid Sellars calls the "manifest image"), in order to regard reality as consisting of material substances and processes interacting in law-governed ways (the "scientific image").[5]

It should be obvious that hermeneutic phenomenology is at odds with naturalism as an approach to the study of humans. First, this sort of phenomenology brackets the uncritical presuppositions that make up common sense and the sciences. Among these presuppositions is the seemingly self-evident assumption that human reality must consist of physical organisms that are products of evolution and interact with their physical surroundings in ways characterizable in terms of scientific generalizations. Note that what is put in question by the hermeneutic approach is not just physicalism, but *any* ontology that assumes that humans are substances of some sort, whether that substance is regarded as physical, psychical, or some combination of the two. What is in question, given hermeneutic phenomenology, is what might be called the *substance ontology* itself.

Second, hermeneutics puts into question the idea that we can gain access to raw, value-neutral, meaning-free "facts" about objective properties of the human. From its perspective, in contrast, the human is

---

[5] Wilfrid Sellars, *Science, Perception, and Reality* (Atascadero, CA: Ridgeview Press, 1963) 5–9 and *passim*.

always meaning-laden, defined by the significances it absorbs from its socio-historical context.

Finally, hermeneutic phenomenology challenges the assumption that empirically discoverable generalizations about causal relations can be discerned in the study of humans. It holds, instead, that insofar as humans are "self-making" or "self-constituting" beings, there is no reason to expect to find fixed, unchanging regularities underlying their behavior. There are indeed what Heidegger calls "essential *structures*" of humans – such characteristics as temporality, historicity, sociability, finitude, thrownness into a world, and projection into possibilities. But these structural aspects of the human cannot be reduced to empirically discovered, law-like causal determinants of objects. They are instead features of what might be thought of as the "scaffolding" or underlying "armature" that makes possible the creative, constantly changing self-interpretations of humans.

Given these claims, it should be expected that the claims of hermeneutic phenomenology might seem outlandish to mainstream naturalist thinkers. But, they may also seem like a breath of fresh air in an area of inquiry that often seems bogged down in dubious "just so" stories, easily refuted "laws of human behavior," and what Charles Taylor calls "wordy elaborations of the obvious."[6]

The structure of human agency and socialization

Following the dictates of phenomenology, Heidegger brackets the ordinary assumption that humans must be regarded as organisms of a special sort, and instead proposes we think of human agency as a special sort of *movement*. For his characterization of human agency, he draws on Aristotle's writings on life and human being. In the *De Anima*, according to Heidegger, Aristotle defines a human as a moving being (*kinein*) who can engage in discursive reflection through *logos*. What makes humans distinct from other animals, on this account, is that they are motivated by and make decisions on the basis of an anticipation of what is to come. "Thereby," Heidegger says, "humans face the possibility of an opposition between [on the one hand] *epithemia*, sheer 'appetite,' impulsive life, which is blind, and [on the other hand] understanding, action grounded in reasons."[7] In other words, what makes humans unique among animals

---

[6] Charles Taylor, *Human Agency and Language, Philosophical Papers, Vol. 1* (Cambridge University Press, 1985) 1.

[7] Martin Heidegger, *Basic Concepts of Ancient Philosophy*, R. Rojcewicz (trans.) from Heidegger's 1926 lecture series (Bloomington: Indiana University Press, 2008) 229. For

is that what motivates them to act originates from two different levels of desire. In a way comparable to other animals, humans act on the basis of first-order desires, ordinary impulses to satisfy some need or urge. When they are hungry, for example, they typically will find something to eat. At the same time, however, they can act on the basis of second-order motivations that are discerned by reason and pertain to the worthiness of their first-order desires. They can ask, for example, whether this food is fattening, and can thereby refrain from eating it if they are concerned about their appearance.

This two-tier structure of motivation, with its opposition between impulse and reflection, "is a possibility open only to those living beings which can understand time. Insofar as a living being is delivered over to impulse, it is related merely to what is immediately there . . . [to] what is present." But humans, because they possess a sense of time, can make present to themselves the future "as the possible and as that for the sake of which they act."[8] Understood as moving beings, as agency, human existence involves a *double comportment*: in our active lives, we can take a stand on our immediate urges and desires through a higher-order understanding of what our lives are all about, that is, through a projected understanding of the "being-a-whole" of our lives as that "for the sake of which" we act.

For Aristotle, what is definitive of the human is the relation between these two levels of motivation in the ongoing movement of life. Aristotle calls the first-order level of agency *poiesis*, mere making and producing, in which the work to be produced, the *ergon*, is distinct from the acting itself – as, for instance, a builder builds a house for someone to live in. In the second level of agency, *praxis*, the work to be accomplished is not something distinct from the action but rather "resides in the doing itself," in "the acting being as such." So, for example, practicing dancing can be for the sake of being a dancer (even though it may have other goals as well). As Heidegger sees it, specifically human actions involve both *poiesis* and *praxis*: for example, a doctor acts to produce health in another (an end distinct from the action), yet at the same time is concerned with being a good doctor (an end contained in the action). In this respect, all action is for the sake of being a person of a particular sort. We are self-making or self-constituting animals.

a related discussion, see C. Guigon, Heidegger's concept of freedom, 1927–1930. In D. Dahlstrom (ed.) *Interpreting Heidegger: Critical Essays* (Cambridge University Press, 2011) 79–105.
[8] Guigon, Heidegger's concept of freedom.

Heidegger appropriates this Aristotelian conception of human agency in providing his initial characterization of Dasein. According to *Being and Time*, Dasein's being (what it is) consists of a "relationship of being," a relation in which Dasein's day-to-day life is always *at issue* for it. In what we do, our lives are at stake for us insofar as they are undertaken and taken up in terms of where we are heading in our lives as a whole. This means that *who* one *is* (one's "being" as a whole) is at issue for one in all one does (one's being as living out one's life). In this sense, our everyday being (*who* we are as agents in the world) is in question for us, and so is something we *care* about in the course of everyday agency. What Aristotle shows us, on Heidegger's reading, is that a human is defined by its capacity to assess and motivate its present actions in the light of some overarching life-plan it has formulated for itself – the "for the sake of which" of all its actions.[9]

But the life-plan that guides a person's active life is not something that resides in his or her head, as if it were a consciously formulated conception of a goal to be attained. If that were the case, then action would be purely instrumental, a matter of producing outcomes according to a preconceived agenda. Instead, the life-project for one's existence is brought to expression and worked out through the concrete stands one takes in actually living out one's life. We find ourselves *thrown* into a world that is not of our choosing, but once we are in that world, we find ourselves faced with an array of possibilities or choices that are laid out in advance by the cultural context in which we find ourselves. On the basis of these possibilities, we can enter into professions, come to embody personality types, develop distinctive sorts of character, and undertake such mundane actions as riding a bicycle, doing the laundry, or reading a novel. Whether we realize it or not, we are always choosing possibilities of action in what we do. Thus, Heidegger says, "Only the particular Dasein *decides* its existence, whether it does so by taking hold or by neglecting. The question of existence [i.e., of who we are] never gets straightened out except through existing [i.e., actually doing things] itself."[10] In this sense, we *are* what we *do*. Deliberation and rationalizing may play a role in this unfolding "happening" (*Geschehen*) of a life, but what is crucial to a person's identity as an agent is not so much what goes on in her mind as the way her actions at any time figure into the composition of her life story as a whole.

Heidegger suggests that much of what we do in "average everydayness" is conditioned by our enculturation into the practices and forms of life of a particular community – the "They" (*das Man*) into which we find

---

[9] Heidegger, *Being and Time*, 32.   [10] Heidegger, *Being and Time*, 33.

ourselves thrown. For the most part, we do what "one" (*man*) does according to the norms and standards laid out by the "anyone" of which we are a member. I buy and wear the clothes that are available in stores, and these are roughly the same clothes that others wear in my social circles and profession. In the grocery store, I pick out the kinds of food most people in my community buy and I prepare and eat them as others do. I drive on the right-hand side of the street at a speed within the range that others drive, generally observing the rules of driving etiquette that are the norm within my community. Being the "They," in the sense of developing the familiar competence in coping with the world we all have, is the result not so much of explicit observation and rule recognition as it is of a largely tacit *attunement* (*Stimmung*) to cultural practices, a matter of getting into sync with the cadences and patterns of life exemplified within the surrounding community.[11] In the process of this enculturation, we become so tuned in to the everyday ways of doing things that much of our lives take the form of doing what "one does," running on automatic, going with the flow. As essentially *being-with* others, we tend to become fairly typical representatives of the They.

Heidegger's most enduring and influential innovation has been his conception of humans as essentially *being-in-the-world*. The hyphens in this expression indicate that this is a "*unitary* phenomenon."[12] To say that being-in-the-world is "unitary" is to say that it cannot be understood as something that is pieced together by connecting two initially separate items, for example, self and world or consciousness and mere things. On the contrary, what the term is meant to describe is that humans are always inextricably bound up with a worldly context, where "world" is to be understood in the existential sense in which we speak of "the world of business" or "the academic world." We find ourselves "always already" enmeshed in significant situations of action that determine not only how anything can count or matter to us, but *who or what we are* as agents in those contexts. In opposition to the Cartesian tradition, Heidegger claims that there is no "I" or "self" distinct from the familiar totalities of relevance in which we dwell. Our relation to the world is first and foremost a matter of hands-on engagement in practical activities within familiar worksites and equipment. It follows that phenomena such as perception and cognitive processing can appear on the scene only derivatively through abstraction from our most primordial practical "dealings." Prior

---

[11] The best account of the development of our familiar know-how of public forms of skilled coping is Hubert L. Dreyfus, *Being-in-the-World: A Commentary on Heidegger's "Being and Time," Division I* (Cambridge MA: The MIT Press, 1991).

[12] Heidegger, *Being and Time*, 78.

to any being as a "self," and prior to any attempt to hook up mind and material world, we exist as the unified totality of meaningful involvement in a shared field of practical significance.

Authenticity as the realization of the potential for personhood

Throughout *Being and Time*, Heidegger maintains a distinction between two fundamental "essential structures" of Dasein. These are (1) being the *They*; and (2) being an *Authentic Self*. Heidegger emphasizes that these essential structures are "potentialities-for-being," not properties or attributes of an object of some sort. To say that they are "potentialities" is to say that they are "ways of being" that may manifest themselves in a variety of ways (including "privative modes" such as rebelling against) but are always there as underlying conditions for realizing oneself as a person.

We have already seen the respect in which Dasein is the They. As irreducibly social beings, we are invariably participants in the wider context of a historical culture, caught up in practical activities we carry out according to norms laid out by our community. This involvement in familiar practical affairs is Heidegger's development of the Aristotelian dimension of *poiesis* or productivity in the two-tiered structure of Dasein's agency. The notion of an "authentic self," in contrast, is somewhat puzzling. The term *seems* to suggest that Dasein has a "self" component in addition to its engaged, communal being-in-the-world. On such an interpretation of the notion, a human being would consist of two items somehow related into the unity of a self. But, I believe that there is another way to understanding the idea of an authentic self. In my view, what Heidegger has in mind with this term is the second dimension of the structure of human active life identified by Aristotle, the dimension of *praxis*. To say that Dasein is always an authentic self, then, would be to say that in all our actions there is, in addition to the action of producing some product, the fact that Dasein's actions are "for-the-sake-of-itself." Every action contributes to constituting one's own being *as* an agent of a particular sort, so that human agency is always and inescapably a matter of self-making. The "authentic self" would refer to this activity of self-making and, derivatively, to the self so made in this activity.

We saw that, for Aristotle, the phenomenon of praxis both presupposes and makes possible the temporal structure of human life. Actions are normally directed toward satisfying needs in the present, of course. But, on Aristotle's view, they are also aimed at realizing and defining the life of the agent as a whole. Or, to put this point differently, we might say that our comportments toward things in everyday action are organized around or directed by a unifying motivational set – the "for-the-sake-of-which" that Heidegger calls "existence." Because our actions are focused on a unifying end – that is, being a person of a particular sort – they are adding up to a whole that has some sort of meaning, whether we recognize this or not. As "being-toward-the-whole," we are constantly drawing on the past for our resources and imparting significance to what we do in the present in terms of where our lives are heading overall. It is this temporally extended, holistic organization of action that Heidegger calls the "authentic self." It should be evident, then, that this "authentic self" is not a *thing* of any sort. On the contrary, it is the temporality of life itself.

Because our agency is always complicit in the project of self-making, each of us has an "authentic" (*eigentlich*, a term implying "own" or "most proper") task set for us, namely, taking over the project of defining our own identity through what we do. This is what Heidegger means when he says,

Dasein has always made some sort of decision as to the way in which it is in each case mine. That entity which in its being has this very being as an issue, comports itself towards its being [its life as a whole] as its ownmost possibility. In each case Dasein *is* its possibility . . . [and because of this] it *can*, in its being, "choose" itself and win itself, [or] it can also lose itself, i.e., never win itself, and only "seem" to do so.[13]

Given the fact that each of us *cares* about our being (that is, we care about what our lives amount to), we can and do take some stance in relation to this being in our everyday being (that is, in doing the things we do). The stance we take in our concrete undertakings is called the *projection* of possibilities through comporting ourselves toward ourselves. Dasein's being is *care* in the sense that it is projected forward into possibilities, already in a world, and dealing with what shows up in its world.[14]

To be "authentic" or "owned," on this view, is to keep this authentic self in focus, even when one is absorbed in the day-to-day business of life. As authentic, we live in such a way that our actions express the fact that we are always constituting ourselves as beings of a particular sort. Authenticity pertains not to *what* we do – it is not a matter of the particular roles we happen to adopt in our worldly existence. Instead, it has to do with *how* we live. The authentic person owns and owns up to being an entity that is engaged in a constant activity of self-construction. In owning

---

[13] Heidegger, *Being and Time*, 68; translation modified.
[14] See Heidegger, *Being and Time*, 237.

3 2783 00131 4411

PRAIRIE STATE COLLEGE
LIBRARY

50   *Charles Guignon*

itself, the authentic Dasein is for the first time genuinely *responsible* for itself: it is capable of being a respondent and giving meaningful responses to questions about what it is doing and why.

Heidegger marks this difference between inauthentic and authentic existence with an expanded characterization of what it is to "choose." As we noted earlier, all of us are making choices all the time. If I drive to work rather than walking, I am choosing to be a driver, regardless of whether or not I realize that I am making this choice. But, even though we are constantly making decisions, we typically do so in such a way that these decisions involve just doing what "one" does as "one" does such things. We choose and act, but we do not really stand behind our choices, nor can we fully stand up for our choices. In contrast to this everyday way of being an inauthentic "they-self," Heidegger suggests, becoming authentic involves "choosing to choose," that is, making a choice to "be-one's-self."[15] This involves resolutely taking responsibility for one's actions and knitting those actions together into a meaningful whole that one can stand up for and own. Although Heidegger does not use the term "person" to refer to the authentic self, we might say that it is only by becoming authentic that a (genetically) human being fully becomes a *person* as Taylor defines this term. The authentic individual is guided by a life-plan (his or her "projection"), has a point of view of his or her own, holds values and makes choices on the basis of those values, and can be a "respondent" in the sense of taking responsibility for his or her actions.

Authentic historicity and involvement in historical events

Heidegger makes it clear that his account of authenticity is motivated by the goal of uncovering the structures of "authentic, primordial temporality," the distinctive time-structure that underlies and makes possible any understanding of any sort of being whatsoever.[16] Whereas inauthentic They-existing tends to be dispersed and distracted, lacking coherence or continuity, authentic existence has the kind of connectedness and unity that lets us see what human lived time is all about. In an earlier work, Heidegger insisted that Dasein is not *in* time, but *is* time: "Dasein, conceived in its most extreme possibility of being, *is time itself*, not *in* time."[17] Dasein's own temporal being makes possible our familiar ways

---

[15] Heidegger, *Being and Time*, 314.
[16] Heidegger tells us that all particular modes of temporality have their "source in temporality which is primordial and authentic" (Heidegger, *Being and Time*, 374–375).
[17] Martin Heidegger, *The Concept of Time*, W. McNeill (trans.) of a 1924 lecture (Oxford: Blackwell, 1992) 13–14.

of understanding entities of various types – for example, objects seen as enduringly present, equipment that shows up as teleologically organized towards goals, mathematical entities that endure "forever," historical events that took place in the past, weather forecasts about the future, and so forth.

The temporal basis for the intelligibility of all entities depends on the distinctive structure of human existence understood as a "happening" or "movement" (*Geschehen*). The primary dimension of human lived time is the *future* (in German the word for "future," *Zukunft*, comes from stems meaning "coming-toward"). Dasein, in its practical life, exists as a continuing thrust forward toward realizing certain goals, a forward-directedness that is itself made possible by its directedness toward its "ownmost" possibility, its life-long "way of being" as *being-towards-death*. This movement towards the future constitutes the "for-the-sake-of-which" of *praxis*: everything we do is done *for* being a person of a particular sort. The commitments and undertakings that define our futurity in turn throw us back onto our *past*, where this "having-been" (*Gewesenheit*) is seen as making up the assets or resources available to us for any sort of action. So, for example, a person's education gains its meaning from the way it is put to use in the project of achieving something for her life. Only through its relationship to futural projects can the past be meaningful and for that reason be carried forward, whether as an asset or as a liability. Finally, the meaningful conjunction of future and past makes possible a *present* in which one's situation can appear as making a specific sort of demand on one, as calling for some specific type of action. Heidegger emphasizes that a genuine life situation (*Situation*) can show up for a person only by virtue of its having a place within the meaningful, interwoven whole of past and future that makes up that person's life story.[18] On this account, then, action must be understood as emerging out of an entire life course, not through an act of will that causes some physical movement (like the tip of a shoe hitting a soccer ball).

As we have seen, the individual's life story is always inextricably embedded in the wider context of the unfolding of a historical culture. As unfolding life-stories, we are both products and producers of history (*Geschichte*, which means both "story" and "history," is related to the word designating human life, *Geschehen*, "happening"). According to

---

[18] Heidegger uses two German words that can be translated by our English word "situation": *Lage* (which means general circumstances) and *Situation* (which is a technical term referring to a life context that is filled with import, and where in a "moment of vision" a life-transforming leap becomes possible). The English translation distinguishes these by using the upper case for the second, existential use of the word. I will follow this orthographic convention by rendering occurrences of *Situation* with the upper case.

Heidegger, Dasein is historical in a dual sense. First, its own existence has a story-shaped structure to the extent that, as in any coherent story, events occurring in the present are intelligible only in relation to (1) where the story as a whole is going; and (2) where the sequence of events is coming from. Because Dasein at any time is the crossing-point of both past and future, Heidegger can say that

Dasein "is" its past, [which] "happens" out of its future on each occasion. What-ever the way of being it may have at the time, and thus with whatever understand-ing it may possess, Dasein has grown up both in and into an understanding of being that has been handed down to it ... Its own past ... is not something that follows along after Dasein, but something which already goes ahead of it.[19]

Second, Dasein's understanding of itself and of entities generally has been shaped in advance by the "tradition" that is transmitted from the past, an understanding that comes to be ingrained in us as part of our competence in participating in the forms of life and linguistic skills of our historical community. This tradition is both our window onto any sort of intelligibility at all and a source of the leveling down of possibilities that blocks creativity and originality. Dasein's relation to tradition is therefore ambivalent: it must respect and even "revere" the possibilities of being that make it the entity it is, while at the same time challenging and rethinking that tradition in defining its own existence.

Heidegger's most substantial account of the being of what we think of as a "person" comes toward the end of *Being and Time* in his discussion of *authentic historicity*. Section 74 of *Being and Time* begins with a reca-pitulation of the account of human existence that has been developed throughout the book. To be human is to be a *thrown projection*, where that means that human beings are distinctive in the fact that they are projections onto possibilities (roles, personality traits, concrete projects, undertakings) who draw their sense of what is "possible" from the range of meanings made accessible by the historical culture into which they find themselves. The meaningful possibilities, which are made accessible to us from the average, everyday understanding of the They, are encoun-tered as a manifold of options available to us. In average everydayness, choosing among them is most commonly a matter of simply following the fads in our current cultural context. As we have seen, the everyday "They-self" tends to be adrift, floating along with what is "acceptable" in its circles, being a team player. In other words, the historicity of Dasein's life is for the most part inauthentic.

---

[19] Heidegger, *Being and Time*, 41.

When Dasein achieves *authentic historicity*, the mode of being that correlates with being a "person," the character of both its thrownness and its projection are transformed. Heidegger says that, in authentic historicity, the They possibilities that provide our sense of what is possible are encountered not as the only way to go, but instead as a *heritage* or *inheritance* (*Erbe*) made up of possibilities of understanding that are genuinely binding on us because they are definitive of who we are in our historical context. This distinctive way of understanding our thrownness is opened up by a clear-sighted grasp of the significance of the fact that we are mortal beings with finite possibilities.

Only by facing up to and embracing [*Vorlaufen in*] death is every accidental and "provisional" possibility driven out. Only being-free *for* death gives Dasein its goal outright and pushes existence into its finitude. Once one has grasped the finitude of one's existence, one is snatched back from the endless multiplicity of possibilities which offer themselves as closest to one . . . so that one's Dasein is brought back to the simplicity of its *fate* [*Schicksals*].[20]

As authentically historical, one's life is taken over as a matter of one's own choosing, and one gains both the lucidity needed to understand what the current situation requires and the focus and resoluteness needed to act in a way for which one is ready to be held responsible. Such an individual takes up a role model from his or her historical past and strives to emulate it in all he or she does. The authentic person, Heidegger says, "choose[s] its hero" and is "free for the struggle of loyally following in the footsteps" of the Dasein that has come before.[21] In doing so, it does not blindly follow some historical precedent. Rather, it exists as a "reciprocative rejoinder" (*Widerruf*) to what has come before, constantly putting it in question, reinterpreting it, and carrying it forward in all it does.[22] An individual becomes a *person* in this strong sense by "repeating" or "retrieving" possibilities of action from the communal history that it now encounters as a shared *destiny* (*Geschick*): "In repetition, fateful destiny can be disclosed explicitly as bound up with the heritage which has come down to us."[23]

Consequences for ethics and politics

As I have presented Heidegger's views, the correlate of what is called a "person" is the authentic individual, the person whose being is characterized by authentic historicity. This conception of personhood obviously

[20] Heidegger, *Being and Time*, 435; translation modified slightly.
[21] Heidegger, *Being and Time*, 437.   [22] Heidegger, *Being and Time*, 438.
[23] Heidegger, *Being and Time*, 438.

sets a very high standard for counting as a person, a standard that enables us to distinguish genetically human beings from those we would call persons. Though this characterization of a person might be criticized as elitist, we should keep in mind how Aristotle made clear the benefits of envisaging an extremely high ideal even if very few could attain it.

Yet, a more serious objection to this image of personhood might be formulated as follows. Everyone knows that Heidegger threw his hat in with the Nazis when they came to power six years after *Being and Time* was published, and it is well known that Heidegger told his friend Karl Löwith in 1936 that it was the concept of historicity he developed in *Being and Time* that "was the basis of his political 'engagement'."[24] So, the troubling question arises of whether there is something essentially fascist or proto-Nazi about the conception of historicity in *Being and Time*.

I have discussed this issue at length in my essay "History and commitment in the early Heidegger."[25] For now, it is enough to say that Heidegger's conception of authentic historicity, with its ideal of a leap of commitment based on one's best understanding of the demands made by the "world-historical Situation" at a given time, no doubt motivated his behavior in 1933. But, this fact does not indicate that the idea of historicity is inherently fascist, or even that by itself it supports any particular political orientation. In fact, the most likely model for the idea of authentic historicity, Martin Luther's "Here I stand" shows only that Luther was willing to follow his conscience and beliefs, following in the footsteps of his heroes, the Christian martyrs of the early Church, to take a stand in the current situation (or "Situation") as he saw it. Moreover, we might see respected figures in recent times as models of authentic historicity. Dr. Martin Luther King Jr., for example, understood the biblical "heritage" of America, and followed in the footsteps of early American pastors in incorporating biblical cadences and terminology into his speeches in order to persuade the American public that racism is a betrayal of America's ideals – its "heritage" and "destiny." American progressives as well as dedicated conservatives often seem to instantiate the idea of authentic historicity in varying degrees. What we do know about Heidegger is that, faced with what most Germans at his time perceived as a choice between international socialism (Bolshevism) and a national socialism, Heidegger sided with the latter. His ugly behavior

[24] Quoted in Richard Wolin (ed.) *The Heidegger Controversy: A Critical Reader* (Cambridge, MA: The MIT Press, 1993) 152.
[25] In H. L. Dreyfus and H. Hall (eds.) *Heidegger: A Critical Reader* (Oxford: Blackwell, 1992) 130–142.

after making that decision should be seen as the result of his own personal opportunism and predilections, not of anything in his philosophy.

The concept of a person has traditionally been bound up with very strong ethical and political convictions. The concept of personalism, which was developed by Max Scheler and by Catholic thinkers such as Emmanuel Mounier and Karol Wojtyla (who later became Pope John Paul II), made fundamental the idea of the absolute value of the person, together with the strong ethical responsibilities that result from that value. To attribute personhood to a being on this account would therefore have important political significance, for it would require thinking of people as having a higher worth than other beings. Heidegger, in contrast, has often been accused not only of failing to develop an ethical theory, but also of failing to say anything that might clarify the relationship between his ontological thought and ethics. Asked by a French student in 1946 about the relationship of his philosophy to ethics, Heidegger wrote a long and obscure essay titled "Letter on Humanism," the main thrust of which is to dismiss the question by suggesting that the entire field of philosophy called "ethics" fails to appreciate how human action is partly dependent on "being" itself.[26]

Heidegger's views are correctly said to be "anti-humanist" to the extent that they put in question the extreme anthropocentrism and correlative denigration of the mundane world often found in various forms of personalism. But does this mean that Heidegger's thought should be understood as anti-ethical? Or, might it mean that he is formulating a different kind of ethics, a type of ethical thinking perhaps closer to radical environmentalism than to mainstream ethics? It is certainly true that Heidegger does not produce any writings on ethics, where "ethics" means formulating tables of values, devising purportedly universal rules for human action, or engaging in casuistry. In his writings, he often gives hints as to why he thinks such undertakings, standing in isolation from any reflection on underlying assumptions, tend to be either fatuous or vacuous. But, if we take "ethics" to include Aristotle's *Nicomachean Ethics*, then we may find something very similar in Heidegger's magnum opus. Aristotle does not spend any time producing rules or principles for action, and he seldom gives us any clue as to how particular moral puzzles should be solved. Instead, his interest is in clarifying what a human agent must be like in order to be an effective moral agent. The *Nicomachean Ethics* deals with personal formation, with the conditions for being able to see what situations call for, and thereby with being able to act as morally

---

[26] See Letter on Humanism. In M. Heidegger, *Martin Heidegger: Basic Writings*, D. F. Krell (ed.) (San Francisco: Harper, 1993) 213–266.

responsible agents. As we have seen, however, Heidegger's *Being and Time* undertakes exactly the same project. In trying to show how an agent can become authentic – that is, in our terminology, can become a *person* – his concern is to show what it takes to be able to make meaningful choices in concrete "Situations" that confront us in extreme moments of choice. In this respect, although we might disagree with Heidegger's account of what a person is, we cannot accuse him of failing to develop an ethics.

Part II

Historical perspectives

4   Historical psychology of persons: categories and practice

Kurt Danziger

Introduction

The fruit of research never falls on previously untilled soil. Not only are there likely to be previous relevant findings, but the target of the research will have a label that incorporates a certain pre-understanding of its nature. The discipline of psychology tries to discover new knowledge about objects that it identifies in terms taken from the common language, terms whose present meaning was established some time in the past.[1] In doing so, the discipline helps to change that meaning, but the change always begins with what was received from the past. Acknowledged or not, the shadow of past transformations of understanding hangs over present-day innovation, circumscribing the conceptual alternatives available for consideration, limiting the direction of steps towards a different future.

Shadows of the past vary greatly in their depth and intensity. Many of the objects that attract current psychological attention are not all that old in terms of human history. Test intelligence, cognitive dissonance, and post-traumatic stress disorder, for example, are inventions of the twentieth century, and claims that they were always there, though unacknowledged, require somewhat arbitrary historical speculations. "Persons," on the other hand, have been recognized as objects worthy of explicit conceptualization for a very long time. The term and its cognates are among the few in modern psychology – "memory" being another – that have a really deep history. A *specifically psychological* understanding of persons emerged relatively late in that history and was effectively superimposed on rich layers of alternative meanings. The relationship between these levels is so murky that serious doubts have been expressed about the usefulness of "person": "The term itself is already a thoroughly abused concept... The list of meanings itself

---

[1] K. Danziger, *Naming the Mind: How Psychology Found its Language* (London: Sage, 1997).

could provide us with a judicial and political history of the English language."[2]

Rather than throw up their hands in despair, most psychologists simply ignore the problem and get on with their empirical work. Raw empirical data always require interpretation before they acquire any psychological meaning, an interpretation that depends on verbal categories with a semantic history. When personality researchers publish their findings, they are assumed to contribute to our knowledge about something that is already believed to exist, something already identified and given a label with a certain sense in common language use. The knowledge in question is assumed to be about something identified as "personality" and not as the immortal soul or as the moral character, to mention only two possible but implicitly rejected alternatives.

Some of those who were most active in founding a viable field of personality psychology, notably Gordon Allport, were only too well aware of the need to differentiate the new psychological conceptualization from various historical alternatives. But once the field became established historical amnesia took over. This has had two unfortunate consequences. First of all, some of the most distinctive characteristics of personality psychology simply became taken for granted, incorporated in instruments whose use transformed conceptual questions into technical issues. As a result, some of the most basic assumptions of the field disappeared from view. Second, as in so much of the discipline, the line separating the new approach from what went before was drawn so sharply that much of what might have been productively assimilated was abandoned to other disciplines or simply consigned to oblivion.

In the last section of the present chapter, I address the first of these issues. The earlier sections attempt some illumination of the second issue. However, given the multitude of meanings attached to "person," it is necessary to set some boundaries. In principle, everything that has ever been implied about the nature of the human individual, for example in works of poetry or drama, could be considered part of the history of this concept. Philosophical or medical works might also carry such implications, even when they do not directly address the topic.

One way of hewing a path through this labyrinthine and potentially boundless territory is to use the history of a key word and its cognates as a marker for explicit use of the concept and as a thread to follow changes of use over time. This does not always work, but it works reasonably

---

[2] H. J. Stam, The dispersal of subjectivity and the problem of persons in psychology. In W. E. Smythe (ed.) *Toward a Psychology of Persons* (Mahwah, NJ: Erlbaum, 1998) 221–244 (241).

well for "person," with one noteworthy exception: at a certain point, the history of "person" virtually disappears into the history of "self." As I have previously given some consideration to this topic, I will deal with it lightly here.[3] For earlier periods, using the Latinate "person" as a historical marker avoids questions of translation and interpretation that would be inappropriate in the present context and are better left to specialist publications.

The history of concepts, especially over longer periods, does not typically follow one uninterrupted course. More usually, there are interruptions, replacements, new beginnings, and above all, there is not one line of development but several that may or may not meet. Concepts of the person are no exception. Over a long period, there were several new starts that added additional layers of understanding to a category that was always complex. Even in Roman times, persons were defined in two different though related contexts, legal and moral. Subsequently, other kinds of person became important, and each section of this chapter provides hints regarding their most significant characteristics. These changes on the level of understanding were usually accompanied by corresponding changes in social practices often linked to legal, religious, medical, and scientific institutions. But this is not an institutional history, and so I have limited myself to drawing attention to changes in *literary* practices involving personal documents, especially autobiographies, and to a crucial scientific practice considered in the final section of the chapter.

Legal persons

Because of its concern for definitions and its close link to social practice legal discourse provides a useful entry point to the history of the concept of "person." In medieval Europe and beyond, legal discourse was strongly indebted to basic principles of jurisprudence that had been codified by the Emperor Justinian in the sixth century AD.[4] One of the basic concepts enshrined in Roman law was that of the legal person. Though not unchanging, this understanding of "person" provided a relatively stable cultural presence against which later developments had to assert themselves. At the end of the seventeenth century the philosopher John Locke, whose writings ushered in a new era for conceptualizing the human individual, still referred to "person" as "a forensic concept."

---

[3] K. Danziger, The historical formation of selves. In R. D. Ashmore and L. Jussim (eds.) *Self and Identity: Fundamental Issues* (New York: Oxford University Press, 1997) 137–159.
[4] "From the eleventh century to the eighteenth and even beyond, the main feature of legal change in western continental Europe was the Reception of Roman law." A. Watson, *The Evolution of Western Private Law* (Baltimore: Johns Hopkins University Press, 2001) 193.

The Justinian Code was itself based on the work of earlier Roman jurists who had developed a set of fundamental concepts that enabled them to systematize the collection of specific laws handed down from previous generations. Many of the relevant pre-Justinian texts have been lost, but an important one was rediscovered in the nineteenth century. Around 160 AD its author, Gaius, had formulated the classical juridical trinity by indicating that "all the law which we use pertains either to persons or to things or to actions" (*de personis, de rebus, de actionibus*).[5] Laws provided a formal regulation of potential conflicts involving these three fundamental entities. The legal person was not a standalone concept but part of a network of concepts designed to represent those aspects of the social order that were the target of formal regulation and legal sanctions. These targets might be actions, as in the case of theft or murder, they might be things that could be inherited and possessed, or they might be persons who assumed obligations involving other persons.

In this context, the criterion of personhood was the capacity to enter into obligations in such a way that one could be held legally responsible for fulfilling those obligations. For this reason, young children were not held to be persons. They were "minors" under the guardianship, *tutela*, of designated adults, usually a father, who was responsible for them and their actions. Women also had the status of minors. So the status of "person" was far from being a universal human characteristic. Slaves (of whom there were many) also lacked this status. They were not minors (who had some rights) but mere possessions that could no more enter into legal obligations than could a domestic animal. However, slaves could be freed through the deliberate choice of their owner, and in due course a freed male slave might even become a legal person. Personhood was something that males could attain, sometimes by good fortune, though more usually by reaching the age of maturity. But when was that? When one could be held responsible for one's obligations, the criterion stipulated. Legal decision making demanded a distinct threshold for personhood but it was not easy to reach agreement on the marker of that threshold. Some authorities favored chronological age, others the bodily signs of puberty.[6]

In this context, the concept of the person singled out a particular minority of the human population as the privileged bearers of special rights and obligations. This minority was also politically privileged. In

[5] D. R. Kelley, *The Human Measure: Social Thought in the Western Legal Traditions* (Cambridge, MA: Harvard University Press, 1990) 49.

[6] T. G. Leesen, *Gaius meets Cicero: Law and Rhetoric in the School Controversies* (Leiden: Nijhoff, 2010).

ancient Rome, they had the status of citizens of the state, and within their household or "dominion" they exercised complete authority. Legal personhood was also part of the political order, though after the disintegration of the Roman Empire the politics of personhood became more fragmented. They also became more complicated because of the growing influence of a Christian Church that functioned as a second source of law, canon law. The Church was committed to a doctrine of universalism that attributed to each and every human individual an immortal soul. In the long run, this meant loosening the exclusivity of the status of personhood and gradually extending some of its benefits to previously excluded categories of people.

Moral persons

Positive law assumes the existence of some sense of right and wrong among those it covers. Ideally, its appeal is to existing concepts of what is just and what is not, and when it conflicts with those concepts it will be ignored or opposed. It often arises out of an existing moral order, and the sanctions it provides are meant to uphold that order whenever it is flagrantly threatened.

In the case of Roman law, we can get quite a good idea of the moral order within which it originated because the period just before and during its systematization produced a significant body of literature dedicated to moral education, literature that was respected in its own time and sometimes influential many centuries later. Moreover, much of it has survived. Some of this literature contains references to the concept of the person, providing us with the context for a crucial change in the use of the Latin term *persona* that had previously referred to the masks worn by actors on a stage. By the first century BC, the theatre was becoming a metaphor and the term is given a more general meaning that is closer to "social role" than to an actor's mask.

The most explicit and most influential example of this development is found in a book of advice directed at his son by the Roman politician, writer and philosopher, Marcus Tullius Cicero (106–43 BC). The title of the book is usually translated as "On Duties" but, as a recent translator points out, "On Obligations" provides a better rendering of the essentially moral connotations of the original.[7] This is no quibble, because it is all too easy for the modern reader to overlook the fact that, once it left the theatre, "persona" was for a very long time a term of moral philosophy.

---

[7] P. G. Walsh, Introduction. In M. T. Cicero, *On Obligations* (Stanford, CA: Stanford University Press, 2000) xvii.

The observation that an actor puts on different masks to play different roles on stage initially served as a metaphor for the way in which each individual faces different obligations in relation to different aspects of the human condition. In this vein, Cicero tells his son that in the conduct of his life he, like others, will have to pay attention to four kinds of responsibility. In the first place, he ought to conduct himself as a rational human being, not as a creature governed by impulse. Second, he needs to take into account the special features of his own make-up and to realize that being true to oneself entails different things for different people. Wise actors do not always opt for the best plays but for those most suited to their talents.[8] Third, the social circumstances of our lives, being born rich or poor, noble or commoner, assuming public office, all impose particular obligations on us that should be respected. Finally, we have to recognize that our own life choices create situations that bring new obligations with them. This happens when we decide on a certain career, for example.

Cicero's attempt at guiding his son is useful for alerting us to the gulf that separates the modern meaning of "persona" from its ancient meaning. The term is still in use today to refer to the way individuals present themselves in a particular social situation, to their literally playing a role. At times this simply amounts to faking it. But this is not what Cicero is advising his son to go in for. Quite the contrary, each of the four *personae* he mentions involves some serious moral purpose. What he takes from the theatrical analogy is not that the actor wearing a mask is some sort of fake but that the same actor is obliged to conform to different requirements in different roles. Each role entails its own set of obligations; the role requirement is given with the role. That is why the idea of a role can serve as an illustration of moral obligation.

What is also important for this understanding of "persona" is the notion of perfectibility. Actors can play their roles well or badly. Some play them superbly. As an actor on life's stage, one ought to perform as well as possible, always trying to improve. This principle sets the tone of the guide books of moral education. For the Stoic philosophers, whom Cicero followed, life offered constant challenges for moral improvement.[9] This is not a significant component in the modern understanding of "persona," but it was critical for the moral understanding of the person as actor.

---

[8] M. T. Cicero, *On Obligations* (Stanford, CA: Stanford University Press, 2000), part I, 114.

[9] P. Hadot, *Philosophy as a Way of Life* (Oxford: Blackwell, 1995).

In this understanding, moral values were experienced as part of the world, not as an individual preference. There is no private subjective stage from which an autonomous self regards the world beyond. The individual person is always embedded in some set of public obligations: "*no* aspect of the person was 'private' in any way meaningful to modern westerners."[10] One's own individuality is not the source of one's values but the source of one set of shared obligations among others. Our individuality does not define us but should be morally respected.

The lives of others could function as models of upright conduct or as bad examples. In his advice manual, Cicero frequently refers to historical figures whose lives and deeds provide specific illustrations of the principles he propounds. A similar intention is also evident in early examples of the genre of biography, though in this case it is the illustration that occupies the foreground and the moral lesson which forms the background. In his collection of *Lives*, Plutarch presented the stories of notable individuals in such a way as to make their actions signify qualities of moral character that could provide lessons for the reader.[11] Only relatively recently did the tradition of moral biography yield to the more modern form that employs a more subjectivized narrative.[12]

In contrast to biography, the genre of autobiography could hardly be said to exist in classical antiquity. In his monumental effort to cover the history of this genre, George Misch could find only eight cases that might be regarded as autobiographies for all the centuries of Greek and Latin antiquity.[13] Most of these were "speeches in self-defence," that is to say, extended descriptions of the circumstances of their lives offered in way of excuse, exculpation, or denial of responsibility by individuals who had been publicly accused of serious transgressions.[14] Such documents are similar to biographies in that there is an attempt to present an individual life as a whole, but such presentations typically take place in a moral or legal context.

---

[10] T. J. Reiss, *Mirages of the Selfe: Patterns of Personhood in Ancient and Early Modern Europe* (Stanford, CA: Stanford University Press, 2003) 237.

[11] Plutarch, *Roman Lives: A Selection of Eight Roman Lives*, R. Waterfield (trans.) (New York: Oxford University Press, 1999); and also Plutarch, *Greek Lives: A Selection of Nine Greek Lives*, R. Waterfield (trans.) (New York: Oxford University Press, 1998).

[12] C. Gill, *The Structured Self in Hellenistic and Roman Thought* (Oxford University Press, 2006).

[13] G. Misch, *A History of Autobiography in Antiquity* (London: Routledge, 1950). This translation covers only a relatively small part of the author's life work on the history of autobiography.

[14] A. Momigliano, Marcel Mauss and the quest for the person in Greek biography and autobiography. In M. Carrithers, S. Collins, and S. Lukes (eds.) *The Category of the Person: Anthropology, Philosophy, History* (Cambridge University Press, 1985) 83–92.

Persons of substance

Morality and the law were not the only contexts in which the original meaning of "persona" was significantly extended. The term was used in texts on rhetoric, an important field in classical antiquity, and also in grammar, where three "persons" were distinguished with respect to the use of verbs: the speaker, the one spoken to, and the one spoken about. This analytic usage was generalized to the interpretation of literary and philosophical texts, for example the Platonic Dialogues, where identification of the persons implicitly playing a role in certain verbal interactions made a difference to the meaning of the text.

This rather specialized usage appears to have played a role in the early development of a field in which questions of "person" and "personality" were to become quite prominent, namely, Christian theology. For a religion whose doctrines relied heavily on sacred texts in a foreign language (Hebrew), the closely related questions of correct translation and exegesis were inescapable. Because in the relevant religious texts divinity takes on at least two forms, father and son, and probably three (the Holy Ghost), the relationship among these forms became a matter of supreme interest for Christian theologians. A religious institution that was fast becoming centralized and autocratic required an explicit dogma against which heresy could be defined, and questions about the relative status of the three forms of divinity soon became central for the early Church Fathers. As they had often been trained in pre-Christian techniques of text analysis, they easily adopted a formulation of these questions in terms of the "persons" of the divine. Trinitarian dogma eventually became crystallized in the formula *tres personae, una substantia* – three persons, one substance – also rendered as one nature.[15] Related debates addressed the dual aspect of Christ which was described in terms of the union of human and divine natures in one person.

In medieval theology, the category of "person" was explicitly limited to individual creatures with the gift of rationality: humans, angels, and God. An essential attribute of human individuals was their immortal soul, and this led to an emphasis on the internal unity, the indivisibility, of the human person.[16] Echoes of this emphasis survive to this day, though its origins are not always recognized.

Though all humans might be granted a soul, their personhood could be qualified. For example, a text dating to 1234 is reported to have stated that it was "through baptism in the Church of Christ that a man

[15] Aurelius Augustinus, *On the Holy Trinity* (Grand Rapids, MI: Eerdmans, 1956).
[16] St. Thomas Aquinas, *Summa Theologica* (New York: Benzinger Bros., 1947).

becomes a person."[17] More generally, human personhood was regarded
as imperfect though potentially perfectible. It was very much a matter of
degree rather than an invariable human attribute. In confessional texts,
individuals constantly compare themselves to persons more perfect than
themselves, to saints and to other exemplary figures from sacred or sometimes secular literature.[18]

One might say that the key variable for personhood was now *worthiness*. Imperfect beings could be accorded various degrees of worthiness,
depending on their moral conduct and their social standing. It was a
quality primarily attributed to certain classes of people, with individuals
being able to claim worthiness on the basis of their actual or potential
membership of these classes. In secular texts, "person" carried a con-
notation of social standing, generally involving elevated rank and due
respect, but occasionally the opposite. It defined individuals in terms of
their place in a hierarchical network of social positions, not in terms of
their unique characteristics. Persons had a singular existence, but this
was not defined in terms of what set them apart from others, their individuality, but in terms of the way in which they exemplified generally
valued human qualities.[19]

Persons apart

Although earlier conceptions of the person never died out completely,
particularly when supported by legal or religious institutions, their prominence gradually declined as a new understanding of the term emerged.
Speaking very broadly, this new understanding can be characterized as
individualistic, though there were many facets to that, and these did not
develop in any synchronized manner, with regard to either place or time.
There is a huge literature of potential relevance to this development, but
there are certain aspects that must be regarded as particularly significant for the later emergence of specifically psychological conceptions of
personhood.

First of all, one encounters an enhanced sense of the separateness
of each individual. By the seventeenth century this receives explicit,
even radical, expression in a new way of depicting the basic relationship
between people. This, in the rather sweeping summary of one French
scholar, is "the epoch in which the individual discovers his isolation."[20] In

---

[17] A. Gurevich, *The Origins of European Individualism* (Oxford: Blackwell, 1995) 90.
[18] M. Carrithers, *The Book of Memory: A Study of Memory in Medieval Culture* (Cambridge University Press, 1990).
[19] Gurevich, *Origins*.
[20] G. Poulet, *Studies in Human Time* (New York: Harper, 1959) 13.

earlier times, it had generally been taken for granted that participation in a life shared with others was the natural state of human beings. Individuals were always embedded in social "circles" of family, kinsfolk, citizenship, friendship, authority relations, and so on.[21] Social status entered into the definition of personhood, as we have seen. In reflective discourse there was a respect for traditional authority that seems misplaced to the modern reader but was often little more than an expression of solidarity with a particular intellectual community. By way of contrast, René Descartes (1596–1650), the prominent seventeenth-century philosopher, does not write as a member of any community: he reports on his own introspective efforts to work out a viable philosophical position and invites his readers to try out these thought experiments for themselves.[22] As one might expect, his philosophy is much less concerned with social being than with what goes on within each separate individual.

His contemporary, Thomas Hobbes (1588–1679), on the other hand, was very interested in working out the social consequences entailed by the essential separateness of each individual. In doing so, he provided a view of the person that was very different from what had gone before. People are naturally solitary, he claims: "Men have no pleasure (but on the contrary a great deal of griefe) in keeping company."[23] Human behavior can be entirely explained in terms of mechanical processes within separate individuals whose natural relation to each other is one of "war of every one against every one." People always want what others have, so they live in fear of each other. However, they are rational enough to grasp that they could escape this state of constant inter-individual strife by coming to some mutual arrangement for limiting their naturally anti-social tendencies. As a result, they enter into "bonds" or contracts reciprocally restricting their power to harm others or obliging them to render certain services to others. This is how individuals are able to live with each other. Peaceful social co-existence is based on contract, not on people's inherently social nature.

In this model, all speech is individual speech and all action is individual action. A person is defined as the owner of the words and actions that belong to him (Hobbes does not consider women). He may enter into "covenants" with other persons regarding these possessions, as he would with any other possessions.[24] He may also delegate another person to

---

[21] Reiss, *Mirages*; also C. Gill, The ancient self: Issues and approaches. In P. Remes and J. Sihvola (eds.) *Ancient Philosophy of the Self* (New York: Springer, 2008) 35–56.

[22] R. Descartes, *A Discourse on the Method of Correctly Conducting One's Reason and Seeking Truth in the Sciences*, I. Maclean (trans.) (Oxford University Press, 2006, orig. 1637).

[23] T. Hobbes, *Leviathan* (Oxford: Clarendon Press, 2006, orig. 1651) ch. 13.

[24] Hobbes, *Leviathan*, ch. 16.

speak or act on his behalf in return for specified services rendered by the other person.

The idea of defining persons in terms of their ability to enter into contracts with other persons was not new, as we saw in the section on legal persons. But relationships governed by formal legal concepts and requirements had remained a relatively small part of the domain of social relationships that linked people to each other. Kinship, a common language, a shared symbolic world, and group loyalties are just some of the frames for human relationships that existed without any involvement of legal concepts. What was new and shocking in the Hobbesian world was the claim that contract was the basis for *all* interaction among individuals, insofar as that interaction was not antagonistic. By expressing this claim in a particularly forthright and brutal way, Hobbes provided a useful foil for arguments purporting to show its limitations. But there was always a lingering suspicion that it did describe, if not a universal human condition, at least a set of beliefs on which many people act much of the time in commercial civilization.[25] One did not need to be a Hobbesian to see the world as populated by separate competitive individuals, each an owner of personal qualities and capacities that could become the objects of contractual arrangements with other individuals. One's identity as a person would then be quite separate from one's social relationships.[26] In broad cultural circles, beliefs of this kind became increasingly taken for granted, and Hobbesian assumptions are readily detectable in contemporary psychology.[27]

Psychologically significant post-Hobbesian developments of social contract theory are usually associated with the names of John Locke (1632–1704) and Jean-Jacques Rousseau (1712–1778). Both accepted the original and fundamental separateness of individuals but, far from being Hobbesian mechanisms, their individuals were endowed with a complex inner life. Increasingly, it is this inner life that comes to dominate conceptions of the person until well into the twentieth century.

After asking what "person" stood for, John Locke provided an answer that relied on a term that had only recently been introduced into the English language, namely "consciousness":

---

[25] For eighteenth-century elaborations, see E. J. Hundert, The European Enlightenment and the history of the self. In R. Porter (ed.) *Rewriting the Self: Histories from the Renaissance to the Present* (London: Routledge, 1997) 72–83.

[26] M. Hollis, Of masks and men. In Carrithers *et al.*, *The Category of the Person*, 217–233.

[27] J. Martin and J. Sugarman, A theory of personhood for psychology. In D. B. Hill and M. J. Kral (eds.) *About Psychology: Essays at the Crossroads of History, Theory and Philosophy* (Albany, NY: State University of New York Press, 2003) 73–87.

For since consciousness always accompanies thinking, and it is that which makes every one to be what he calls self and thereby distinguishes himself from all other thinking things, in this alone consists personal identity, i.e. the sameness of a rational being: and as far as this consciousness can be extended backwards to any past action or thought, so far reaches the identity of that person.[28]

Here, being a person was defined, not in terms of an individual's social being, as had been the case in the past, but in terms of inner, private being. What makes me a person is my constant awareness of myself as the same conscious entity now and in the past. On this view, moral accountability does not define personhood but is itself a consequence of acting consciously. Individuals are to be held responsible for their actions only insofar as they acted in full consciousness of what they were doing.

In the years preceding the appearance of Locke's *Essay*, members of some Protestant sects had already been promoting a marked inward turn of religious experience.[29] And there had been many examples of soul searching among Christians before that.[30] But Locke's philosophy was a secular one. The conscious self he posited as a person's core was not to be equated with the Christian immortal soul. It was a this-worldly phenomenon open to empirical inspection like any other natural phenomenon. Not surprisingly, Locke's views were taken very seriously in the course of the European Enlightenment but aroused resistance among defenders of more traditional doctrines.

The secular inward gaze had the potential of developing in two very different directions. One could adopt Locke's own sharply analytical attitude to private experience and dissect consciousness into its elements. That was the path of David Hume and a long succession of (mostly British) associationists. But on this path the individual person tended to disappear behind a curtain of general psychological laws that applied

[28] J. Locke, *An Essay Concerning Human Understanding* (New York: Dover, 1959), Book II, ch. 27, 449. The excerpt is from the second edition originally published in 1694.
[29] Well known English examples are provided by Richard Baxter (1615–1691) and John Bunyan (1628–1688). Their writings were analyzed from a perspective that is particularly relevant in the present context in K. J. Weintraub, *The Value of the Individual: Self and Circumstance in Autobiography* (University of Chicago Press, 1978), ch. 10. For a more general account of seventeenth-century tendencies to privatize attempts at achieving salvation, see especially N. Luhmann, The individuality of the individual: Historical meanings and contemporary problems. In T. C. Heller, M. Sosna, and D. E. Wellbery (eds.) *Reconstructing Individualism: Autonomy, Individuality and the Self in Western Thought* (Stanford University Press, 1986) 313–325. The emergence of autobiography as "a cultural practice" and its relation to earlier practices, such as diary keeping, is covered in M. Mascuch, *Origins of the Individualist Self: Autobiography and Self-identity in England, 1571–1791* (Stanford, CA: Stanford University Press, 1996).
[30] This aspect is stressed in M. Carrithers, An alternative social history of the self. In Carrithers *et al.*, *The Category of the Person*, 234–256.

to everyone. Far more consequential for later conceptions of the person were the pre-occupations of a complex cultural phenomenon that became known as Romanticism. Several of these pre-occupations became part of a common understanding of personhood that persisted long after Romanticism's ascendance.

What remained was first of all an insistence on the *singularity* of individual experience that ran counter to virtually all previous discourse on the subject of the person. Of course, people had long been aware of the fact that no two individuals had exactly the same feelings or precisely the same personal qualities. But those had been regarded as rather trivial matters, not at all the sort of consideration that might affect one's conception of what it meant to be a person. Very few individuals had ever written accounts of their lives that a post-Romantic reader would recognize as genuine autobiographies. Some had written accounts of their deeds and public achievements, others of their religious lives. But almost always the focus had been on the *exemplary* nature of their experience, not on its *unique* nature. This applied even to figures such as St. Augustine (354–430 AD) who had the writing skills of a good autobiographer but who used them in his *Confessions* to illuminate his religious conversion and his beliefs so as to provide a guide for others to follow.[31]

Rousseau's *Confessions*, published in 1782, are utterly different.[32] He is quite fascinated by his own individuality, by the unique quality of his life and person, by the nuances of his inner life. Not that he had any great deeds to dwell on; quite the contrary, he was a miserable misfit and he revels in it. What gives value to his person is an essential individuality that is there, irrespective of any social entanglements. This individuality is not to be confused with the Christian soul, for Rousseau was neither a religious person nor was he "confessing" to a religious audience. He was simply giving expression to a soon to be generally held belief that to be unique was not an exceptional quality bestowed on "great men" but an essential aspect of common personhood.

Closely linked to Rousseau's highly developed sense of individuality was his awareness of his past. He takes his readers through the experiences that were important to him over the years, even the early ones. These were not matters that had any public significance; he relates them because they illustrate what kind of person he came to be. Though an essential core is implied, his individuality is not presented as something fixed but as

---

[31] Aurelius Augustinus, St. *Confessions*, H. Chadwick (trans.) (Oxford University Press, 1991). On Augustine's narrative talent and the way he employed it, see J. Olney, *Memory and Narrative: The Weave of Life Writing* (Chicago University Press, 1998).

[32] J.-J. Rousseau, *The Confessions of Jean-Jacques Rousseau*, J. M. Cohen (trans.) (Harmondsworth: Penguin, 1953).

something that can only be understood as developing over a lifetime. In this respect, too, his autobiography marked the appearance of a new dimension in common conceptions of personhood. Human individuals were increasingly felt to be characterized by their history, by the unique succession of events and experiences that had formed them. Alongside the much older idea of a public and collective history there now emerged the notion of a private history that each and every person could lay claim to.

There had been older accounts representing personal experience as a path to a religious goal, an outcome taking individuals *beyond* themselves. In the late eighteenth century and beyond individuals became increasingly wrapped up in their own history. Only now did autobiography develop as a recognized literary genre with its own conventions and clichés.[33] Childhood was paid a hitherto unheard of degree of attention and early memories began to be taken seriously. Self-disclosure was no longer unseemly.[34] Having a potentially revealing inner, private life became an important part of being a person.

The life history that now identified a particular person was always thought of as something to be *narrated*: its coherence was the coherence of a narrative. It could be looked to for help in making sense of a life, not only one's own life but also that of others. In the course of the nineteenth century, psychiatric case histories slowly began to take on some of the characteristics that had become common in autobiographies. In its early days, psychiatry, especially German psychiatry, preserved the moral significance of the revelations uncovered by probing life histories. But such tendencies were soon submerged by the medical imperative of ordering personal lives in terms of the categories of "symptoms" and "diseases."[35]

The medicalized person

By the end of the nineteenth century, there was widespread recognition of a kind of person that had been unknown a century earlier, a person with a personality disease. Certainly, there had long been people regarded as mad, and sporadic attempts had been made to keep them from interfering with decent citizens. But even in the eighteenth century, madness was only gradually coming to be regarded as primarily a medical problem.

---

[33] L. Anderson, *Autobiography* (London: Routledge, 2001).

[34] M. Sheringham, *French Autobiography Devices and Desires: Rousseau to Perec* (Oxford: Clarendon Press, 1993).

[35] G. Verwey, *Psychiatry in an Anthropological and Biomedical Context* (Dordrecht: Reidel, 1985).

In any case, madness, defined in terms of an individual's loss of reason, placed the afflicted in an altogether different category from ordinary humans, whose capacity for reason had been a defining feature of personhood since antiquity, recognized even by the likes of Thomas Hobbes. The mad were a category apart, aliens among human persons. Their sad fate was likely to call for religious rather than medical ministration.

Gradual secularization of human affairs favored the medicalization of madness, and in due course that led to the emergence of physicians who specialized in the care of the insane. Initially, this branch of medicine was closely linked to special institutions for the segregation of the insane, asylums, but in the course of the nineteenth century some doctors, often identified as neurologists, began to treat people with "nervous complaints" in their regular consulting rooms.[36] This represented a major breach in the wall separating the insane from other people, for here were patients who had not lost their capacity for reason but were unable to use that capacity to repair seriously disturbed personal lives. Once they had consigned themselves to medical care, such patients would have their situation described in terms of the already common medical categories of diseases and their symptoms.

For some time, this form of medicalization could continue without creating any problems for the definition of personhood. An individual could easily be regarded as a rational and moral being who was simply unfortunate in being plagued by some disorder located in his or her nerves. However, during the latter part of the nineteenth century some alienists in France, and then in America, began to publicize a kind of disorder that seemed to affect the personality as a whole and not just some specific function. These were cases of so-called alternating or multiple personality, where the same individual would at different times manifest completely different personal characteristics, attitudes, modes of expression, emotional tendencies, preferences, memories, and so on.[37] Often, a particular personality exhibited at one time would appear to have no knowledge of the same individual's alternate personality exhibited at a different time.

These were extraordinary phenomena, but their effect was greatly magnified by the fact that their existence was not kept hidden in obscure

---

[36] J. Goldstein, *Console and Classify: The French Psychiatric Profession in the Nineteenth Century* (Cambridge University Press, 1987).

[37] Among numerous historical accounts of these developments, see especially I. Hacking, *Rewriting the Soul: Multiple Personality and the Sciences of Memory* (Princeton, NJ: Princeton University Press, 1995); and G. P. Lombardo and R. Foschi, The concept of personality in 19th-century French and 20th-century American psychology. *History of Psychology* **6** (2003) 123–142.

medical publications but broadcast to an appreciative lay audience by members of the medical profession and by accomplished popularizers, such as T. Ribot, whose *Diseases of the Personality* reached a broad audience in several languages.[38] In days gone by, the phenomena of alternating personality would have received a supernatural interpretation, but now they could be accepted as part of the natural world to be elucidated by scientific medicine.

Those elucidations quickly led to a rupture in what had become the orthodox western understanding of personhood, the selfed person. According to this widely accepted Lockean orthodoxy, the coherence of the self that formed the core of personhood depended upon the continuity of conscious memory. Whenever I think and act, I am aware that it is I who thinks and acts, and this awareness provides the thread that holds my thoughts and acts together as those of one and the same person. So went the Lockean mantra. But in alternating personalities the thread was clearly broken. What might be happening?

Whatever the specific details of the explanations offered by medically trained experts (and a few others), the Lockean conception of the person had to be changed. An early view, linked to the prominent French philosopher and clinician, Pierre Janet (1859–1947), turned a label for the new phenomena into an explanation: dissociation.[39] Denying the continuity, the mutual accessibility, of all self-conscious states, it regarded the person as an assembly of mental contents with more or less permeable boundaries between them. Going much further, Sigmund Freud (1856–1939) proposed a division of the mind into the familiar conscious part and a much larger unconscious part. Some of the latter was accessible to consciousness but most of it was protected by a strong barrier that could only be penetrated under special conditions, such as occurred in dreaming or under the influence of particular psychotherapeutic techniques.[40] The self was reduced to just a part of this organization of the personality, and only some of it was conscious. Far from offering a universally valid concept of the human individual, the image of the consciously selfed person had become a difficult ideal imperfectly realizable by a minority prepared to invest considerable time and effort.

[38] T. Ribot, *Les Maladies de la Personnalité* [*Diseases of the Personality*] (Paris: Alcan, 1885).
[39] P. Janet, *L'Automatisme Psychologique: Essai de Psychologie Expérimentale sur les Formes Inférieures de l'Activité Humaine* (Paris: Alcan, 1889).
[40] S. Freud, *Introductory Lectures on Psycho-analysis* (London: Allen and Unwin, 1922). This is a translation, by Joan Riviere, of lectures delivered at the University of Vienna in 1915–1917 that represented Freud's first extended public systematization of his ideas. The Freud literature is of course enormous and only its existence can be hinted at here.

In the early years of the twentieth century, a new concept of the person was fast gaining credibility. The quality of unity, long the essence of individual personhood, was no longer to be taken for granted. In its place there appeared a variety of constructions that had in common a view of the person as fragmented into diverse segments whose communication with each other was always problematic. The identification of these segments varied, as did the account of their relationship to each other. In the most influential cases, including those of Freud and Carl Jung (1875–1961), the segments of the personality were not seen in one plane but as stacked on top of each other, with more power concentrated at the lower, generally unconscious, levels. Instead of unity, a dimension of *depth* was now an essential characteristic of personality.[41] Sometimes, as in the Freudian version, the deepest layer had a biological basis.[42]

What was absent from these conceptions was any faith in the pre-established harmony among the segments constituting the person. At best, a degree of harmony lay at the end of a long process, but the normal state of affairs was one of internal conflict that could easily become manifest in perpetual unhappiness, personal crisis, uncontrolled action, and diverse individual oddities identified in the language of medical symptoms. The boundary between madness and the essential rationality of the ordinary person had become frayed to the point of disappearance.

The dissected person

Even at the height of its influence, the depth psychological conception of the person was far from being the only model on offer. A major reason for this is to be found in the extraordinary fractionation of knowledge that began in the nineteenth century and continued at an accelerating pace thereafter. There was of course a huge increase of systematized public information, but this accumulation depended on a division of labor among many groups of knowledge producers, each of which specialized in a particular kind of product. One after another, these groups broke away from older, much broader and looser associations to form the "disciplinary" structures familiar to us today. In each case this entailed a sharpened focus on a delimited subject matter and a commitment to particular norms and practices of investigation that varied among disciplines. This was a highly efficient way of facilitating the accumulation of

---

[41] The term "depth psychology" seems to go back to the Swiss psychiatrist Eugen Bleuler (1857–1939), Freud's exact contemporary, who also invented the term "schizophrenia."

[42] F. J. Sulloway, *Freud: Biologist of the Mind* (New York: Basic Books, 1979).

knowledge, but it also led to its dispersal among diverse groups that generally had little incentive for communicating with each other. Economists, historians, sociologists, and psychologists, to name only the biggest groups in the human sciences, were able to develop and maintain separate conceptions of the person to suit their particular agenda. The fact that major disciplines often fragmented internally tended to compound the problem.

Ironically, psychology as a discipline was about the last of the human sciences to make room for the person. For the founders of experimental psychology the human person was not on the agenda. Their interest was strictly in *general* regularities of human functioning, such as visual space perception, sensory judgment, reaction time, and so on. Persons did not exist for them as potential objects of investigation. *Individual differences* in psychological functions did exist, but these were treated as error terms: what was psychologically significant was the general regularity of individual experience and action, not the differences among individuals.[43] Yet, about half a century after its emergence, the modern discipline of psychology did find room for a sub-discipline, identified as "personality psychology," that elaborated its own concept of the human person. For that to happen, *inter-individual* differences would have to be reconceptualized as a source of information about individual persons.[44]

This depended on dissecting human personality into distinct components that were common to all individuals. The Romantic vision of the person as a unique whole would have to be replaced by a more anatomized image of the individual as an assembly of characteristics shared with other individuals. In the nineteenth century, phrenologists, and later graphologists, had already worked with distinct components of the person that could be assessed by specialists. Enhanced social mobility had opened a new spectrum of occupational choices that would benefit from reliable knowledge of an individual's specific characteristics.[45] But the earlier attempts at providing such knowledge remained qualitative and never gained scientific respectability.

[43] K. Danziger, *Constructing the Subject: Historical Origins of Psychological Research* (Cambridge University Press, 1990).

[44] With very few exceptions, the sub-discipline of personality psychology long ignored the social embeddedness of personhood and avoided the study of individual lives. It quickly distinguished itself from its disciplinary rivals by relying very heavily on the statistical analysis of individual differences. See N. B. Barenbaum and D. G. Winter, History of modern personality theory and research. In O. P. John, R. W. Robins, and L. A. Pervin (eds.) *Handbook of Personality Theory and Research* (New York: Guilford Press, 2008) 3–26.

[45] R. Cooter, *The Cultural Meaning of Popular Science: Phrenology and the Organization of Consent in Nineteenth-century Britain* (Cambridge University Press, 1984).

A technological advance laid the basis for a *science* of individual differences.[46] As part of his life-long effort at establishing a science of heredity, Francis Galton (1822–1911) turned the focus of social statistics from the *average* person to the inter-individual differences that existed between persons. He and his acolyte, Karl Pearson (1857–1936), worked out relatively simple techniques for analyzing these differences, provided of course they were formulated quantitatively. If one had several measurements, e.g., of visual acuity, strength of hand grip, and speed of reaction, from the same set of individuals, one could obtain statistical correlations among these measures based on the inter-individual differences within the set of individuals. At the beginning of the twentieth century, Charles Spearman (1863–1945) was already applying these techniques to analyzing tests of intelligence. An important personal quality had been measured and identified. Could something similar be achieved with other personal qualities? There was never any doubt about the real existence of intrinsic qualities ascribed to socially separate individuals, the problem was how to isolate and identify them as potentially scientific objects.

Measuring quantitative differences between individuals always required some scale on which all individuals of interest could be assigned a position. That meant selecting personality components that could plausibly be regarded as common to all these individuals. Physical characteristics, such as height and weight, provided the prototype for such components, and the simple psycho-physical measurements used in Galton's "anthropometry" hewed closely to these models. The challenge for a Galtonian science of personality was to find components that were psychologically more significant and yet could be made to fit the requirements of the technology.

One way of meeting this challenge was to turn from attempts at direct measurement of personal performance to the analysis of language about personality. Here the term "trait" played a key role. Like "personality," this was not a widely used term in English at the time the "new psychology" got off the ground. But, promisingly, its use straddled the moral and the scientific realm. One spoke of character traits, but the term also occurred in biology, especially the new science of heredity and its ugly sister, eugenics. An early systematic attempt at producing a collection of trait names resulted in *The Trait Book*, published by the Eugenics Record Office in 1919, which contained a list of about 3,000 traits "that might conceivably be hereditary according to the principle of unitary

---

[46] For a detailed critical account of this development in relation to conceptions of the person, see J. T. Lamiell, *Beyond Individual and Group Differences: Human Individuality, Scientific Psychology, and William Stern's Critical Personalism* (London: Sage, 2003).

characteristics."[47] With this kind of use, the term was acquiring a meaning that was far more radically elementaristic than its use in the context of human character could ever be. A person's character was understood to constitute some kind of whole, so that any of its "traits" would be one feature of that whole. For the then science of heredity, on the other hand, a unitary trait was the expression of a somatic element that had an existence irrespective of any superordinate organization. When Gordon Allport made traits (or rather trait names) the basis of the new psychology of personality, he indicated these units were to be seen as features of a whole and not as independently defined elements.[48] However, his view did not prevail, and the most influential version of personhood associated with this branch of twentieth-century psychology took a radically elementaristic form that was historically unique.

In this construction of "personality," human individuals each possess a large number of discrete attributes that are identifiable by the fact that natural languages have words for them. By further assuming that such attributes do not change their identity because they form part of a different collection of attributes in each individual, and are also measurable, it becomes possible to assign a value for each individual on each attribute or trait. This generates a set of individual differences that can be analyzed by means of classical Galtonian techniques and their later developments. The mathematical analysis yields a somewhat indeterminate mathematical result that must be subjected to non-mathematical criteria and then given some meaningful and relevant interpretation in order to be regarded as evidence for the existence of "personality factors" common to all human individuals. Agreement on what these are was not easily achieved, but in the late twentieth century a degree of consensus emerged that there were just five, no more and no less.

Modern psychology also accommodated personality studies that did not follow this path but shared conceptions of the person with some of the older traditions already discussed. Depth psychology inspired much work in the earlier phases of personality psychology, and a turn to life history writing emerged later.[49] However, within twentieth-century psychology, a truly novel conception of the person is to be found only in the approach

[47] G. W. Allport, *Personality: A Psychological Interpretation* (New York: Holt, 1937) 236.
[48] I. A. M. Nicholson, *Inventing Personality: Gordon Allport and the Science of Selfhood* (Washington, DC: American Psychological Association, 2003).
[49] Three broad conceptual approaches are identified in D. P. McAdams, A conceptual history of personality psychology. In R. Hogan, J. Johnson, and S. Briggs (eds.) *Handbook of Personality Psychology* (San Diego: Academic Press, 1997) 3–39. For a recent overview of the history of this field, see F. Dumont, *A History of Personality Psychology: Theory, Science and Research from Hellenism to the Twenty-first Century* (New York: Cambridge University Press, 2010).

that became established as the "taxonomy" of individual traits.[50] In this case, certain assumptions about natural language provide a basis for defining individuals by their place in a linguistic network.

Empiricists in the natural sciences have usually begun with things (or phenomena) and then given them names or provided verbal descriptions, usually according to some system. However, since the emergence of personality psychology as a distinct sub-discipline in the 1930s many of its most prominent representatives have pursued an empiricism of words as the royal road to a knowledge of persons. Gordon Allport believed that "men experience a desire to represent by name such mental processes or dispositions of their fellows as can be determined by observation or by inference."[51] Therefore, culling from a dictionary 18,000 words that might conceivably be applied to persons seemed to be a worthwhile undertaking.[52] Allport and others condensed the list of applicable words and employed it as a basis for naming attributes on which individuals could rate themselves or others. Individual differences obtained in this way could then be analyzed as described above. Half a century later, the rationale for this path of nominal empiricism had become more explicit: "Those individual differences most salient and relevant in people's lives will eventually become encoded into their language; the more important such a difference, the more likely is it to become expressed as a single word."[53]

Single words are the elements of dictionaries. Indeed, in this conception the dictionary functions not only as a source of material but also as a silent metaphor for the individual person. Dictionaries break natural language into a list of separately defined units, much as the taxonomy of traits analyzes a living personality. In both cases, there is a problematic relationship between a dissected anatomy and a functioning whole, natural language in the one case, and individual personality in the other.

Languages, of course, are not collections of separate written words. They involve structural features, overlapping semantic fields and pragmatic functions. Correlations in the application of linguistic units are therefore to be expected, not least when people use language to talk about each other. Treating such correlations as an unproblematic reflection of

---

[50] In this historical study I exclude developments of the last two decades. For an historically important overview of the lexical taxonomic approach, see O. P. John, A. Angleitner, and F. Ostendorf, The lexical approach to personality: A historical review of trait taxonomic research. *European Journal of Personality* 2 (1988) 171–203.

[51] Allport, *Personality*, 304.

[52] G. W. Allport and H. S. Odbert, Trait names: A psychological study. *Psychological Monographs* 47 (1936) no. 211.

[53] John et al., The lexical approach to personality, 174.

the thing talked about implies a hidden linguistics that reduces language to its representative functions and ignores its internal coherence.[54] It also implies a pre-established conception of what is to be discovered when one investigates persons scientifically.

Looked at in a more distanced historical perspective, the striking feature of much of twentieth-century personality psychology is the strength of its faith in the objective reality of whatever it is attempting to uncover. From its beginnings, this endeavor was spurred on by the conviction that the techniques of Galtonian science would yield a significant body of non-trivial, non-artefactual psychological knowledge about the single human individual as an entity. Such convictions are by no means rare in the history of the human sciences, and without them little might ever be achieved. In the late nineteenth century, for example, there was such a conviction about the promise and achievability of a science of memory, and that certainly brought to light some things that were previously well hidden. Some philosophers refer to this kind of conviction as "deep knowledge," a sort of knowledge of what to expect before there is any real knowledge.[55] One might think of it as a knowledge niche. A confluence of deep cultural traditions regarding individuals, a more recent fad for outing "personality," a loss of moral certainties, faith in the power of dissection and of measurement, competition among disciplines: these and other factors seem to have produced a niche in which a novel conception of the person could flourish.[56]

---

[54] C. Taylor, Language and human nature. In C. Taylor, *Human Agency and Language: Philosophical Papers I* (Cambridge University Press, 1985) 215–247; F. de Saussure, *Course in General Linguistics* (New York: Philosophical Library, 1959).

[55] Hacking, *Rewriting the Soul*.

[56] The twentieth century was marked by a culture of personality chatter. Everyone, not merely persons of great accomplishment, was now assumed to have a "personality" easily described in words. Adjectival checklists for purposes of personnel selection appeared early. Entertainment and self-help literature regularly invited its consumers to engage in exercises of self-rating and self-evaluation. Talk about personal characteristics that previous generations would have considered inappropriate, embarrassing, or unseemly was now everywhere. In this respect the modern cultural history of "personality" resembled that of sexuality; see M. Foucault, *The History of Sexuality I: An Introduction* (New York: Random House, 1978).

5   Persons and historical ontology

Jeff Sugarman

In a late essay, "What is Enlightenment?," Michel Foucault frames his approach to the study of human subjectivity retrospectively as "an historical ontology of ourselves."[1] In his analysis of Kant's answer to the question posed by the essay's title, Foucault detects an innovation in philosophical thought pivotal for his own program of work. It is Kant's use of history. Unlike his predecessors, Kant does not characterize his era in terms of a totality to which all thought must be oriented or by deciphering signs that signal the future. Instead, Kant elaborates the significance of the Enlightenment by the ways it differs from the past. In Kant's depiction, the Enlightenment is a means of escape from a history of human "immaturity." This immaturity is lack of will. It is most apparent, Kant admonishes, in the habit to accede to authority rather than apply one's own powers of reason given within the limits of necessary and universal *a priori* structures of knowledge. Kant attributed to the Enlightenment a new conception of human autonomy made evident by an historical shift in understanding the relations that connect will, authority, knowledge, and the use of reason.

However, it is not Kant's interpretation of the Enlightenment that Foucault finds compelling. Rather, it is the manner in which Kant reflects on the status of his own project. Kant describes the significance of Enlightenment thought not just in terms of knowledge, but also, the time in which he is writing and how contrasting the present with the past shapes the substance of his reflections. For Kant, the present stands "at the crossroads of critical reflection and reflection on history."[2]

Foucault's attention also was drawn to Kant's focus on limits, especially those interpreted as bordering and indispensable to our constitution as autonomous subjects. Foucault adopted the Kantian approach to critique as analysis and reflection on limits, but with a crucial difference.

---

[1] M. Foucault, What is Enlightenment? In P. Rabinow (ed.) *The Foucault Reader* (London: Penguin, 1984) 32–50 (45).
[2] Foucault, What is Enlightenment? 38.

According to Foucault, Kant did not go far enough to situate himself within historical limits. While using history to outline the meaning of the present, what Kant failed to recognize were the limits that constrained his own thinking. These limits were neither universal nor necessary. Rather, they were historical and contingent. In contradistinction to Kant, Foucault pursued critique directed not to articulating the limits by which we were defined as rational or moral agents, but instead, showing where limits might be transgressed and transformed by historical particularity and contingency. "[I]f the Kantian question was that of knowing what limits knowledge has to renounce transgressing," Foucault wrote, "the critical question today has to be turned back into a positive one: in what is given to us as universal, necessary, obligatory, what place is occupied by whatever is singular, contingent, and the product of arbitrary constraints?"[3] History transforms all it touches and it is a history of particulars, not universals.

Among the lessons Foucault draws from Kant is that the ways in which we have come to recognize, interpret, and act on ourselves as subjects, only can be understood historically. We constitute ourselves at a particular place and time, with means and materials that bear the particularities of their own unique historical formations and that mark us distinctively as the kinds of persons we are. This is the sort of object Foucault has in mind for an historical ontology of ourselves. The task for historical ontology is to reveal the conditions of a complex and often contradictory past – the historical *a priori* – in which possibilities for human knowing and subjective existence are shaped. Further, by tracing the limits within which we find ourselves and using history to call them into question, Foucault offers that we might invite productive possibilities for thinking and being other than what we are.

In this chapter, I elaborate historical ontology as an approach to the study of personhood. Having briefly described historical ontology as it germinated in Foucault's work, I turn to two of Foucault's intellectual heirs: Ian Hacking and Nikolas Rose. Hacking and Rose have adopted and extended historical ontology in their critical examinations of the role of psychology and other of what Rose terms the "psy" disciplines (i.e., psychology, other social sciences, psychiatry, and related domains of clinical medicine) in the formation of various features and kinds of personhood.[4] A striking implication of their work is that failing to take into account the constitutive influence of historical, social, cultural, and

---

[3] Foucault, What is Enlightenment? 45.

[4] N. Rose, *Inventing Ourselves: Psychology, Power, and Personhood* (Cambridge University Press, 1998) 2.

political institutions has led to fixing features of persons to human nature rather than to characteristics of institutions within which we become persons. After describing and illustrating Hacking's and Rose's approaches, I turn to discussion of implications for psychological investigations of personhood.

Ian Hacking: persons as moving targets

According to Hacking, we experience ourselves as persons only by doing so under certain descriptions.[5] Personhood consists in taking up and acting in terms of the descriptions available to us. When persons become aware of how they are described and classified within their groups, societies, and cultures, they experience themselves in particular ways as a result, forming and altering the kinds of persons they are. However, individuals also can react against the ways in which they are classified. What is more, sometimes they are able to change those systems of classification and this, in turn, creates further descriptions and possibilities for personhood.

Hacking calls this interaction between systems of classification and those classified "the looping effect."[6] When the looping effect occurs and individuals change the ways in which they describe themselves, Hacking insists that they no longer are the same kinds of persons they were before. New languages of description and classification can bring about new possibilities for action and new kinds of persons. This means there can be a variety of descriptions of personhood and, consequently, many different kinds of persons.

Our practices of naming are interactive with what we name.[7] Thus, in contrast with traditional nominalism that denies any correspondence between language and the structure of the world, Hacking observes that language can be generative and transformative. There can be a relation. From the fourteenth century, traditional nominalism has defended that structure is derived from language, from names and other means by which we interpret the world. The world does not come to us structured as categories. Traditional nominalists insist that naming is a human practice,

---

[5] I. Hacking, *Historical Ontology* (Cambridge, MA: Harvard University Press, 2002).

[6] I. Hacking, The looping effect of human kinds. In D. Sperber, D. Premack, and A. J. Premack (eds.) *Causal Cognition: A Multidisciplinary Debate* (Oxford: Clarendon, 1995) 351–383.

[7] Hacking asserts this to be the case with both "human" and "natural" kinds although he now no longer believes the classifications of human and natural to be useful. See I. Hacking, Natural kinds: Rosy dawn, scholastic twilight. Paper presented to the Royal Institute of Philosophy (London, 2006, February 17).

the products of which (e.g., concepts, categories, classifications) exist only in language or human minds. However, Hacking claims, human beings are distinctive in the ways they use and respond to language. Names mark us and work on us. The kinds of persons we are told we are, told to be, treated as, by which we recognize ourselves, with which we identify, against which we compare ourselves, and so forth, have a constitutive influence. The kinds of persons we understand ourselves and others to be are tied up with practices of naming. Consequently, Hacking declares a new form of "dynamic" nominalism is required.[8]

Concepts, classifications, and the descriptions they enable, are integral to how we experience and understand our lives and how we choose to act. However, intentions are not features of actions; nor are actions fixed by intentions. Rather, following Anscombe, intentions are features of "actions under descriptions."[9] The distinction is important, Hacking points out, because it explains how an action can fall under multiple descriptions. The further implication is that with new descriptions, new intentional attributes can be assigned to an action and performing the same action now can be doing something entirely different. Discussing one's most intimate problems and fantasies with a complete stranger was socially unacceptable, if not unthinkable, during the Victorian era. Freud developed the talking cure in the late nineteenth century and now we pay to do it. What it is to be a patient, to require or request treatment, to be qualified to provide treatment, to have a disorder, to be cured, and so on, have expanded to include psychological descriptions. What it means to tell one's most guarded secrets to a stranger, what it is believed can be accomplished by doing so, and the kinds of persons who now are capable of participating in these kinds of interchanges, are radically different. Hacking contends that when actions are re-described, people not only may be doing something different, but being something different. As Hacking explains the effects of dynamic nominalism, "numerous kinds of beings and human acts come into being hand in hand with our invention of the ways to name them."[10] Moreover, "making up people" requires particular historical and socio-cultural settings.[11]

Hacking's investigations of historical ontology have attended primarily to the kinds of persons who have been made objects of scientific study by the psy disciplines. He takes special interest in those afflicted by what he calls "transient mental illnesses" and the kinds of persons formed by

---

[8] Hacking, *Historical Ontology*, 106.
[9] G. E. M. Anscombe, *Intention* (Oxford: Blackwell, 1957) 11.
[10] Hacking, *Historical Ontology*, 113.
[11] This is Hacking's phrase. See *Historical Ontology*, 99.

psychiatric diagnosis.[12] Transient mental illnesses have a characteristic trajectory. They appear suddenly, are recognized as a disorder afflicting numbers of people, are sustained for some time, but then disappear. For Hacking's purposes, they make for compelling illustrations of historical ontology.

Hacking outlines a "banal framework of five elements" comprising the contours of his investigative approach: classification, people, institutions, knowledge, and experts.[13] "Classification" is the identification and description of actions or features of persons with reference to a disorder. "People" are those who fall under the description. There are "institutions" that support, regulate, and perpetuate disciplinary and professional knowledge regarding the disorder and its treatment. "Knowledge" refers to claims and assumptions made, reported, taught, revised, and spread about the disorder, not only in disciplinary and professional circles, but also to the general public. "Experts" are those deemed qualified to produce knowledge and whose job also is to evaluate and apply it in their practices. There are, of course, strong connections among these elements. Experts rely on institutions to legitimate their knowledge, maintain their status as experts, and grant them authority over people classified of given kinds. Hacking offers the framework to be clear that there is much more to historical ontology than simply what or how things come to be named and the interaction between classifications and those classified. However, Hacking finds the framework banal in that ontological inquiry demands attention to historical particularities and, in his words, there is "no reason to suppose that we shall ever tell two identical stories of two different instances of making up people."[14]

Making up people: multiple personality disorder

To illustrate the framework, Hacking instantiates his account of multiple personality disorder.[15] This is elaborated in his book, *Rewriting the Soul.*[16] In the book, Hacking traces the emergence, proliferation, and eventual disappearance of multiple personality as a psychiatric diagnosis from the mid to late twentieth century. Hacking finds multiple personality a compelling example of the dynamic interaction between naming and the

---

[12] I. Hacking, *Mad Travellers: Reflections on the Reality of Transient Mental Illness* (Charlottesville, VA: University of Virginia Press, 1998) 1.
[13] I. Hacking, Kinds of people: Moving targets. The Tenth British Academy Lecture (London, 2006, April 11) 5.
[14] Hacking, Kinds of people, 5.   [15] Hacking, Kinds of people.
[16] I. Hacking, *Rewriting the Soul: Multiple Personality and the Sciences of Memory* (Princeton, NJ: Princeton University Press, 1995).

historical appearance of a new kind of person. His historical ontology reveals how multiple personality disorder became viable as "a culturally sanctioned way of expressing distress" and how it "provided a new way to be an unhappy person."[17]

According to Hacking, in the absence of the classification, individuals were incapable of experiencing themselves or interacting with others as a multiple personality. Around 1970, a few startling cases appeared. Psychiatrists began to diagnose multiple personality as a disorder. Some of these cases were sensationalized in books and film, and knowledge of the condition soon spread to the general public. A dramatic rise in the numbers of people manifesting symptoms followed. Symptoms also began to change. Initially, patients presented with two or three alters. But within a decade patients were showing up with a parade of alters. By 1980, the mean was 17. It became common practice for therapists to elicit alters. Patients obliged, producing not only more alters, but also memories of childhood sexual abuse assumed to be the etiology of the disorder. The International Society for the Study of Multiple Personality was founded along with a patient liaison group. Multiples became a hot topic for television talk shows. There were weekend training programs for therapists, support groups for multiples, and a split bar for multiples looking for a singles scene.

Multiple personality disorder entered the nomenclature of the *Diagnostic and Statistical Manual of Mental Disorders* (DSM-III) in 1980 and was firmly established as a way of classifying people within a decade. Hacking writes,

[By] 1992, there were hundreds of multiples in treatment in every sizable town in North America. Even by 1986 it was thought that 6000 patents had been diagnosed. After that, one stopped counting and spoke about an exponential increase in the rate of diagnosis since 1980. Clinics, wards, units, and entire hospitals dedicated to the illness were being established all over the continent. Maybe one person in twenty suffered from a dissociative disorder.[18]

Hacking asserts that with multiple personality disorder, "A wholly new kind of person came into being, the multiple, with a set of memories and set of behaviors."[19] However, controversy arose among academics and clinicians over issues of validity and reliability of the diagnosis. There also was concern over damage to patients resulting from "fringe" treatments. The diagnosis fell into disfavor and multiple personality disorder was removed from the DSM-IV published in 1994. Hacking elaborates how, with the replacement of multiple personality disorder by dissociative

---

[17] Hacking, *Rewriting the Soul*, 236.
[18] Hacking, *Rewriting the Soul*, 8.   [19] Hacking, Kinds of people, 6.

identity disorder, not only is it now assumed that patients do not possess a repertory of completely distinct personalities but, moreover, they no longer act and experience themselves in quite this way. The name has changed and, along with it, the kind of person it made possible.

There are highly significant historical, social, and cultural conditions that shaped the space of possibility in which multiple personality became a way of being a person. Hacking provides a richly detailed account of the historical interplay among institutions, knowledge, and experts in which multiple personality, memory, and child abuse gradually became objects of expert knowledge, intervention, and institutional authority. For instance, there was the development of "the new sciences of memory" beginning in the nineteenth century – neuroanatomy and the attempt to localize brain functions; the efforts of Ebbinghaus in establishing psychology as a laboratory science built on measurement and statistics, and in initiating the experimental study of memory; and there was the invention of psychoanalysis. Preceding psychoanalysis, there was the creation of a descriptive vocabulary among French psychologists and psychiatrists in theorizing the link between memory and mental illness – somnambulism, animal magnetism, and hypnosis, and the English contribution, double consciousness. There was the emergence of a conception of normal memory and, importantly, the use of science to sever memory from its presumed connection with the soul. Double consciousness contradicted the idea of an indivisible soul and Hacking detects that among the purposes of the new sciences of memory was displacing spiritual beliefs about the soul with scientifically obtained, objective knowledge of memory. Hacking's historical ontology elaborates how this cluster of ideas came into being and created a space of possibility for the emergence of descriptions that led people to conceive themselves in new ways. Hacking is convinced that "the multiple personality of the 1980s was a kind of person unknown in the history of the human race."[20]

Through a wide array of examples (e.g., adolescence, autism, child abuse, fugue, genius, homosexuality, multiple personality disorder, obesity, poverty, suicide, and teenage pregnancy), Hacking has illustrated how new classifications of people, especially those advanced by the human sciences, are implicated in supporting the actions and experiences characteristic of the individuals classified and, in so doing, help reify the classification.[21] Such classifications not only expand possibilities for human action and experience, and create new kinds of personhood,

---

[20] Hacking, Kinds of people, 6.
[21] For specific sources see Hacking, The looping effect, for adolescence, child abuse, suicide, and teenage pregnancy; Hacking, *Rewriting the Soul*, for multiple personality disorder; Hacking, *Mad Travellers*, for fugue; and Hacking, Kinds of people, for autism and homosexuality.

but also come in and out of fashion. According to Hacking, making up people does not take a universal form. We are constituted as persons at a particular place and time, within an historically distinctive constellation of conditions conducive to persons of certain kinds. Hacking's account reveals the dangers of ahistoricism. Multiple personality came to matter at a particular place and time, and its designation as a "disorder" is bound inextricably to this context. It is easy to imagine how under different conditions, multiple personality might never have surfaced as a disorder, let alone escalated to epidemic proportions.

We tend to consider psychological properties and the ways we classify them as fixed and definitive. This is bolstered by the further assumption that the psy disciplines are progressing ever closer toward an accurate final account of the nature of persons and those properties in which their psychology consists. However, in light of Hacking's account, these assumptions are highly problematic. This is because persons are "moving targets." As Hacking explains,

They are moving targets because our investigations interact with the targets themselves, and change them. And since they are changed, they are not quite the same kind of people as before. The target has moved. That is the looping effect. Sometimes our sciences create kinds of people that in a sense did not exist before. That is making up people.[22]

This also insinuates that much psychological theorizing and research mistakenly has assumed its concepts, categories, and classifications correspond to definitive properties of a fixed and timeless human nature rather than to historical, social, cultural, and institutional features of the contexts within which we develop as persons.

Nikolas Rose: persons as governable subjects

Rose, like Hacking, uses history to demonstrate that we have an orientation to ourselves peculiar to our place and time.[23] The subject of the psy disciplines is not always and already there, lying hidden in nature and awaiting discovery by the right method. For Rose, an ontology of ourselves only can be pursued from an historical perspective. As Rose states: "Our ontology is historical: it is both temporal and spatial. What humans

---

[22] Hacking, Kinds of people, 2.
[23] See N. Rose, Assembling the modern self. In R. Porter (ed.) *Rewriting the Self: Histories from the Renaissance to the Present* (New York: Routledge, 1997) 224–248; Rose, *Inventing Ourselves*; N. Rose, *Governing the Soul: The Shaping of the Private Self*, 2nd edn (London: Free Association Books, 1999); and P. Miller and N. Rose, *Governing the Present: Administering Economic, Social and Personal Life* (Cambridge: Polity, 2008).

are – perhaps better, what human beings are capable of, what we can do –
is variable, historical, situational – not an originary 'being' but a mobile
'becoming'."[24] Rose also agrees that experience of ourselves as persons
only is possible "under a certain description" and that we have come to
rely on forms of psy description and discourse to acquire awareness of
our own characteristics and means to articulate them in self-identifying
ways.[25] Adamant that persons and selves exist only in relation to names
and descriptions given them, and within institutional arrangements and
practices that incorporate those names and descriptions, Rose argues that
their history should be told in those terms.

Of particular interest to Rose is the historical development of psychological expertise in liberal societies. However, the sort of history Rose
practices runs in the tradition of Kant, Foucault, and Hacking. Rose uses
history to confront the present. Rose wants to show how psychological
expertise serves political interests; more specifically, in what ways the psy
disciplines produce knowledge and interventions connected to a kind of
selfhood integral to the functioning of contemporary liberal democracies. This is a self presumed to exist as a discrete entity bounded by its
body; possessed of uniquely individual experiences, beliefs, desires, and
potentialities; and autonomous and self-governing. However, not only
does human autonomy vary with the ways we understand ourselves. It
does so in lockstep with institutions that justify their regulation of conduct on this very self-understanding. As Rose illustrates, it is "law, with
its notions of responsibility and intent; morality, with its valorization of
authenticity and its emotivism; politics, with its emphasis on individual
rights, individual choices and individual freedoms."[26]

It is within this context that the psy disciplines have become prominent
as instruments of institutional control by administering classifications of
human difference: normal, disordered, educable, employable, admissi-
ble, legally responsible, capable of leadership, and so forth. Through an
array of knowledge and expertise, exercise of institutional authority and
practical technologies, the psy disciplines affirm certain sorts of personhood and selfhood, while refusing others. Rose builds a case implicating
the psy disciplines in the formation of a self-understanding expressly
characteristic of persons in advanced liberal democracies. It is a self-
awareness indispensable to this kind of governance, Rose contends. By
articulating specific kinds of persons and selves, the psy disciplines have

---

[24] Rose, Assembling the modern self, 234.
[25] Rose, Assembling the modern self, 234.
[26] N. Rose, Power and subjectivity: Critical history and psychology. In C. F. Graumann and
K. Gergen (eds.) *Historical Dimensions of Psychological Discourse* (Cambridge University
Press, 1996) 103–124 (103).

been complicit in making our self-understanding an object on which others can act. Moreover, Rose embraces the Foucaultian insight that the technologies through which we are controlled by others can be turned toward ourselves and thus become means of self-control. The psy disciplines have come to be a vital means of making us intelligible to ourselves. This intelligibility, however, not only enables individuals to govern themselves, it also provides effective and efficient means of social and political control.

Rose's purpose is not to impugn the psy disciplines. His aim is to make us aware that the psy disciplines are far from politically neutral. Rather, they are intimately involved in assembling the kinds of "governable subjects" required of modern liberal democracies.[27] The psy disciplines have furnished a complex of techniques for the exercise of political and personal control that conforms with western liberal notions of individual freedom and autonomy. As a quick case in point, the sorts of technologies designed by psychologists for measuring public opinion gave rise to a conception of the "opinionated person" living in an "opinionated society."[28] But then, people came to fit the demands of the research. They learned to be the kind of person who has opinions and expresses them freely. There is a looping effect. But, it takes place through technologies employed by the psy disciplines that are suited to persons and selves with a specific ideological structure.

It should be noted as key to Rose's thesis, that the ascent of the psy disciplines is attributed neither to arbitrary authority nor elaborate conspiracy. Rather, the psy disciplines have succeeded through widely unquestioned acceptance by both experts and the lay public that disciplinary knowledge and professional practice are founded scientifically on the real nature of human persons as psychological subjects. However, the ways in which the psy disciplines facilitate a correspondence between political and personal interests are not coincidental either. As Rose explains, "These technologies for the government of the soul operate not through the crushing of subjectivity in the interests of control and profit, but by seeking to align political, social, and institutional goals with individual pleasures and desires, and with the happiness and fulfillment of self."[29]

Governing in advanced liberal democracies, according to Rose, operates through its subjects, by structuring a field of action in which individuals govern themselves. This manner of government is effective to the

---

[27]   Rose, *Governing the Soul*, vii.
[28]   T. Osborne and N. Rose, Do the social sciences create phenomena? The example of public opinion research. *British Journal of Sociology* **50** (1999) 367–396.
[29]   Rose, *Governing the Soul*, 261.

extent that it is able to co-opt citizens in sustaining certain social, political, and economic aims and structures. In advanced liberal democracies this is not accomplished by coercion. Rather, it occurs indirectly through social practices: by implementing technologies consistent with a conception of persons as autonomous subjects with responsibility and choice, by acting on them through the value they place in their liberty, and by granting powers to social institutions that are at some remove from formal political authority. Advanced liberal democracies harness individual freedom as a form of control that is regulated indirectly through social practices. Rose refers to this as "government at a distance."[30]

The enterprising self

To illustrate Rose's historical ontology of persons as governable subjects, I will summarize one strand of a large corpus of work. The theme is concerned with a kind of person he names "the enterprising self" and the participation of psychology in its emergence and persistence. Here Rose elaborates an observation made originally by Foucault.[31] Foucault identified enterprise as a political form that was becoming generalized beyond institutions to all conduct, including the shaping of personal life. Rose believes the enterprising self has become dominant in advanced liberal democracies by the historical development of a particular relation between a state government and individuals' self-government.

According to Rose, contemporary "advanced liberalism," as established during the last thirty years of the twentieth century, is the product of a series of shifts in the practices of liberal democracies. In Rose's historical ontology, these shifts can be distinguished by the ways persons were conceived as governable subjects by the state. Classical liberalism was defined largely by its separation of state responsibility from private life, the market, and civil society. Nonetheless, the state relied on philanthropy and external institutions (e.g., churches, charitable societies, trade unions) in order to meet the needs of its citizens. During the latter half of the nineteenth century, the extent to which mounting needs of citizens were exceeding the capacities of these social institutions was becoming rapidly apparent. In response, the state began to broaden its reach to new domains of responsibility – urban planning and sanitation, medical care, and education. In nineteenth-century liberalism, persons were comprehended as "political subject[s] thought to be motivated by a

---

[30] Miller and Rose, *Governing the Present*, 16.
[31] See M. Foucault, *The Birth of Biopolitics: Lectures at the Collège de France 1978–1979* (Basingstoke: Palgrave Macmillan, 2008).

calculus of pleasures and pains" and as "possessor[s] of physical capacities to be organized and dominated through the inculcation of moral
standards and behavioral habits."[32] Political subjects were persons of
need and whose liberty was to be contained.

Rose postulates that for the first half of the twentieth century, liberalism subscribed to "the social point of view."[33] The state was to
assume greater responsibility for insuring the welfare of individuals. This
approach appealed as the way to rescue private enterprise from the perils
of communism and runaway market capitalism. At its core was a new
contract between citizens and the state formulated in the language of
social welfare and solidarity, and predicated on a conception of citizens
as social persons with social needs, social rights, and social responsibilities. There were now mutual obligations. As Rose demarcates them, "the
individual was a locus of needs that were to be socially met if malign consequences were to be avoided, but was reciprocally to be a being to whom
political, civil, and social obligations and duties were to be attached."[34]
A rash of social programs was implemented: social insurance; child welfare; social, physical, and mental hygiene; universal education; public
broadcasting and forms of popular entertainment.

In Rose's analysis, what was common to these initiatives was an
endeavor to form responsible citizens who would channel their freedom
through an institutional matrix of social norms. Citizens no longer are
to be dominated in the interests of production and control. Rather, they
are steered by structures that align their ambitions and pursuits with
institutional objectives and activities. Individuals were to regulate themselves. But they did so primarily in terms of choices made in family life,
work, leisure, lifestyle, and cultivating their personality, all of which were
articulated and framed by political values and institutional structures. A
morality of stoicism in the service of the collective good was being eroded
by an orientation to personal choice and self-fulfillment that nonetheless
cohered with state notions of solidarity and social welfare.

Rose relays how, in the 1970s, social welfare as policy was attacked from
across the political spectrum.[35] A chorus of critics alleged it was bureau-
cratic, inefficient, patronizing, patriarchal, ineffectual in addressing social
inequalities, and that it impinged on fundamental rights and freedoms.
From this criticism arose Reaganomics in the US and Thatcherism in
the UK. By the mid 1980s, a new political rationality emerged in which
the neoliberal notion of "enterprise" became central. The language of

---

[32] Rose, *Governing the Soul*, 10.
[33] Miller and Rose, *Governing the Present*, 85.   [34] Rose, *Inventing Ourselves*, 164.
[35] See Rose, *Inventing Ourselves* and Miller and Rose, *Governing the Present*.

enterprise captured a new relation between the economic well being of the state and personal choice. This relation consisted in an economic conception of citizens as consumers, and of consumption as a key element of entrepreneurship in the venture of one's own life. "Consumers were considered, as in a sense, entrepreneurs of themselves, seeking to maximize their quality of life through the artful assembly of a lifestyle put together through the world of goods."[36] Rose claims that consumerism transformed citizenship from a passive to active form. A machinery of design, manufacturing, and marketing infused products with meanings and connected consumption to the active pursuit of a personally meaningful life. Consumer goods became the instruments through which enterprising persons were to be honed as governable subjects. At the same time, consumer choice could be exploited as a mechanism for economic growth. Markets replaced political planning as the tool with which to regulate economic activity.

According to Rose, the vocabulary of enterprise proved highly useful in translating technologies of the market into the various domains of individual and collective life. In enterprise culture, persons now were individuals who actively administered themselves as an economic interest, who sought to establish and add value to themselves through personal investment (e.g., in education or insurance), who managed their lives in ways to maximize returns, and who expressed their individual autonomy through consumer choice. In making an enterprise of its life, the enterprising self is active and calculating: "a self that calculates about itself and that acts upon itself in order to better itself."[37]

The language of enterprise also bridged private and organizational life. In the workplace, self-enhancement was promoted through a profusion of seminars and training courses. To be a better worker or manager was to become a better self, as stipulated by "the values of self-realization, the skills of self-presentation, self-direction, and self-management."[38] The notion of work was reconceived. Work no longer was burden, tedium, and constraint of one's freedom. Instead, it became the vehicle for the enterprising self to pursue a sense of personal meaning, individual accomplishment, and self-expression. The idea of bettering oneself through work was not new. However, what was new was that the structure of the enterprising self as an autonomous individual propelled by self-enhancement became the way to address organizational problems and "ensure dynamism, excellence, and innovation by activating and engaging the self-fulfilling aspirations of the individuals who make up the

---

[36] Miller and Rose, *Governing the Present*, 49.   [37] Rose, *Inventing Ourselves*, 154.
[38] Miller and Rose, *Governing the Present*, 50.

94   *Jeff Sugarman*

workplace."[39] In the case of enterprising selves, the autonomous sub-
jectivities of productive citizens became the major economic resource.
The autonomy of enterprising selves was fixed to state economic growth
through consumer choice.

Accompanying these shifts in liberal governance was the growth of "the
experts of subjectivity": the psy disciplines.[40] According to Rose, while
these forms of expertise were not invented by the state, they abetted
governmental control with techniques that aligned individuals' commitments and choices with political and economic goals. However, the psy
disciplines facilitate government at a distance. They function between
formal political authority and citizens by guiding them toward being persons of particular kinds. In the case of neoliberal democracies, these are
persons for whom autonomy, responsibility, and choice are the defining
features of their freedom and, thus, the goods by which they orient their
lives, goods that also serve the economic interests of the state.

In charting the rise of psychological expertise, Rose infers that the con-
solidation and ascendancy of psychology as a discipline resulted from the
effectiveness of its contrivances for observing, differentiating, classifying,
and administering individual variability. It already was recognized by the
time psychology emerged as a discipline in the latter half of the nineteenth
century that the well being of the state required effective organization and
disposition of its resources, including its populace. It also was known that
prosperous government relied on methods of rational calculation. Part of
what is entailed in such methods, Rose submits, is that they represent the
elements of the domain to be governed (i.e., persons) in ways that make
them intelligible and subject to analysis, so that problems can be solved or
averted and desired ends achieved. This representation, Rose delineates,
has two vital features: vocabularies that render the objects of government
intelligible and means to inscribe them.[41] Rose deciphers how, in the
case of liberal democracies, disciplinary and professional psychology was
well suited to these two projects.

As Rose documents in considerable historical detail, psychological language (from the nineteenth century vernacular of moral pathology and
degeneracy to the massive psychological lexicon that had accumulated
by the 1980s) and means of inscription (e.g., statistics, diagnostic categories, tests, surveys, polls, questionnaires, experiments, and therapeutic
interventions) were mobilized to make subjectivity an object of rational
government and to codify the rationalities of liberal forms of governance

---

[39] Miller and Rose, *Governing the Present*, 194.
[40] Rose, *Inventing Ourselves*, 165.   [41] Rose, *Inventing Ourselves*.

into everyday life.[42] Thus, for example, among a plethora of psycho-therapies popular in the 1980s – from Rogers' client-centered therapy to Perls' Gestalt therapy, from psychoanalysis to Berne's transactional analysis, and from Janov's primal therapy to T-groups – Rose finds in common the moral injunction to work on the self to improve one's quality of life, to realize one's autonomy, to achieve one's potential, and to be responsible for one's life and one's choices.[43]

Rose's account reveals how psychological expertise is related intimately to political reasoning in advanced liberalism and significantly, for the purposes of illustrating historical ontology, that this form of government relies on rendering governable subjects of a specific kind: enterprising selves. The fundamental issue for this style of governance concerns provisions for making these kinds of persons, who express their autonomy and freedom by seeking to fulfill themselves in the domains of daily life, responsible to government through their choices. This is accomplished by the shaping of a field of action in which persons are reconfigured by an economized conception of enterprise that alters previous understandings of individual freedom and autonomy. In this way, individual autonomy becomes not the antithesis or boundary of advanced liberal governance, but rather, the very target and instrument of political control. It is not merely that we are free. In enterprise culture, we are obliged to exercise our freedom by understanding and enacting our lives specifically in terms of autonomy, responsibility, and choice.

Rose demonstrates how advanced liberalism operates through government at a distance, facilitated by a particular relation between persons and varieties of expertise. In the case of psychology, this relation occurs where languages and techniques of inscription practiced by psychologists interface with the enterprise-related goods of self-enhancement, self-mastery, and increasing the value of one's life through acts of choice. The languages and techniques of inscription devised and disseminated by psychologists are important for the ways they induce us to become persons of a certain sort who define and conduct themselves in ways aligned with governmental aims and forms of administration. Rose radically re-envisions how the understanding of personhood and selfhood ought to be pursued. The pressing question is not how to converge on singular, unified conceptions of personhood and selfhood. Rather, Rose believes it is more instructive: "to examine the ways in which psychology has participated in the construction of diverse repertoires for speaking about, evaluating, and acting upon persons that have their salience in different sites and in relation to different problems and have a

---

[42] Rose, *Inventing Ourselves*.   [43] Rose, *Governing the Soul*.

particular relationship to the types of self that are proposed in contemporary practices for the administration of individuals."[44]

A word about agency

Foucault argued in his earlier work that if the subject is produced by institutional structures and practices then it cannot have the sovereign autonomy and causal agency proclaimed in modern liberal democracies. Foucault firmly rejected the autonomous and disengaged subject of the Enlightenment. But toward the end of his life, it appears he attempted to reconcile agency as a kind of self-formation capable of limited forms of critique and resistance.[45] Foucault granted, "perhaps I've insisted too much on the technology of domination and power. I am more and more interested in the interaction between oneself and others and in the technologies of individual domination, the history of how an individual acts upon himself, in the technology of self."[46] Foucault came to assert human freedom, albeit a freedom within limits. As he described his project, "I shall thus characterize the philosophical ethos appropriate to the critical ontology of ourselves as a historico-practical test of the limits we may go beyond, and thus as work carried out by ourselves upon ourselves as free beings."[47]

Hacking and Rose, like Foucault, argue that persons are formed within institutional orders. And, similarly to Foucault, they repudiate any theory of the essential person. However, Hacking and Rose part company on the issue of agency. Rose sides with the earlier Foucault, insisting that agency is entirely unnecessary for personhood. The origin of human choice, action, and experience is not the autonomous actor. Rather, Rose claims, it is persons' "constant movement across different practices that subjectify them in different ways."[48] This stream of activity does not require agents born with the impulse to realize their autonomy. As Rose states: "It needs no account of the inherent forces within each human being that love liberty, seek to enhance their own powers or capacities, or strive for emancipation, that are prior to and in conflict with the dreams of

[44] Rose, *Inventing Ourselves*, 64.
[45] See N. Gordon, Foucault's subject: An ontological reading. *Polity* **31** (1995) 395–414; T. McCarthy, The critique of impure reason: Foucault and the Frankfurt School. *Political Theory* **18** (1990) 437–469; and J. Sawicki, *Disciplining Foucault: Feminism, Power, and the Body* (London: Routledge, 1991).
[46] M. Foucault, Technologies of the self. In L. H. Martin, H. Gutman, and P. H. Hutton (eds.) *Technologies of the Self: A Seminar with Michel Foucault* (Amherst, MA: University of Massachusetts Press, 1988) 16–49 (19).
[47] Foucault, *Enlightenment*, 47.   [48] Rose, *Inventing Ourselves*, 35.

civilization and discipline."[49] Rose denies any capacity for agency beyond that produced as an institutional effect. Clearly, certain capacities for thought and action need to be developed. However, these capacities only are acquired through an elaborate course of development in which they are cultivated purposefully to fit sanctioned forms of expression. Rose resolves, "Our own 'agency' then is the result of the ontology we have folded into ourselves in the course of our history and our practices."[50] For Rose, agency provides no psychological capital whatsoever,

> For all the desires, intelligences, motivations, passions, creativities, will-to-self realization, and the like folded into us by our psychotechnologies, our own agency is no less artificial, no less fabricated, no less unnatural – and hence no less real, effective, confused, technical, machine-dependent – than the problematic agency of the robots, replicants, and monstrous symbioses that Donna Hardaway uses to think of our existence.[51]

In contrast to Rose, Hacking defends that persons are agents capable of exercising some degree of self-determination with respect to their choices and actions. Like the later Foucault, Hacking is unwilling to surrender the concept of human agency. Persons are biophysical beings constituted by their descriptions and classifications. It may be the case, Hacking admits, that we are highly constrained by biophysical and socio-cultural conditions. Acknowledging his existentialism, Hacking holds, however, that whatever of our personhood is determined by constraints of which we are unaware or powerless to change, at least some of what we are and become owes to the choices we can make. As Hacking describes,

> We push our lives through a thicket in which the stern trunks of determinism are entangled in the twisting vines of chance. Still, you can choose what you do, under the circumstances. The choices that you make, situated in the thicket, are what formed you and continue to form you. Responsibility is in part taking responsibility for that being you become, as consequence of choosing.[52]

The looping effect requires not only that we are responsive to the descriptions others have of us, but also that what we are is partially constituted by our own particular interpretations and understandings of ourselves. Because human psychological beings are self-aware and reflective, at least some of the time, their courses of action and ways of being are affected not only by the classifications of their societies and cultures, but also by their own conceptions of, and reactions to, such

---

[49] Rose, *Inventing Ourselves*, 35.
[50] Rose, *Inventing Ourselves*, 189.   [51] Rose, *Inventing Ourselves*, 189.
[52] Hacking, I. Between Michel Foucault and Erving Goffman: Between discourse in the abstract and face-to-face interaction. *Economy and Society* **33** (2004) 277–302 (282).

classifications.[53] Thus, for example, the experience of racial discrimination is not simply a social construction but is constituted partially by one's own interpretation and understanding of the significance of being a victim. In order to experience racial discrimination, one needs to have been immersed in socio-culturally available descriptions that lend intelligibility to experiences and actions. However, much also depends on the unique experiential history of the particular person – an ontological history in which choice figures largely.

Further, the interpretations and reactions of classified individuals often result in changes to systems of classification. People can refuse the psychological, psychiatric, political, medical, legal, educational, or religious classifications imposed on them. Removal of homosexuality from the DSM-II was largely a consequence of political activism by the gay community who objected to being classified as mentally ill. Individuals are capable, at least potentially, of taking matters into their own hands. The self-determining properties of persons owe to their agency: "the deliberative, reflective activity of a human being in framing, choosing, and executing his or her actions in a way that is not fully determined by factors and conditions other than his or her own authentic understanding and reasoning."[54]

The socio-cultural determinism Rose accepts seems difficult to defend. The forms and meanings conveyed by socio-cultural orders and practices are not fixed and static. They change over time. The ongoing change evinced in individual and collective life would not be possible if institutional structures and practices were fully determinate of human action and experience. In order for sociopolitical structures and practices to change, they must be at least partially open-ended in ways that permit individuals to develop new descriptions, classifications, and possibilities for action and experience that can contribute to sociopolitical transformation. While institutional structures and practices enable individuals to develop psychological capacities to transform these very structures and practices, the provision of such possibility is not determination.[55] Our conceptions of agency may vary in degree and type, are influenced by specific sociopolitical conceptions and are always open to revision and change. However, persons are able to interact with, and resist, those

[53] J. Sugarman, Historical ontology and psychological description. *Journal of Theoretical and Philosophical Psychology* 29 (2009) 5–15.
[54] J. Martin, J. Sugarman, and J. Thompson, *Psychology and the Question of Agency* (Albany, NY: SUNY Press, 2003) 82.
[55] See Martin et al., *Psychology and the Question of Agency*, for arguments in support of this claim.

classifications and practices devised to describe, study, and control them, precisely because they have agentive capability.

Psychology and the historical ontology of ourselves

Hacking's and Rose's work shows that the disciplinary and professional practices of psychologists are not ontologically innocent. They create a space of possibility and field of action in which features and kinds of persons appear as objects of concern, achieve ontological stability, and become targets of expert intervention. By interpreting persons as isolated individuals, evoking various performances from them, measuring these performances, subjecting them to quantitative comparisons and evaluations, inscribing them with language, ordering them in systems of classification, and making aspects of them amenable to therapeutic intervention, psychologists have rendered stable and transparent features and kinds of persons that might have remained undetected or, perhaps in some cases, non-existent.

The consequence is that life in advanced liberal democracies is infused with psychological language, psychological entities, and psychological authority. Our conduct, characteristics, and proficiencies are understood in psychological terms. Dysfunctions and deviations are set against scientifically derived standards of normality and made troubling yet intelligible to both those afflicted and others charged with their administration. With a growing system of diagnostic classification, a host of human maladies are readily identified, from pathological shyness (i.e., social anxiety disorder) to a pathological penchant for confrontation (i.e., oppositional defiance disorder). Shyness and being overly confrontational have obvious disadvantages in enterprise culture.

At the same time, psychologists advance particular features and kinds of personhood. Currently in the US, for instance, there is a widespread campaign for "positive psychology" advertising that we can learn to be happy by cultivating six core virtues and twenty-four character strengths.[56] These strengths and virtues – abstracted from their sociocultural particularity and presented in a system of classification along with interventions to inscribe them – pave the road to fulfillment. But true to enterprise culture, such self-cultivation appears to require endless consumption of psychological expertise.

Psychological description is not a simple matter of representation. It is a constitutive and defining feature of persons. When certain descriptions

---

[56] See J. Sugarman, Practical rationality and the questionable promise of positive psychology. *Journal of Humanistic Psychology* **47** (2007) 175–197.

prove useful in making our actions and experiences intelligible and in pursuing our various purposes, they can become "objectified" in the practices and conventions of cultures and societies. Such practices and conventions supply normative criteria by which the actions of individuals are sanctioned and censured. But also, descriptions of persons and selves are taken up by individuals to recognize, examine, and evaluate their personal experiences, beliefs, feelings, memories, goals, and conduct. We live our lives within and through psychological descriptions and norms they provide. As such, they become constitutive of the kinds of persons we are, and the kinds of cultures and societies we inhabit.

Historical ontology confronts psychological objects and issues with history. It reveals the historical conditions of possibility in which personhood and selfhood take various shapes. However, it is not limited to descriptive claims. It intimates normative interests. Historical ontology opens up and makes visible spaces of possibility, fields of action, their sociopolitical and historical particularity and contingency, and that of the objects investigated. By implication, there is the possibility to be otherwise, to have other options and choices. As agents, we have the capacity not only to adopt and wield psychological descriptions, but also, to react to them, to revise them, and to transform them. This, for Foucault, is the purpose of a historical ontology of ourselves: "seeking to give new impetus, as far and wide as possible, to the undefined work of freedom."[57]

[57] Foucault, What is Enlightenment? 84.

6   Critical personalism: on its tenets, its historical obscurity, and its future prospects

James T. Lamiell

In a letter dated January 6, 1933, the German philosopher and psychologist William Stern (1871–1928) congratulated his friend and colleague, the Freiburg philosopher Jonas Cohn (1869–1947), on the publication of his book *Wertwissenschaft* (*The Science of Values*).[1] Stern wrote:

> I hope that, beyond the pleasure of seeing the finished book lying there in front of you, you will have the additional pleasure of sensing its impact on others near and far. For even if the immediate present is not exactly favorable for works of such a fundamental nature, which without being radical or laden with delusions of grandeur nevertheless address themselves to the most decisive issues of humanity, still we must hope that such times will return, because, otherwise, all of our objectives and accomplishments of the past fifty years will have been in vain! History simply cannot be so senseless![2]

Of course, the "immediate present" to which Stern referred was one dominated by Germany's severe economic woes and political unrest. Just three weeks after this letter was written, the ruinous reign of the Nazis officially began, leading to an epoch of the twentieth century perhaps more senseless than anything Stern would ever have been able to imagine.[3] But even well prior to the outbreak of the first world war in 1914, the intellectual climate in psychology was becoming inhospitable to works of the sort that Stern regarded as being of a "fundamental nature." Included among such works would certainly have been those of his own in which he set forth that comprehensive system of thought, or *Weltanschauung*,

---

[1] Translations in the text are my responsibility unless otherwise noted. J. Cohn, *Wertwissenschaft* (Stuttgart: Frommans, 1932).

[2] H. E. Lück and D.-J. Löwisch (eds.) *Der Briefwechsel Zwischen William Stern und Jonas Cohn: Dokumente einer Freundschaft Zwischen Zwei Wissenschaftlern* (Frankfurt am Main: Peter Lang Verlag, 1994) 166–167.

[3] In an essay published after the second world war, Stern's son, Günther Anders, wrote of how his father's nearly unshakeable belief in the basic goodness of other people, and of the world generally, blinded him to the danger signs that were clearly present in Germany well before Hitler came to power. See Bild meines Vaters, in the second unrevised edition of W. Stern, *Allgemeine Psychologie auf Personalistischer Grundlage* (Den Haag: Nijhoff, 1950) xxiii–xxxii.

that he called "critical personalism." Moreover, and decidedly contrary to Stern's clearly expressed hopes, the re-establishment of an intellectual climate more hospitable to such works did not soon happen, and, one might argue, still has not happened. As a result, critical personalism is a conceptual framework that has remained unknown to several generations of psychologists.

In recent years, however, the present author and a small but growing number of others have been seeking to revive interest in and appreciation for Stern's works.[4] The present contribution extends that effort. More specifically, my objectives in this work are to review the primary tenets of critical personalism, to discuss some reasons for its historical obscurity, and to consider the prospects for a revival of personalistic thinking in contemporary psychology. Though I have devoted some attention to each of these topics in various earlier publications, the editors of the present work have requested a contribution by me that discusses all of these matters in one piece.[5]

On the conceptual foundations and primary tenets of critical personalism

The letter to Jonas Cohn quoted above was written more than thirty years after he wrote the following, also in a letter to Cohn, on July 31, 1900:

Dear friend . . . I am gradually becoming more a philosopher than a psychologist, and am carrying around with me so many ideas that will take me many years to formulate . . . I believe that what we need above all is a comprehensive worldview, one that relates the psychological and the physical . . . that is anti-mechanistic; that is vitalistic-teleological; one in which modern natural science dogma is reduced

---

[4] See, for example, W. Deutsch (ed.) *Über die Verborgene Aktualität von William Stern* (Frankfurt am Main: Peter Lang Verlag, 1991); see also J. T. Lamiell, William Stern: More than "the I.Q. Guy." In G. A. Kimble, C. Alan Boneau, and M. Wertheimer (eds.) *Portraits of Pioneers in Psychology*, *Vol. 2* (Washington, DC, and Mahwah, NJ: American Psychological Association Books and Lawrence Erlbaum Associates, 1996) 72–85; G. Bühring, *William Stern oder Streben nach Einheit* (Frankfurt am Main: Peter Lang Verlag, 1996); J. T. Lamiell and W. Deutsch (eds.) Psychology and critical personalism: A special issue. *Theory and Psychology* **10** (2000) 715–876; J. T. Lamiell and L. Laux (eds.) Personalistic thinking: A special issue. *New Ideas in Psychology* **28** (2010) 105–262; J. T. Lamiell, *Beyond Individual and Group Differences: Human Individuality, Scientific Psychology, and William Stern's Critical Personalism* (Thousand Oaks, CA: Sage Publications, 2003); J. T. Lamiell, William Stern (1871–1938) und der "Ursprungsmythos" der differentiellen Psychologie. *Journal für Psychologie* **14** (2006) 253–273; M. Tschechne, *William Stern* (Hamburg: Ellert and Richter Verlag, 2010); J. T. Lamiell, *William Stern (1871–1938): A Brief Introduction to His Life and Works* (Lengerich, Germany: Pabst Science Publishers, 2010).

[5] See works cited in note 4.

to its true – that is, relatively inferior – value. This is a huge task, but I will work on it as I can.[6]

Lest the first line of this passage mislead, Stern never believed that one concerned to understand human nature should – or even could – be a philosopher *or* a psychologist but not both. On the contrary, he firmly believed that a proper understanding of human nature would require a combination of philosophical and psychological considerations that would inform and complement each other.[7] That said, the feature of the above-quoted passage that is most directly relevant to our immediate concerns is Stern's expression of the firmly anti-mechanistic stance from which his thinking proceeded. This stance is recognized first and foremost in the distinction he drew between *persons*, on the one hand, and *things*, on the other.

Persons versus things

The person–thing distinction is the conceptual cornerstone of critical personalism, and was articulated clearly by Stern in the first volume of the three-volume series, titled, aptly enough, *Person and Thing*:

A person is an entity that, though consisting of many parts, forms a unique and inherently valuable unity and, as such, constitutes, over and above its functioning parts, a unitary, self-activated, goal-oriented being... A thing is the contradictory opposite of a person. It is an entity that likewise consists of many parts, but these are not fashioned into a real, unique, and inherently valuable whole, and so while a thing functions in accordance with its various parts, it does not constitute a unitary, self-activated and goal-oriented being.[8]

Proceeding from this distinction, Stern's next task was to explain how *critical* personalism differed from two other "-isms" that he sought to counter: *naïve* personalism, on the one hand, and *im*personalism, on the other.

Naïve personalism, in Stern's view, is essentially a simplified Cartesian dualism, according to which mind is properly understood to exist as an immaterial substance quite separate from a person's material body.

---

[6] Lück and Löwisch, *Briefwechsel*, 33.
[7] See, for example, the opening passage in Stern's monograph, *Die Psychologie und der Personalismus* (Leipzig: Barth, 1917). My English translation of that work is published as Psychology and personalism. *New Ideas in Psychology* 28 (2010) 110–134.
[8] W. Stern, *Person und Sache: System der Philosophischen Weltanschauung. Erster Band: Ableitung und Grundlehre* (Leipzig: Barth, 1906) 16. See also: W. Stern, *Person und Sache: System der Philosophischen Weltanschauung. Zweiter Band: Die Menschliche Persönlichkeit.* (Leipzig: Barth, 1918); and W. Stern, *Person und Sache: System des Kritischen Personalismus. Dritter Band: Wertphilosophie* (Leipzig: Barth, 1924).

"This," Stern wrote, "is the conception of personality as we encounter it in folk beliefs about the mind."[9]

Impersonalism, by contrast, is a view according to which the individual is merely "a congeries; physically a sum of atoms; psychologically a bundle of perceptions . . . a mechanical by-product of elements [whose functioning is] determined by the general laws governing all occurrences. On this view, the individual is no person, but a 'thing'."[10]

Contra naïve personalism (and dualism more generally), Stern advocated a conception of the person as a *psychophysically neutral* entity. His argument was that while one can sensibly refer to both mental and physical aspects of a person's functioning, such discourse itself presumes an entity that is, ontologically speaking, both *prior* to, and *neutral with respect* to any and every discursive partitioning of that entity, including but not limited to a partitioning into "the mental" and "the physical." In critical personalism, that entity just *is* the psychophysically neutral person. "The primary fact of the world," Stern argued, "is not that there are both physical and mental aspects [to personal functioning], but rather that there are real persons . . . The distinction between the mental and physical is of a secondary order."[11]

Contra impersonalism, Stern advocated and defended at length just those features of genuine personhood, as opposed to thingness, that he had set forth in the definition given above. "*Ich werte, also bin ich . . . Wert*," he declared: "I evaluate, therefore I am . . . value."[12] Deliberately formulated as a variation on Descartes' "*Cogito ergo sum*" (I think therefore I am), this declaration lies at the core of the person–thing distinction. To "e-valuate" literally means to send out, project, or radiate value, analogous to the way in which the sun radiates light and warmth. Hence, just as the sun is the source of light and warmth on planet earth, so are persons the source of the values that permeate human life. Furthermore: in order for an entity to "radiate" value, value must in some sense be regarded as proper to or inherent within that entity to begin with. This, Stern believed, is true of persons but not of things. The latter can be evalua-*ted*, passively, but they cannot themselves actively e-valu*ate*.

---

9   Stern, *Die Psychologie und der Personalismus*, 6.
10 Stern, *Die Psychologie und der Personalismus*, 6–7.
11 Stern, *Ableitung und Grundlehre*, 204–205. In this same vein, Stern noted elsewhere that "the distinction between the physical and mental aspects of a person's functioning is something secondary, often isolating the two simply for the purposes of scientific considerations." See W. Stern, Personalistische psychologie. In E. Saupe (ed.) *Einführung in die Neuere Psychologie* (Osterwieck am Harz: A. W. Zickfeldt Verlag, 1927) 165–175. The quoted passage appears on page 167.
12 Stern, *Wertphilosophie*, 34.

Persons, on this view, are thus properly regarded as inherently value-able, whereas things are only contingently valuable.

Building upon this fundamental distinction between persons and things, Stern elaborated his conception of persons as **unitary, self-activated**, and **goal-oriented** beings.

The person as *unitas multiplex*. In discussing the unitary nature of persons, Stern often invoked the Latin expression *unitas multiplex*.[13] His point was to recognize the multi-faceted complexity of persons without compromising a firm theoretical grasp of the fundamental coherence of personal being. The wholeness or unity that Stern was at pains to capture is not, as he put it, "simple simplicity, but neither is it mere colorful multiplicity. It is instead a unity containing the multiplicity" – the *unitas multiplex*.[14]

He believed that fidelity to the concept of *unitas multiplex* required a perspective according to which the otherwise chaotic and overwhelming abundance of the rudimentary sensory-perceptual "givens" of psychological experience, *phenomena*, are rendered coherent through meaningful *acts* that are in turn lent temporal continuity by *dispositions* that are the more or less enduring inclinations of an *I* that is, ultimately, a projection of the psychophysically neutral *person*. It is this "I," Stern stated, that "experiences phenomena, executes acts, and owns dispositions."[15]

It is significant that in his quest for a maximally inclusive expression for the many entities – phenomena, acts, dispositions – that the unitary "I" experiences, executes, and owns, respectively, Stern rejected the term "elements." He did so because that term suggests a theoretical appeal to "discrete entities the existence of which is not dependent upon the unity. This would give priority to the simple entities over the whole."[16] As a consequence of this, Stern opted for "the neutral and not yet theory-laden expression 'moment':... *Every whole is the unity of its moments.*"[17]

---

[13] See, for example, Stern, *Die Psychologie und der Personalismus*.

[14] W. Stern, *Studien zur Personwissenschaft, Erster Teil: Personalistik als Wissenschaft* (Leipzig: Barth, 1930) 13.

[15] Stern, *Die Psychologie und der Personalismus*, 31.

[16] Stern, *Studien zur Personwissenschaft*, 13.

[17] Stern, *Studien zur Personwissenschaft*, 13, emphasis added. It was in full accordance with the spirit of this terminological commitment that Stern would voice his one reservation about Gestalt psychology, a conceptual framework with which he was otherwise in substantial agreement. His worry was that an over-emphasis on Gestalts *per se* would lead to a mistaken regard for Gestalts themselves as the "elements" of experience. Thus was Stern at pains to emphasize (p. 17): "Keine Gestalt ohne Gestalter" [*There is no Gestalt without a Gestalt-ing person*].

The person as self-activated and goal-oriented. Within critical personalism, it is because persons are seen as e-valuating entities that they must be regarded as both self-activated and goal-oriented.

Since persons are by their very nature evaluative, it is unnecessary to postulate any outside force that prompts them into the making of evaluations. Persons are the *authors* of evaluations, and not simply the "conduits" of evaluative outcomes that are somehow determined by extra-personal (e.g., "situational") factors and only "mediated" – if at all – by "cognitive mechanisms" of some sort. To view persons as the authors of evaluations is just to regard them as self-activated entities, and not merely as the loci of meditational mechanisms.

Of course, goals or objectives play a role in any evaluative process, and in recognition of this point, critical personalism postulates two broad goal categories, or goal "systems," as Stern preferred to call them: self goals (*Selbstzwecke*) and foreign goals (*Fremdzwecke*), i.e., goals set by entities other than the self.[18]

Self goals are in turn sub-divided into self-maintenance (*Selbsterhaltung*) and self-development (*Selbstentwicklung*). Pursuit of these goals manifests what Stern referred to as the "autotelic" nature of personal being. The rationale for the "auto" portion of this term is obvious. The "telic" portion was chosen by Stern quite deliberately to draw attention to his insistence upon the necessity of a teleological perspective in order to achieve a scientific understanding of persons as opposed to things. Stern was fully aware that his commitment in this regard placed him squarely at odds with the vast majority of his contemporaries. However, he also believed that a teleological perspective would be indispensable in any attempt to grasp human nature with fidelity, and he even went so far as to label the widespread avoidance of such a perspective "teleophobic."[19]

In connection with his elucidation of *Fremdzwecke*, i.e., the goals of entities other than oneself, Stern wrote: "The person who would pursue only his/her own narrow individual goals would be an extension-less point in emptiness. Only goals extending beyond the self give the person

---

[18] There is no presumption in critical personalism that evaluation is always a conscious process. See, for example, Stern, Personalistische psychologie, esp. footnote 2 on p. 166. This point will be further clarified below.

[19] See Stern, *Die Menschliche Persönlichkeit*, 270. Readers familiar with the works of Joseph F. Rychlak (b. 1928) would not be mistaken to surmise a substantial compatibility between Rychlak's ideas and those of Stern, though to the best of the present author's knowledge Rychlak had no direct familiarity with Stern's works. See J. F. Rychlak, *A Philosophy of Science for Personality Theory*, second edn (Malabar, FL: Krieger, 1981). See also J. F. Rychlak, *The Psychology of Rigorous Humanism*, second edn (New York University Press, 1988).

concrete content and living coherence with the world. Autotelie encounters *heterotelie*."[20]

Heterotelic goals can be further classified into three sub-categories: (1)
the strictly heterotelic, which from the point of view of the focal person are
the goals of other persons; (2) the *hypertelic*, which are the collective goals
of supra-personal entities such as family, a people, religious institutions,
the community, etc.; and (3) the *ideotelic*, which are the non-personal
goals of abstract ideals such as truth, justice, etc.[21]

**Introception, person-world convergence, consciousness, and
self-determination**. Speaking again from the standpoint of the focal
person, heterotelic goals become *syntelic* to the extent that they are
actively appropriated by that person and thus made part of his/her own
(autotelic) goal system. "Only in this way," Stern argued, "is it possible
that the acceptance of supra- and non-personal goals nevertheless does
not signify any de-personalization or degradation of the personality into a
mere thing and tool, but that, on the contrary, the personality becomes,
through its embodiment of the outer goals in its own self-activity, a
microcosm."[22]

In the language of critical personalism, this process of actively appro-
priating goals that are initially outside of the focal person's self system is
called *introception*, and it is a particular form of a broader process that is of
central significance in critical personalism, namely, the process of person-
world *convergence*. The world, on this view, is not simply the source of
forces that impinge upon the passive person and impel his/her thoughts,
behaviors and development in this direction or that, but is rather a kind of
arena where, in some ways and at certain times, the realization of one's
goals is constrained or impeded, but in other ways and at other times
facilitated.

It was in terms of the dynamics of person-world convergence that
Stern came to articulate his conception of consciousness and self-
determination. He argued that to the extent that the world is fully conso-
nant with and hence entirely accommodating of the person's objective(s)
at any given point in time, convergence proceeds outside of awareness. It
is simply a moment of life through which the person passes.

Life (*das Leben*) is a precondition for experience (*ein Erlebnis*), but not
all that is lived is consciously experienced. On the contrary, it is out of

---

[20] Stern, *Die Psychologie und der Personalismus*, 46, emphasis added.
[21] Stern did note that such goals cannot properly be regarded as completely non-personal,
since they would have to be, or have been, embodied in persons at some point in
time. Hence, their adoption by a given individual must be regarded as, in some sense,
"syntelic," a notion to be discussed presently.
[22] Stern, *Die Psychologie und der Personalismus*, 47.

the tension resulting from some degree of mismatch between personal objectives and world affordances that the world (*die Welt*) becomes an environment (*eine Umwelt*) in which the person not only lives (*lebt*) but consciously experiences (*erlebt*) something. Moreover, just because every experience is an occurrence requiring evaluation by the person within the framework of his/her goal system, part of the meaning of an experience is to be found in the alternative possible actions to which that experience gives rise. The plural "actions" is used here advisedly, since, in Stern's view, the directionality "is not of a straight, linear sort (for that would amount to a firm given, a predestination), but is instead a kind of radiating cone whose breadth accommodates a multiplicity of possibilities."[23] The person's "consciousness of freedom," Stern argued, "is the precipitate of this relationship between directedness and ambiguity that characterizes all psychological experience."[24]

The nature of personal(ity) characteristics. Of central relevance to most thinkers' understanding of individuality/personality (the latter term has long been the more favored) is the notion of more or less enduring personal qualities or characteristics. Such a notion is found within critical personalism as well, so a few words here about Stern's understanding of such qualities or characteristics are in order.

Most fundamental in this regard is that tenet of critical personalism according to which all characteristics of personality are properly regarded not as fixed determinants, whether partial or complete, of behavior or states of psychological being (as was true of the *Vermögenspsychologie* that, already by Stern's time, had been discredited), but rather as *potentialities*. "Dispositions," the broadest of the terms used by Stern in this context, "are not special forces but instead only partial radiances of a unitary, goal-oriented entity," and hence "mere potentialities which require supplementation to be carried over into action."[25] That supplementation is precisely what is supplied by the world in which the individual lives, including (but not limited to) that portion of the individual's meaningful world, i.e., his/her *Umwelt*, that is constituted of other persons. In this case, the "personal" converges with the extra-personal to form the inter-personal.

Stern was of the view, informed by his many years of closely observing his own children, that some dispositions can manifest themselves very early in life, as characteristics of temperament (*Anlagen*), but it is here perhaps more than anywhere else where Stern would underscore the need

[23] Stern, *Studien zur Personwissenschaft*, 15, parentheses in original.
[24] Stern, *Studien zur Personwissenschaft*, 2.
[25] Stern, Personalistische psychologie, 167.

to conceive of dispositions as potentialities.[26] It is only through extended interaction with the world that the range of such potentialities can gradually become constricted, so that what is initially but a mild tendency in one direction but allowing for many other possibilities can become a relatively firm inclination. It was specifically for such firm inclinations that Stern reserved the term "trait" (*Eigenschaft*), and it was in the spirit of this postulated progression from temperamental tendencies to firmer traits that Stern observed that an adult "can exert an influence on the directions taken by a young child's temperamental tendencies, but must find a way to come to terms with a more developed individual's emergent traits."[27]

It bears re-emphasis here that not even as a genuine trait in the critically personalistic sense of the term does a personal disposition become fully determinant of an individual's behavior or psychological state of being. On the contrary, an individual's dispositional inclinations are never fully determinant of his/her actions, but instead are ever in need of supplementation by the world in order for one or another of the potentialities they incorporate to be actualized. Stern wrote:

There is no pattern of life or of experience, no condition or mode of behavior of the person that could be derived exclusively from dispositions, just as there is no such item that could be uniquely determined by the milieu. The milieu has an effect only because *susceptibility* to its influence is pre-established in dispositions. For their part, dispositions must be supplemented; they eventuate into explicit action only because the environmental situation affords them the prompting or the material for doing so.[28]

Living and experiencing are ever and continuously matters of person-world convergence.

On the reasons for critical personalism's historical obscurity

In a letter to Jonas Cohn dated March 9, 1904, when Stern was hard at work on the first volume of *Person and Thing*, he wrote:

[26] See H. Behrens and W. Deutsch, Die Tagebücher von Clara und William Stern. In W. Deutsch (ed.) *Über die Verborgene Aktualität von William Stern* (Frankfurt am Main: Peter Lang Verlag, 1991) 19–36. See also Lamiell, *William Stern, A Brief Introduction*.
[27] W. Stern, "*Auf Anlagen kann man wirken; mit Eigenschaften muss man rechnen.*" Personalistische psychologie, 167.
[28] W. Stern, *General Psychology From the Personalistic Standpoint*, H. D. Spoerl (trans.) (New York: The Macmillan Company, 1938).

All of my recent empirical work is but something to keep me busy during the course of the semester. The quiet vacation days have been and are dedicated above all to my true life's work, the worldview project. If things go well, I hope to be able to publish the first volume by the end of the year... Only very few people will understand it, and hardly anyone will agree with it. It is difficult and quite off the beaten path, but nevertheless I believe in its future.[29]

Its future was not something that Stern would live to see. He died in April of 1938, and in an appreciation written soon thereafter, Gordon Allport (1897–1967) could only forecast, with a hint of bravado, that critical personalism would "one day have its day," and that its day would "be long and bright."[30] That day has yet to come.

The divorce of psychology from philosophy

Up until *Psychology and Personalism* was published, in 1917, Stern had deliberately given his philosophical writings a low profile in psychological circles. His own commentary on that fact in the introductory pages of *Psychology and Personalism* is revealing. Speaking of himself in the third person, Stern wrote that

the author has, up to now, produced primarily works of empirical psychology which, though based on a certain philosophical standpoint whose features were quite apparent to knowledgeable readers, were nevertheless not explicitly and systematically incorporated into the psychological considerations. On the other hand, and quite independent of his specialized psychological works, this same author has sought to establish the system of a philosophical worldview he has called "critical personalism." The author was always aware of an organic connection between these two domains of work, but this connection was so little apparent to others that many preferred to regard his preoccupation with a worldview as "anti-psychological," as a dalliance that at best would have no bearing on, and might even do damage to, the psychological works.[31]

The last point made by Stern in this passage is entirely plausible given the rise to favor among psychologists of a positivistic-empiricistic outlook on their discipline. For by the time that *Psychology and Personalism* was published, proceedings toward a divorce of psychology from philosophy had been underway for no less than two decades, and the positivistic-empiricistic contours of that development are clearly visible in the *fin de siècle* writings of none other than Stern's own mentor at the University of

[29] Lück and Löwisch, *Briefwechsel*, 58.
[30] G. W. Allport, William Stern: 1871–1938. *The American Journal of Psychology* 51 (1938) 770–773, 773.
[31] W. Stern, *Die Psychologie und der Personalismus*, 2–3.

Berlin and then senior colleague at the University of Breslau, Hermann Ebbinghaus (1850–1909).[32]

Consider, for example, Ebbinghaus' critique of Wilhelm Dilthey's (1833–1911) famous call for a *verstehende Psychologie*.[33] In that work, Dilthey advocated a psychology devoted to *understanding* behavior by interpreting its meaning in consideration of the larger socio-cultural context within which it transpires. This he contrasted with the dominant *erklärende Psychologie* aimed at *explaining* behavior in the cause–effect terms of natural science.

Resolutely committed to the continued prosecution of psychology strictly on the terms of natural science, Ebbinghaus trained his arguments against Dilthey's views squarely on the latter's conception of causal explanation as something requiring an explication of the specific mechanisms through which causes realize their effects.[34] Against this view, Ebbinghaus wrote:

> It may be that most natural scientists hold to the assumption that the external world can be explained in mechanistic fashion, but the scientific status of their work is not dependent on this idea. One should recall the writings of E. Mach, who never tired in his efforts to [establish that] the mechanical explanation of things is not a necessary component of genuine and truly scientific investigations. Rather, when such occurs at all, it is a supererogatory matter, so to say.[35]

The E. Mach to whom Ebbinghaus referred in this passage was, of course, the physicist *cum* philosopher Ernst Mach (1838–1916), whose ideas concerning science and scientific explanation were strongly influenced by the positivism of Auguste Comte (1798–1857) and would in turn influence the logical positivists of the Vienna Circle. Continuing his critique of Dilthey, Ebbinghaus wrote:

> [To see how Mach's ideas apply in psychology], one need look no further than to the law of association. Psychologists see a causal relationship in the co-occurrence of two sensations based on the fact that, over a series of instances, the mental

---

[32] See W. Wundt, *Die Psychologie im Kampf ums Dasein*, zweite Auflage (Leipzig: Kröner, 1913). In the foreword to that work, Wundt warned that, were the contemplated divorce to take place, "philosophy will lose more than it will gain, but psychology will be damaged the most" (p. *i*).

[33] W. Dilthey, *Ideen über eine beschreibende und zergliedernde Psychologie*. *Sitzungsberichte der Akademie der Wissenschaften zu Berlin, zweiter Halbband* (1894) 1,309–1,407.

[34] See e.g., H. Ebbinghaus, *Psychology: An Elementary Textbook*, Max Meyer (trans.) (Boston, NY: D.C. Heath and Co. Publishers, 1908). Ebbinghaus insisted that psychology should continue to follow the course set by natural science: "In order to understand correctly the thoughts and impulses of man, we must treat them just as we treat material bodies [in natural science], or as we treat the lines and points of mathematics," p. 9.

[35] H. Ebbinghaus, *Über erklärende und beschreibende Psychologie. Zeitschrift für Psychologie* 9 (1896) 161–205.

image of one produces the other. No one claims on the basis of such a relationship that the effect must somehow be contained within the cause, or that there must be some sort of quantitative equivalence between the two. Indeed, however one might construe the process, it is difficult to understand what might be meant by such a claim.[36]

Here, Ebbinghaus was quite explicitly advocating an essentially positivistic conception of scientific explanation in psychology, and, as is well known, one major objective of the positivists – indeed, perhaps *the* major objective – was to rid science of all traces of metaphysics. This was an objective that Stern never embraced – not even during his days as a student of Ebbinghaus. On the contrary, in a *Selbstdarstellung* or intellectual autobiography published in 1927, Stern recalled that upon his matriculation at the University of Berlin (today the Humboldt University) in 1888, he bemoaned his discovery there that most of the philosophers were interested either in the history of philosophy or in epistemology.[37] "It was," he stated ruefully, "as if the concept as well as the word 'metaphysics' had been banned, regarded as the ruins of a by-gone historical era."[38]

Tellingly, Stern went on to state in the *Selbstdarstellung* that it was not until much later in his scholarly life that he would realize what a loss it had been for him to have failed during his student days to avail himself more fully of the tuition of Ebbinghaus' intellectual adversary, Dilthey.[39] As was true of Stern himself, Dilthey did not share Ebbinghaus' positivistic antipathy toward metaphysics, and, in other ways as well, Stern's nascent worldview was, already by then, much more compatible with the views of Dilthey than with those of Ebbinghaus.

It was, however, the positivistic/empiricistic perspective that gained the upper hand as psychology moved into the twentieth century. Stern's friend and countryman Hugo Münsterberg (1863–1915) argued in his 1900 book, *Foundations of Psychology*, that while questions of an essentially personalistic nature, i.e., questions concerning values, ethics, esthetics, etc., should by no means be ignored, they must also be recognized as falling strictly within the domain of philosophy and ever beyond the reach of an empirical psychology.[40] Thus, while Münsterberg

[36] Ebbinghaus, Über erklärende und beschreibende Psychologie, 186.
[37] W. Stern, Selbstdarstellung. In R. Schmidt (ed.) *Philosophie der Gegenwart in Selbstdarstellung, Vol. 6* (Leipzig: Barth, 1927) 128–184. W. Stern's English translation of this work was published as: William Stern, S. Langer (trans.). In C. Murchison (ed.) *A History of Psychology in Autobiography, Vol. 1* (Worcester, MA: Clark University Press, 1930) 335–388.
[38] Stern, William Stern: *History in Autobiography*, 131.
[39] See Stern, William Stern: *History in Autobiography*, 132.
[40] H. Münsterberg, *Grundzüge der Psychologie* (Leipzig: Barth, 1900).

was no positivist (he did not deny the meaningfulness of metaphysical questions), he certainly advocated a psychology that would keep its collective nose in the empirical data, so to speak, and leave the metaphysical questions to the metaphysicians (philosophers). To Stern, this attitude was unsatisfactory, and he explicitly stated as much in a letter to Jonas Cohn dated November 11, 1900. Stern wrote that he had been reading Münsterberg's *Foundations of Psychology*, and commented:

I find myself very sympathetic toward the seriousness and urgency with which Münsterberg takes up questions of philosophical principles ... Nevertheless, his solution does not satisfy me. He has left us still with the problem of reconciling the "two truths." One cannot without contradiction be an ethical idealist in metaphysics and a mechanist in psychology.[41]

Of course, nowhere in early twentieth-century psychology was the antimetaphysical perspective more strongly represented than in the behavioristic school of thought initiated by J. B. Watson (1878–1958). In his view, behaviorism meant the end not only for metaphysics but for philosophy more generally:

With the behavioristic point of view now becoming dominant, it is hard to find a place for what has been called philosophy. Philosophy is passing – has all but passed, and unless new issues arise which will give a foundation for a new philosophy, the world has seen its last great philosopher.[42]

In this light, it is not difficult to understand why Stern would claim in his last major work that the personalistic framework was broad enough to accommodate all of the then extant perspectives in psychology with the exception of behaviorism.[43] Among its other implications, this claim may be seen as a reaffirmation, in 1935, of a philosophical conviction that Stern had made explicit quite early on in his scholarly career, in a work that, while not published until 1915, was authored in 1901.[44] Stern attributed the publication lag in part to his youthful uncertainty, but also in part to his realization that the intellectual climate at the time, the very climate that his mentor Ebbinghaus was fostering, was simply not favorable for a work that would link metaphysical considerations to psychology.

Early in the work just mentioned, titled (in translation) "Preliminary Considerations for a Worldview," Stern wrote:

[41] Lück and Löwisch, *Briefwechsel*, 39.
[42] J. B. Watson, *The Ways of Behaviorism* (New York: Harper and Brothers, 1928) 14.
[43] Stern, *Allgemeine Psychologie*.
[44] W. Stern, *Vorgedanken zur Weltanschauung* (Leipzig: Barth, 1915).

A worldview is more modest than the old metaphysics, but it is also more demanding than skepticism and positivism. A worldview renounces the notion of metaphysical knowledge in the sense of absolute truth, but it affirms the metaphysical impulse toward the greatest possible unification of all convictions and evaluations, and it strives to satisfy this impulse to the fullest degree humanly possible.[45]

Given that these words were penned in 1901, when Stern was but 30 years of age, it seems warranted to say that his understanding of the proper role of philosophical considerations in psychology was, from the very start, far out of step with the views of most of his contemporaries within psychology. As if that were not problematic enough, developments in the domain of method would further undermine critical personalism's prospects within the mainstream of the discipline. Ironically, these developments took place largely within an investigative framework that was formally initiated by Stern himself.

Psychologists' uncritical embrace of statistical concepts and methods

Stern's early call for a "differential" psychology. In his highly influential *Psychology and Industrial Efficiency*, published in 1913, Hugo Münsterberg wrote:

As long as experimental psychology remained essentially a science of the mental laws common to all human beings, an adjustment to the practical demands of daily life could hardly come into question. With such general laws we could never have mastered the concrete situations of society, because we should have had to leave out of view the fact that there are gifted and ungifted, intelligent and stupid, sensitive and obtuse, quick and slow, energetic and weak individuals.[46]

Already by the turn of the twentieth century, pressure was mounting within psychology for greater attention to matters of practical concern outside of the discipline, in the schools, military, business and industry, health care and so on, and the "pure" psychology defended by Wundt seemed wholly inept in the face of such concerns.[47] It was precisely because Wundt-ian investigative methods were aimed at the discovery of the *general* laws of consciousness – i.e., laws that are "common to all" (*allen gemein*) – that those methods were not well suited to accommodate

[45] Stern, *Vorgedanken*, 4.
[46] H. Münsterberg, *Psychology and Industrial Efficiency* (Boston and New York: Houghton-Mifflin, 1913) 9–10.
[47] See K. Danziger, *Constructing the Subject: Historical Origins of Psychological Research* (Cambridge University Press, 1990).

individual and group differences.[48] This was the source of the difficulty of which Münsterberg wrote.

What was needed, then, was a framework within which it would be possible to investigate systematically just those between-person and between-group differences that the early experimentalists were deliberately ignoring. As it happened, the pioneering work of Francis Galton (1822–1911) and Karl Pearson (1857–1936) in the study of intelligence differences had already provided the rudimentary technical wherewithal for doing this, so there was nothing to prevent the expansion of investigative boundaries beyond the study of intelligence differences into other substantive domains such as abilities, interests, personality characteristics, etc. Rather than investigating individual research subjects one by one (an approach to psychological research logically mandated by the quest for knowledge of general laws in the sense defined above), the quantitative methods developed and refined by Galton and Pearson could be used to investigate large numbers of research subjects simultaneously, with the objective of determining the statistical characteristics of those variables with respect to which individuals and groups were being differentiated.[49] More specifically, the focus would be on the population means and variances of measures of the attributes or characteristics of interest, and, most importantly, on population level correlations between such measures and criterion variables of practical interest.

These are the ideas that served as the basis for the establishment of a "differential" psychology alongside the general-experimental psychology that Wundt had founded, and, wearing his psychological hat, William Stern was the person most responsible for this development. His 1900 book, *On the Psychology of Individual Differences*, was the first systematic attempt in this direction.[50] With the publication eleven years later of *Methodological Foundations of Differential Psychology*, the new subdiscipline assumed a secure and clearly defined place within the field as a whole.[51]

In the 1900 book, Stern identified the three central tasks of differential psychology as those of: (1) determining the most fundamental

---

[48] In addition to his general experimental psychology, Wundt also envisioned a cultural psychology (*Völkerpsychologie*) that would be pursued outside of laboratories designed for experimental investigation. In a 1914 publication, Stern explicitly identified the differential psychology, entailing what he termed "test experiments," as a third alternative positioned between Wundt's general-experimental psychology and his cultural psychology. See W. Stern, Psychologie. In D. Sarason (ed.) *Das Jahr 1913: Ein Gesamtbild der Kulturentwicklung* (Leipzig/Berlin: Teubner, 1914) 414–421; see in particular p. 416.

[49] See Lamiell, *Beyond Individual and Group Differences*, esp. ch. 2.

[50] Stern, *Über Psychologie der Individuellen Differenzen*.

[51] Stern, *Die Differentielle Psychologie*.

dimensions of between-person differences; (2) discovering the sources of those differences (presumably in some combination of nature and nurture); and (3) explicating the effects or consequences of those differences in various domains of human endeavor (school, work, personal life, etc.). By the time that his second differential psychology text was published, in 1911, Stern's outlook on the field had become more nuanced, to the point where he found it necessary to distinguish four basic research schemes proper to the discipline.[52]

Within the first of those four, "variation" research, one would investigate a single attribute variable in terms of the distribution of measures of that attribute across individuals within a population ("one attribute, many individuals"). The second scheme, "correlation" research, would be devoted to the study of the co-variation(s) in measures of two or more individual differences variables within a population ("two or more attributes, many individuals"). Both of these research schemes, Stern noted, are properly understood as yielding empirical knowledge of *attribute variables*.

The third research scheme is one Stern called "psychography" (*die Psychographie*). In that scheme, one would study a single individual in terms of two or more attributes ("one individual, many attributes"), while the fourth scheme, "comparison" research, would enable comparisons of individuals, each of whom has been represented in terms of an array of attributes ("two or more individuals, many attributes"). It is within these latter two research schemes – and not within either of the first two – where knowledge of individuals would be secured. Even here, Stern sounded a cautionary methodological note:

So as to eliminate right from the start a possible misunderstanding, it must be emphasized that psychography can never substitute for biography. On the contrary, the biographer of the future will make use of a psychographic schema or rely on already available psychograms of his subject only as preliminary work alongside of archival and other source material. It is only through a synthetic and artistically empathic processing of such material that a genuine biography can be produced.[53]

As this passage suggests, Stern was fully cognizant of the methodological implications of his personalistic worldview for the conduct of psychological research, and this is why he could state with full justification in the 1927 *Selbstdarstellung* that "even [in 1900] I could see that true individuality, the understanding of which was my ultimate objective,

---

[52] Stern, *Die Differentielle Psychologie*, see esp. p. 18.
[53] Stern, *Die Differentielle Psychologie*, 329.

cannot be grasped through the channels of differential psychology."[54] The reason for this, Stern argued, is that differential psychology of necessity fractionates the individual into a collection of attributes and hence fails to do justice to the *unitas multiplex* of personhood. As he would repeatedly emphasize:

All research into the isolated details of specific aspects of the functioning of persons must be organized from the standpoint of their relationship to the whole; every particular must be located with reference to the whole. That is, its determination by the whole and its significance for the whole must be made clear. The principle of "whole-relatedness" (*Ganzheitsbezogenheit*) must be regarded as the central theme of personalistic research.[55]

Later in the same work from which this passage is taken, Stern acknowledged that the task of relating all of the investigated particulars to the whole would not have to be, and indeed could not be, carried out in fact in every single investigation. Trying to do that, he noted, "would render the more specialized work unspeakably difficult or even illusory."[56] By the same token, however, he stressed that every methodological concession to the practical necessity of isolating discrete aspects of experience for investigation is a provisional application of elementalistic *methods* that neither requires nor scientifically justifies an elementalistic *theoretical account* of whatever has been discovered through the exercise of those methods.[57] Moreover, ultimate fidelity to the principle of whole-relatedness would require the use of interpretive methods (not merely the search for cause–effect relationships), and Stern designated the challenge of developing sound interpretive methods as "one of the most urgent tasks of scientific psychology."[58] Alas, despite Stern's repeated insistence on this and related points, the majority of his contemporaries continued to move in a direction that was incompatible with his personalistic convictions.[59]

Differential psychology's fateful wrong turn. In what was arguably the single most untoward misstep in twentieth-century psychology, mainstream thinking within differential psychology managed to obscure the distinction Stern had drawn in 1911 between knowledge of individuals, on the one hand, and knowledge of attribute variables in terms of which

[54] Stern, William Stern: *History in Autobiography*, 142.
[55] Stern, *Studien zur Personwissenschaft*, 2.   [56] Stern, *Studien zur Personwissenschaft*, 31.
[57] The failure to grasp this distinction is one of the unfortunate legacies of the methodological empiricism that has for so long prevailed in mainstream psychology.
[58] Stern, Personalistische Psychologie, 175. The insistence on the development of and appreciation for interpretive/qualitative research methods is prominent even in the highly quantitatively-oriented *Die Differentielle Psychologie* book of 1911. For a further discussion of this point see Lamiell, *Beyond Individual and Group Differences*.
[59] See Lamiell, Ursprungsmythos; see also Lamiell, *William Stern: Brief Introduction*.

individuals have been differentiated, on the other. Instead, the over-whelming majority of investigators within the field proceeded in accor-dance with a view articulated by E. L. Thorndike (1874–1949) in a treatise on "individuality" also published in 1911.[60] On the latter's view, knowledge of variables with respect to which individuals have been differ-entiated just *is* knowledge of the individuals who have been differentiated in terms of those variables.

In Thorndike's 1911 book, this view is manifest explicitly in his con-tention that the correlation between measures of two traits within a group of individuals is an empirical indicator of "the extent to which the amount of one trait possessed by an individual is bound up with the amount he possesses of some other trait."[61] The fatal problem here is that unless correlations of the type Thorndike was discussing are perfect, i.e., equal to +/− 1.00 – which of course is never empirically the case – his claim that such correlations are indicative of some individual-level empirical factuality is simply not true. Less-than-perfect reliability co-efficients are *not* empirical indicators of temporal (in)consistency in individuals' behavioral manifestations of putative personality characteristics.[62] Less-than-perfect validity coefficients are *not* empiri-cal indicators of the predictability of individual behavior.[63] Probabilistic claims to knowledge about individuals based on population-level statisti-cal evidence are *not* logically warranted.[64] Despite all of this, mainstream thinking in the psychology of personality has long since accorded – and continues to accord – fully with Thorndike's claim, in all of its many superficially different renditions, and it is only for this reason that the study of individual differences variables can even *appear* adequate as a means of securing scientific knowledge about individuals.[65]

But it is appearance and nothing more. What "personality psychology" has become in the hands of those legion investigators who have labored for decades in the intellectual patrimony of Thorndike is, finally, a species of demography. If the work can be said to be "psychological" at all, that

[60] E. L. Thorndike, *Individuality* (New York: Houghton-Mifflin, 1911).

[61] Thorndike, *Individuality*, 21.

[62] W. Mischel, *Personality and Assessment* (New York: Wiley, 1968).

[63] D. J. Bem and S. Allen, On predicting some of the people some of the time: The search for cross-situational consistencies in behavior. *Psychological Review* **81** (1974) 506–520; S. Epstein, The stability of behavior: I. On predicting most of the people much of the time. *Journal of Personality and Social Psychology* **37** (1979) 1,097–1,126.

[64] R. R. McCrae and P. T. Costa, Jr., Trait explanations in personality psychology. *European Journal of Personality* **9** (1997) 231–252.

[65] See Lamiell, *Beyond Individual and Group Differences*, esp. ch. 7. See also J. T. Lamiell, Individuals and the differences between them. In R. Hogan, J. Johnson, and S. Briggs (eds.) *Handbook of Personality Psychology* (New York: Academic Press) 117–141.

is only because the labels assigned to the variables under investigation have a psychological "ring." Labels notwithstanding, the work is, at its core, demographic in nature. The knowledge generated is not knowledge of persons at all, but rather knowledge of between-person variables. By definition, a between-person variable cannot be defined for any individual person. Such variables, and all correlations based on them, can be defined only for *populations* of persons, and the quest for knowledge of populations is precisely what demography is.[66]

Had Stern's contemporaries and their successors in differential psychology properly grasped and scrupulously respected his altogether valid distinction between knowledge of individuals, on the one hand, and knowledge of individual difference variables ("attributes") on the other, then the need for genuinely personalistic inquiry of the sort Stern repeatedly called for would have remained starkly apparent no matter what the empirical accomplishments of researchers studying individual differences.[67] But because this did not happen, neither psychographic research (in the specific sense described above) nor any other form of inquiry logically suited to the production of knowledge of persons has ever been seen by a critical mass of personality investigators as in any way fundamental to the discipline's scientific agenda. Still less has there ever been any widespread recognition of the need for a sound theoretical and philosophical framework within which to orient oneself properly *vis-à-vis* the empirical knowledge yielded by studies of attributes, on the one hand, and of individuals, on the other. This is true despite Stern's clear admonition on just this point in the foreword of the 1911 *Methodological Foundations* text:

That my conception of the structure of the human individual and of psychological differentiation is not uninfluenced by my fundamental philosophical convictions is obvious. But since this book is devoted to the founding of an empirical science, I have reduced the philosophical aspects of the work to a minimum. For the justification of ideas many of which are discussed here only too briefly, the reader is referred to my philosophical book. But I hope that the usefulness of the present work is not dependent upon agreement with the author's philosophical assumptions (which on many points deviate in non-trivial ways from the currently prevailing opinions).[68]

Alas, it appears that for reasons discussed earlier, all too few of Stern's contemporaries or successors ever made their way to his philosophical

---

[66] See J. T. Lamiell, Statisticism in personality psychologists' use of trait constructs: What is it? How was it contracted? Is there a cure? *New Ideas in Psychology*, in press.

[67] Lamiell, Individuals and the differences between them.

[68] Stern, *Die Differentielle Psychologie*, p. v. The "philosophical book" mentioned by Stern in this passage would have been Volume 1 of *Person and Thing*.

works. As a result, twentieth-century differential psychology became something quite other – and much less – than what Stern the critically personalistic differential psychologist envisioned, and his "philosophical works" became essentially invisible.[69] So the question begs: might there be a place for personalistic thinking in twenty-first century psychology?

On critical personalism's once and future prospects within psychology

Enduring impediments

In taking up the question just posed, it is worthwhile to keep in mind that in Stern's own time, critical personalism was quite favorably received in certain scholarly circles, most notably philosophy and pedagogy.[70] Moreover, and as already noted, Gordon Allport was one prominent figure within psychology who urged his contemporaries to give careful consideration to Stern's writings.[71]

Nevertheless, it is sobering to realize that the major twentieth-century impediments to personalistic thinking discussed in this work remain in place.[72] In the light of this fact, it is, admittedly, difficult to see how Stern's ideas could fare any better in the foreseeable future than they have fared in the past.

Consider: as of August, 2011, the Society for Theoretical and Philosophical Psychology, which is Division 24 of the American Psychological Association (APA), had an official membership count of 376, whereas the average membership across the fifty-five officially recognized divisions of the APA is 1,161.[73] Only four of the fifty-five divisions have memberships smaller than Division 24. These numbers suggest the relative paucity of interest within the APA in broad theoretical and philosophical questions as opposed to relatively narrow fields of specialized empirical inquiry.

Moreover, it would appear that across those fields of specialization, the "cult of empiricism" decried by Toulmin and Leary fully a quarter

---

[69] Lamiell, Ursprungsmythos; Lamiell, *William Stern: Brief Introduction*, esp. ch. 2.
[70] See Lamiell, *William Stern: Brief Introduction*, ch. 8.
[71] G. W. Allport, The personalistic psychology of William Stern. *Character and Personality* 5 (1937) 231–246.
[72] See J. T. Lamiell, On sustaining critical discourse with mainstream personality investigators: Problems and prospects. *Theory and Psychology* 17 (2007) 169–185.
[73] These data were provided to the author by Keith Cooke of the American Psychological Association on August 11, 2011.

of a century ago still dominates.[74] Results of a recently published study indicate that much of the contemporary university-level instruction in research methods in psychology implicitly endorses a positivistic conception of inquiry in the discipline, reflecting, in a worrisomely uncritical fashion, the view that "empirical methodology is more fundamental to establishing a discipline as a science than is speculative theory, integrative theory, or conceptual analysis."[75]

Within the narrower sub-discipline of personality psychology, the mainstream intellectual atmosphere is certainly no better, and it is arguably worse. There continues to be widespread agreement with the view that the merits of trait-based explanations for behavior are properly decided not through deliberations that incorporate "philosophical discourse and formal logic," but instead strictly "on the basis of computer-generated p-values."[76] The prevailing view continues to be that "a real understanding of causes is evident in some level of prediction and control,"[77] that "we scientists are the experts in this game,"[78] and that the job of philosophers, if indeed there is one, is merely "to explain how we [psychologists] manage to make reasonably correct inferences."[79] The anti-philosophical ethos fostered by such views is no more hospitable to critical personalism (or any other philosophically informed system of thought) now than it was in the early decades of the twentieth century, when the tenets of that ethos – tenets that are themselves philosophical – were first widely embraced.

Daunting along these same lines is the content of a 1999 response to a publisher's request to review a detailed prospectus for the present author's 2003 book *Beyond Individual and Group Differences: Human Individuality, Scientific Psychology, and William Stern's Critical Personalism.* The prospective reviewer declined, writing:

The philosophical and historical approach taken by [the author] was of no interest to me and, I suspect, is of little interest to most people in the field . . . I suggest that you have someone more attuned to his philosophical predilections review this manuscript . . . Sorry that I could not be of greater assistance to you. I tried

---

[74] S. Toulmin and D. E. Leary, The cult of empiricism in psychology, and beyond. In S. Koch and D. E. Leary (eds.) *A Century of Psychology as Science* (New York: McGraw-Hill, 1985) 594–617.

[75] R. E. Costa and C. P. Shimp, Methods courses and texts in psychology: "Textbook Science" and "Tourist Brochures". *Journal of Theoretical and Philosophical Psychology* 31 (2011) 25–43.

[76] McCrae and Costa, Trait explanations; the quoted passage appears on page 248.

[77] McCrae and Costa, Trait explanations, 249.

[78] McCrae and Costa, Trait explanations, 249.

[79] McCrae and Costa, Trait explanations, 249.

to read the manuscript and I found it of no interest and of little relevance to the kinds of issues I address in my work.[80]

These comments notwithstanding, the book in question was eventually published, and one reviewer of the work did express appreciation for its historical component. In the end, however, that same reviewer conceded his doubt that adherents of traditional thinking would rise to the personalistic challenge that the book presents.[81] Some confirmation of those doubts can be seen in another review of the same book, in which the reviewer dismissed the author's critique of conventional statistical thinking in personality psychology as "sophistry."[82]

A possible future

However bleak the immediate prospects for critical personalism might seem to be in the light of the *status quo* just described, current and continuing developments within psychology might yet present more favorable opportunities.

A strong case can be made for the argument that psychology is dying – if, indeed, it is not already dead, as Gazzaniga has declared.[83] For many contemporaries, this death, whether pending or *fait accompli*, is attributable to advances in disciplines seen to be more fundamental in the hierarchy of sciences – most prominently evolutionary biology and neuroscience. However, even well before the great proliferation of interest in (and research funding for) work grounded in those disciplines, psychology had unwittingly begun its own demise from the opposite end of the spectrum of the behavioral sciences, by embracing statistical modes of inquiry suited not to the knowledge objectives of a genuine *psychology* at all, but, as argued earlier, suited only to knowledge objectives of demography, or what the Belgian scholar Adolphe Quetelet (1796–1874) envisioned under the name "social physics."[84]

Yet for as long as there is a critical mass of scholars – to say nothing of the lay public – with an abiding desire to understand not mere *parts*

---

[80] Anonymous comments of a prospective reviewer of the prospectus for the book Lamiell, *Beyond Individual and Group Differences.*

[81] J. Valsiner, Toward a new science of the person. *Theory and Psychology* **15** (2005) 401–406.

[82] W. K. B. Hofstee, *Unbehagen* in individual differences – a review. *Journal of Individual Differences* **28** (2007) 252–253. For a reply to the charge of sophistry, see Lamiell, Statisticism.

[83] M. S. Gazzaniga, *The Mind's Past* (Berkeley, CA: University of California Press, 1998).

[84] See T. M. Porter, *The Rise of Statistical Thinking: 1820–1900* (Princeton University Press, 1986).

of persons, such as brains, and not mere *aggregates* of persons, such as experimentally created "treatment groups" or representatively selected population "samples" – but *persons per se*, there will be reason to consider critical personalism as one possible framework for conceptual analysis and empirical inquiry.[85] By its very nature, the framework cannot possibly be undermined by developments in brain science, nor can it be superseded by any species of demography, not even one that uses psychological terms to label its variables. Because of this, it is perhaps not overly optimistic to suggest that within a genuine *psychology* the need for which will surely endure after the brain scientists have gone their way, and after the psycho-demographers have finally been widely recognized for what they are – and are not – personalistic thinking might have its day after all.

[85] See M. R. Bennett and P. M. S. Hacker, *Philosophical Foundations of Neuroscience* (Oxford: Blackwell Publishing, 2003).

Part III

Social-developmental perspectives

7   Conceiving of self and others as persons: evolution and development

John Barresi, Chris Moore, and Raymond Martin

In common language and experience, at least in English, "self" and "other" are opposing terms for the same kind of thing, an individual human being or person.[1] Like "I" and "you," they are deictic terms that shift with the user. I am a "self" to me and an "other" to you, and you are a "self" to you and an "other" to me. In order for us to use these terms, we must be able to recognize that you and I are both persons – that we are equivalent in this way. But our personhood is experienced differently by each of us. Your experience of your personhood is an experience of your self and my experience of my personhood is an experience of my self. Our experience of each other's personhood is that of an-other person.

Given the differences in our experience of self and other, how is it that we come to understand both selves and others as persons and can learn to apply deictic terms such as "I" and "you" so easily that even 2-year-olds can have a conceptual understanding of themselves and others as the same kind of things, selves and persons, and are able to ascribe at least some psychological attributes equally both to themselves and others? The two major current theories of how we understand mental phenomena in ourselves and others – simulation theory (ST) and the theory theory of mind (TT) – have difficulty explaining the ease with which children acquire this understanding, given how the asymmetry in our access to information about mental states of self and other is dealt with in these theories.[2] As a consequence, recently there has been a renewed interest

[1] We wish to thank Jack Martin and Mark Bickhard for their editorial assistance. Separate grants from Social Sciences and Humanities Research Council (SSHRC) of Canada to John Barresi and Chris Moore supported research for this chapter.
[2] D. Premack and G. Woodruff, Does the chimpanzee have a theory of mind? *Behavioral and Brain Sciences* **1** (1978) 515–525, originated the label "theory of mind" (ToM); A. Goldman, *Simulating Minds: The Philosophy, Psychology and Neuroscience of Mindreading* (Oxford University Press, 2006) provides a recent review of the two major theories. A third type of theory focuses on intersubjectivity and interpersonal relations. Our own view falls within this third approach; see, J. Barresi and C. Moore, Intentional relations and social understanding. *Behavioral and Brain Sciences* **19** (1996) 107–122, and, especially, The neuroscience of social understanding. In J. Zlatev, T. Racine, C. Sinha,

128   *John Barresi, Chris Moore, and Raymond Martin*

in theories that focus on the person rather than on mental states. These theories maintain that there is a constitutive link between our ability to apply psychological terms to self and to other. We could not learn to apply mental concepts to self without also learning how to apply them to others. Likewise for the reverse relation, our ability to recognize psychological states of others is intimately tied to our ability to recognize them in ourselves. These person theories maintain that there is a direct non-causal, necessary connection between mental events and their expression. Thus, mental events are not hidden within the organism with only contingent causal relations to their behavioral expressions. Rather, they are transparent in their expression. While the enormous figure of Wittgenstein stands in the background of this alternative approach, much of the inspiration for these theories is Peter Strawson's non-dualist account of persons.[3]

Strawson insists that we cannot do without two ways of viewing ourselves and others, a first- and a third-person perspective, and that whatever concepts we use to describe self must also be equally useful in describing others. In his view, this requires that we understand our selves and others as persons, where persons are objects with material properties that apply to all objects (M-predicates) as well as psychological properties that apply specifically to persons (P-predicates). He views the concept of person as a primitive and essential one that necessarily precedes any notion of a conscious or mental self. He points to a number of contradictions that arise when we attempt to view ourselves as conscious selves, or minds, on criteria that are independent of our bodies and also try to attribute analogous conscious selves to others based on their behavior. Such attempts always give rise to some form of a mistaken dualism in describing persons, though not always dualisms of substance. Unless material and mental predicates can both be ascribed to the same individual entity we can make no coherent sense of their application equally to self and other.

Strawson provides a useful summary of the problems that arise when one tries to provide a general theory of mind that gives priority to the first-person perspective of self (like ST) and is generalized to others, or

and E. Itkonen (eds.) *The Shared Mind: Perspectives on Intersubjectivity* (Amsterdam: John Benjamins, 2008) 39–66.
[3] See A. Avramides, *Other Minds* (London: Routledge, 2001); J. L. Bermúdez, *The Paradox of Self-consciousness* (Cambridge, MA: MIT Press, 1998); J. Dow, On the joint engagement of persons: Self-consciousness, the symmetry thesis and person perception. *Philosophical Psychology* (in press); A. Newen and T. Schlicht, Understanding other minds: A criticism of Goldman's simulation theory and an outline of the person model theory. *Grazer Philosophische Studien* **79** (2009) 209–242; A. Seemann, Person perception. *Philosophical Explorations* **11** (2008) 245–262; and P. F. Strawson, *Individuals* (New York: Taylor and Francis, 1959).

gives priority to the third-person perspective of others (like TT) and is generalized to self:

Just as there is not in general one primary process of learning, or teaching oneself, an inner meaning for predicates of this class (P predicates), then another process of learning to apply such predicates to others on the strength of correlation, noted in one's own case with certain forms of behavior, so – and equally – there is not in general one primary process of learning to apply such predicates to others on the strength of behavior criteria, and then another secondary technique of exhibiting a new form of behavior, viz. first-person P-utterances.[4]

Strawson says that both of these pictures are refusals to note the unique logical character of P-predicates – that these predicates, or properties of persons, are known and ascribable in different ways from the first- and third-person perspective:

It is essential to the character of these predicates that they have first- and third-person ascriptive uses, that they are both self-ascribable otherwise than on the basis of observation of behavior of the subject of them, and other-ascribable on the basis of behavioral criteria... In order to understand this type of concept, one must acknowledge that there is a kind of predicate which is unambiguously and adequately ascribable both on the observation of the subject of the predicate and not on this basis in one's own case.[5]

Strawson says that without the possibility of concepts of this type we could have no concept of person that applies equally to self and other.

Like Wittgenstein before him, Strawson claims that there are non-causal internal relations between the first-person perspective and information that we have about P-properties in our own case, and the third-person perspective and information that we have about P-properties in the case of others, so that we learn to apply these concepts by linking experiential information associated with both points of view. However, not all instances of P-properties are the same. Some are more directly observable and public, like "walking," while others are more private, like "thinking." Nevertheless, if it were not possible to ascribe at least some instances of each type successfully from both a first- and a third-person perspective, it would not be possible to form and apply concepts of P-predicates at all. Thus, applying these concepts requires being able to apply them equally to self and other. This is possible, Strawson claims, only if our notion of person is more primitive than our notions of mind or body, and this notion of person that applies equally to self and other provides the ground for ascription of psychological predicates to self and other.

[4] Strawson, *Individuals*, 104.   [5] Strawson, *Individuals*, 104–105.

In advancing this view, Strawson claims to be engaging in what he calls "descriptive metaphysics," which requires an analysis of how our everyday world presents itself to us as humans. He is not trying to provide a solution to the epistemological problem of knowledge of other minds since he sees the problem itself as incoherent. He says that once this problem is made coherent by explaining correctly how our concepts of mind are even possible, it dissolves. He also claims that his remarks on our acquisition of knowledge of P-properties in self and other are not intended "as *a priori* genetic psychology," though he provides several hints that we will discuss here on how developmental psychologists might proceed.[6] He wants only to make intelligible the conceptual scheme that we actually have. His solution is to show how our concept of person requires that both material and mental properties be ascribed to the same concrete individual and that the meaning of mental properties ascribed to self and to other are the same, though the grounds for ascribing these properties vary due to differences in our perspectives of self and other. In what follows, we agree with Strawson's assessment of the problem and argue for a unified concept of person of a Strawsonian sort as the basis of commonsense psychology.

From Strawson to a developmental psychology of persons and selves

On Strawson's account of our acquisition of mental concepts, our acquisition of mental concepts presupposes that we have a prior intuition that persons are different from other objects. This intuition is not yet the acquisition of the concept of person as individual objects to which material and psychological predicates apply. Nor does this intuition provide concepts of psychological predicates. However, Strawson does provide two hints as to how a genetic or developmental psychology might proceed from this basic intuition to ascriptions of psychological properties. The first of these is to point out that some psychological predicates that we apply to self and other are so simple that the distance between the grounds for first-person ascription and third-person ascription is small. In the case, for instance, of simple actions, like walking or writing, physical movements and psychological properties are intermingled and inseparable. When we see someone walking, we immediately perceive the intentionality of this goal-directed activity as being the same as our own intentionality in walking. So, the gap between self and other is almost negligible in simple actions limited in their goal or object directedness.

---

[6] Strawson, *Individuals*, 109.

Strawson suggests that here is where we might begin to understand how we bridge the gap between our different ways of knowing self and other, thus making a first step toward understanding psychological concepts in the same way for self and other. We will consider shortly how this idea fits within a developmental psychology of psychological ascription.

Strawson's second hint is his suggestion that individual ascriptions of psychological, or intentional, terms to self and other are not the only ways in which we ascribe such terms. In the case of activities involving forms of joint action, such as football (aka soccer), where the individual participates not so much with respect to individual intentions, but with respect to intentions or purposes of the group, Strawson briefly defends the intelligibility of the notion of "group mind." Each participant, though varying in physical behavior, shares a common intention or goal with other members of the same team. One can safely say that there is one goal here, not multiple goals, and this goal is a property of the group, a "we" goal that is singular, but nevertheless shared by individuals. In this case, there is no issue about whether there are different concepts being applied to self and other based on different criteria. It is a single concept of what *we* are doing that is applied, but understood in a first-person manner for self and in a third-person manner for others. Thus, there is a perfect match in the intention as experienced in the first-person and as experienced at the very same time in the third-person, and hence no gap in the content of the intentional state attributed to self and other based on different criteria. In what follows, we will see how this suggestion cashes out in a developmental psychology of our understanding of self and other as persons, and also show how joint cooperative activity and shared goals may have played a significant role in the evolution of the concept of person.

These two ideas of Strawson seem to have guided some recent attempts by philosophers to provide a Strawsonian "person theory" account of development that is opposed to traditional theory of mind (ToM) approaches of ST and TT.[7] What we wish to do here is to be more explicit about how our own intentional relations theory (IRT) relates to Strawson's views and, in particular, to these two ideas. The result will be an updated account of IRT, in light of more recent developments both empirical and theoretical in psychology as well as to developments in other disciplines, such as comparative psychology, evolutionary biology,

---

[7] Dow, On the joint engagement of persons; and Seemann, Person perception. In his article, Dow cites our own work as representing a person theory approach to the development of understanding of mental phenomena of persons. Indeed, Strawson's view, along with Wittgenstein's, did inspire us in developing our theory; see endnote 2 in Barresi and Moore, Intentional relations and social understanding.

Table 7.1 *A multi-level framework of social understanding of intentional relations*

Level	Type	Represents	Information
1	Separate	Only self activity	First-person current of self
		Only other activity	Third-person current of other
2	Interpersonal	Joint agent	First-person current of self and third-person current of other
		We-activity	First-person current and third-person imagined
3	Personal	Embodied agent	
		– self	First-person imagined and third-person current
		– other	First-person imagined and third-person imagined
4	Mental	Mental agent	

and philosophy. In the present section, we will focus on the Strawsonian aspects in our model of human development. In subsequent sections, we will focus on phylogenetic origins of person concepts, and the potential evolutionary source and primary function of our concept of person.

The basic question that we put forward in our original article on IRT is: How is it possible for organisms like us to represent intentional activities (actions, emotions/motivations, and epistemic activities) of self and other in the same way, when the information that we process involving our own object-directed activities (called *intentional relations*) is of a radically different kind from the information that we process of the activities of another individual?[8] Our solution, which we supported by a review of both phylo- and ontogenetic phenomena, is that we can come to a common understanding of the intentional activities of self and other only by recognizing matches between our own actions and the actions of others. In certain shared activities with others, in which mutual imitation often occurs, we recognize that matched intentional relations directed at objects appear in two forms depending on whether viewed from a first- or third-person perspective – forms that can be united into a single unified concept of the activity.

In our model (Table 7.1), we distinguish four levels in understanding of intentional relations that are of particular importance. On the first level, there are representations that help organisms recognize intentional activities of others different from the representations that guide their

[8] Barresi and Moore, Intentional relations and social understanding.

own activities. With respect to their own intentional relations, organisms process information primarily about objects toward which their activities are directed, with minimal, and primarily implicit, information about themselves. By contrast, the information that they process of other organisms, primarily those of their own species, is directed at the animate movements of these others, with less attention and understanding of the objects toward which these agents are directing their activities. Thus, at this level, representations of their own activities differ from their representations of others. We view most organisms other than humans as operating at this level. Though they may acquire an understanding of the activities of others that goes beyond mere behavior toward intentional understanding, their representations of their own and other individuals' activities do not unite and form a single unified conceptual representation that can be applied equally to self and other. Most organisms never develop a concept of self that is on a par with their concept of other organisms. On our account, this means that they cannot apply to their own intentional activities the conceptual representations that they apply to the activities of others; and conversely, any conceptual representation that they have of their own activities cannot be applied equally to the activities of others. This is not to deny that there may be low-level representations that they may apply fairly equally to self and other; but these representations cannot be at the level of the whole organism as engaged in intentional activity. This must be the case because they do not have a representation of themselves as a whole organism that is in the same form as their representations of other organisms.

At our second level, we focus on joint activities in which it is possible to match one's own to another organism's activities directed at objects. In humans, this begins to occur in infants at about 9 months, in triadic relations with adults, where they engage in joint activities of various sorts directed at a variety of objects and not merely engage in face-to-face interactions directed at each other. We see this kind of joint activity as the primary ground upon which the infant comes to form an understanding of intentional activity directed at objects from both a first- and third-person perspective. It is this kind of joint engagement in a common activity, where attention is paid both to the other actor as well as to the objects of engagement, which enables the formation of a concept of common intentional activity that is bidirectional with respect to the perspective of each agent.

Joint engagement of this sort provides the means for eventual understanding of self and other as persons. Moreover, it also provides the ground for entry into the uniquely human world, which is socially constructed rather than a natural inheritance of the species.[9] However, at this age the infant has no more than an intuition that there is something special about interacting with other humans compared to inanimate objects and other beings. There is some evidence to suggest that the beginnings of the concept of person originate at this time, at least in recognizing other humans as members of a single category as well as in the special manner in which these infants interact with members of that category.[10] These infants are capable of perceiving similarities in body parts of self and other that can be matched in imitative actions, which can be used to bridge the gap between intentional actions of self and others. Yet, they are still a long way from having a concept of individual person that they can apply both to self and other to which can be ascribed Strawsonian M- and P-properties. However, the basis for eventually forming such a concept is laid down in these interactions of joint activity directed at objects.

From the ninth to the eighteenth month, the infant goes through a rapid series of changes in understanding of joint activities and eventually achieves an understanding (presumably with Strawsonian unified concepts) of certain forms of intentional relations as properties of individual agents or persons including self.[11] The 9-month-old's engagement in joint activities starts off primarily in a passive role in the context of an adult's scaffolding of the joint activity, but as time moves on the infant becomes active in maintaining the activity. The infant's initial knowledge of the joint activity is sufficiently rich to perceive that she and the other individual are engaged with each other in an interaction involving some other object, but not rich enough to think of herself and the other equally as persons with particular intentional relations directed toward each other and toward the object. In terms of shared experience of the joint activity, this must be built up as the infant learns to behave in a coordinated fashion in the context of the scaffolded activity. In some cases,

[9] J. Barresi, Some boundary conditions on embodied agents sharing a common world. In I. Wachsmuth, M. Lenzen, and G. Knoblich (eds.) *Embodied Communication in Humans and Machines* (Oxford University Press, 2008) 29–52; M. Tomasello, M. Carpenter, J. Call, T. Behne, and H. Moll, Understanding and sharing intentions: The origins of cultural cognition. *Behavioral and Brain Sciences* **28** (2005) 675–735.

[10] L. Bonatti, E. Frot, R. Zangl, and M. Mehler, The human first hypothesis: Identification of conspecifics and individuation of objects in the young infant. *Cognitive Psychology* **44** (2002) 388–426.

[11] C. Moore, Representing intentional relations and acting intentionally in infancy: Current insights and open questions. In G. Knoblich, I. Thornton, M. Grosjean, and M. Shiffrar (eds.) *Human Body Perception from the Inside Out* (New York: Oxford University Press, 2006) 427–442; and C. Moore and J. Barresi, The construction of commonsense psychology in infancy. In P. Zelazo, M. Chandler, and E. Crone (eds.) *Developmental Social Cognitive Neuroscience* (New York: Psychology Press, 2009) 43–62.

this involves imitation of adult actions, or vice-versa, imitation by an adult of an infant's actions. Turn-taking in actions and roles may sometimes occur in these situations. Whether the joint activity is a spontaneous form of play, or some repeated form of a more structured activity like "clean up" of toys, the infant gradually begins to understand basic rules of the activity, which allow it to determine whether the shared activity is occurring in a regular fashion. It is at this point that the infant can appreciate the "normative" quality of the joint activity and engage more actively in maintaining the joint activity. She can anticipate what the adult will or should do next and even lead the adult to do it through various communications that have become part of the activity – such as pointing to a new object to pick up after a previous object has been put away. The development of these skills shifts the form of joint activity from one that is primarily controlled by the adult's scaffolding behavior to one that is more collaborative and negotiated.[12]

There is a gradual shift during this period of development, from an appreciation of the "we" aspect of the experience, with its bipolar forms of representation of common actions of self and other that can be matched and integrated, toward a capacity to perceive diversity in the activities of self and other. Unified concepts of intentional activity that at an earlier stage could be used only when applied to joint actions of self and other, now can be applied individually to self or other. This is achieved through imagined rather than active sharing. When not engaged in joint action with an adult, the infant imagines being involved in the activity that she now understands that the adult is engaged in; or vice-versa, can imagine the adult as involved with her in her own activity. This makes it possible eventually for the infant to conceive of the intentions of others from a first- as well as third-person point of view even when she is not involved in the activity, and also to represent her own intentions as if another person were also engaged in the activity and observing her performance. Thus, the first- and third-person aspects of the activity can now be unified in interpreting the action of individuals, as well as in conditions of joint action.

The outcome of these processes of development is the formation of a concept of person as an embodied agent that can engage in a variety of intentional relations that are object or goal directed. This concept of person and of a person's properties, both material and psychological, can be applied to both self and other. It appears as level 3 of our model in Table 7.1. We propose that at this level the toddler of around age 2 has a reflective capacity to represent self as a fully embodied agent

---

[12] Tomasello *et al.*, Understanding and sharing intentions.

engaging in the same kinds of intentional activities as others. Moreover, the child can also represent other individuals as experiencing from a first-person perspective the same experiences that the child has when performing these intentional activities. In accordance with Strawsonian requirements, there is a perfect symmetry in the representation of intentional actions ascribed to both self and other. The child now understands the other as another self, and the self as another other. As a consequence the child is now able to use deictic terms like "I" and "you" in an appropriate manner, and begins to experience forms of self-consciousness like embarrassment that he could not previously experience because they require a level of representation of the self as a whole agent who is the possible object of another's attitudes.

When engaged at this age in joint activity, the toddler can now readily shift roles, because he can imagine the first-person perspective of the other in complementary positions in any activity.[13] Instead of experiencing one's own role only in a first-person format, and the role of the other only in a third-person format, the child now represents both roles in an integrated format with both first- and third-person aspects. Thus, the child sees their activity as that of two agents engaged in intentional activities, where both agents and their independent roles are understood so as to allow the child to take on either role if that were required. At this time, the child can also show empathy for the other, not only with respect to his own view of the situation they are in, but also with respect to the other's particular stable desires and interests, some of which have been formed in previous joint activity.[14] Mutual imitation becomes a game to play between peers in acquiring a better knowledge of how particular intentional relations appear from a first- and third-person position.[15] Moreover, negotiating roles and choosing the direction of collaborative activity and play becomes increasingly a part of interactions not only with adults, who continue to scaffold normative requirements of culturally constituted activities, but also with peers in creative joint activities.

In sum, an infant's achieving the ability to ascribe some psychological predicates equally to self and other begins in face-to-face interpersonal interaction, which lays the foundation for the infant's differentiating persons from other objects. It then builds up as an understanding of mental phenomena in general out of sharing experiences with others in joint

---

[13] cf. J. Martin and A. Gillespie, Chapter 8, this volume.

[14] M. Tomasello and H. Moll, The gap is social: Human shared intentionality and culture. In P. M. Kappeler and J. B. Silk (eds.) *Mind the Gap* (Berlin/Heidelberg: Springer Verlag, 2010) 331–349.

[15] M. Nielsen, The imitative behaviour of children and chimpanzees: A window on the transmission of cultural traditions. *Primatologie* (in press).

activities. Thus, both joint activities and simple actions enter into an understanding of how what appears in one way for self and another way for other can be united in a single concept of the activity – accessible in different ways for self and other. Intentional activities that the infant can ascribe equally to self and other thus start out with simple actions in which objects are directly involved and then progress to more complex intentional relations, such as emotions directed at objects in the immediate environment of the infant and adult, and then to epistemic relations such as seeing an object or not based on direction of gaze and what can be seen from a particular position. Desires based on previous emotional expressions as well as knowledge based on previous experience can also be represented at this level. However, the psychological properties that can be ascribed by the toddler at level 3 of our model are not yet meta-representational intentional properties, which have content that can be true or false.

Level 4 of our model makes these latter meta-representations possible. Instead of the concept of person as an embodied agent that persists through time, this level 4 concept is of a person, who is a mental agent, with beliefs and desires that can change, but would persist if not revised due to encounters with new experiences that provide a rational basis for change. This kind of mental agent and the associated person concept, match closely the Lockean model of personal identity based on a continued consciousness that links the past, present, and future self through time. Because this level does not provide new insights into Strawson's particular approach to person concepts, but plays a crucial role in distinguishing our human concept of person from related concepts in other animals, we will postpone discussing this level more fully until later in this chapter.

The phylogenesis of persons and selves

In considering personhood from a phylogenetic perspective, the key issues are: When does a common conception of self and other as individual embodied agents of the same kind first appear? Why does it first appear at this time? And is this common conception as elaborate as our own human concepts of persons and selves?

One form of evidence indicating the possibility that an animal can represent itself and others in a similar way appears when it is able to recognize itself in a mirror, especially the capacity to recognize a mark placed on a body part hidden from normal vision and to respond to it when placed before the mirror. While this test does not guarantee a concept of itself equivalent to that of others, it does indicate, along with the use of mirrors to recognize other individuals, that the animal can treat the reflections in a mirror of itself and another equally as indicating a current physical appearance of a particular individual. Perhaps surprisingly, there are few animals that can recognize their full bodies in a mirror, though many can recognize other individuals in the mirror and can use the mirror for other purposes.[16]

Animals that pass stringent forms of the mirror test include great apes (gorillas, orangutans, chimpanzees, and bonobos), cetaceans (e.g., dolphins and killer whales), elephants, and at least one species of bird (magpie).[17] All of these species have relatively large brain/body ratios. Moreover, there is evidence that most of them have the converse capacity to imagine the first-person perspective of others, something that again is unusual among non-human animals. For instance, great apes, cetaceans, and elephants show fairly strong evidence of empathy, not only responding to the expressed distress of kin, but also to unexpressed situational needs of non-kin.[18] There is also evidence to suggest that great apes and dolphins can imagine the visual viewpoint and knowledge of others.[19] Taken together, these findings suggest that such animals have comparable conceptions of self and other, conceiving of each from both a first- and a third-person point of view.

A question that remains to be answered is whether these two views of self and other are integrated? If not integrated, then there may not be a single form of representation, but two separate forms, that can be applied to both self and other. Thus, instead of level 3 of our model in Table 7.1, these animals may be only at level 1, albeit a more sophisticated level 1 than that of other organisms.[20] Alternatively, they may operate in some domains of intentional understanding at level 3 (what Moore calls

---

[16] This procedure was developed by G. G. Gallup Jr., Chimpanzees: Self recognition. *Science* **167** (1970) 86–87. It should be noted that infants only begin to recognize themselves in the mirror at 18 months, when they first show a variety of other evidence that they have concepts of person and self that they can apply equally both to self and other (level 3 of our model). This makes the test a particularly appealing one to evaluate whether other animals develop something like our concepts of person and self.

[17] G. G. Gallup Jr., J. R. Anderson, and S. M. Platek, Self-recognition. In S. Gallagher (ed.) *The Oxford Handbook of Self* (Oxford University Press, 2010) 80–110.

[18] F. B. M. de Waal, Putting the altruism back into altruism: The evolution of empathy. *Annual Review of Psychology* **59** (2008) 279–300.

[19] J. Call and M. Tomasello, Does the chimpanzee have a theory of mind? 30 years later. *Trends in Cognitive Science* **12** (2008) 187–192; B. Hare, From hominoid to hominid mind: What changed and why? *Annual Review of Anthropology* **40** (2011) 293–309; L. Marino, R. C. Connor, R. E. Fordyce, L. M. Herman, P. R. Hof *et al.*, Cetaceans have complex brains for complex cognition. *PLoS Biology* **5** (2007) 966–972.

[20] We have suggested that this may be the situation for autistic individuals. In effect, the two forms of representation mimic ST and TT, because of their first- and third-person forms. See Barresi and Moore, The neuroscience of social understanding.

"intentional islands"), but remain at level 1 in other domains.[21] This may occur because of limited experiences of shared intentional relations at level 2, which are necessary for domain general understanding of intentional relations at level 3. We believe that this latter alternative is more likely to be the case, at least with respect to the chimpanzee.

Evidence that chimpanzees are at level 3 of our model comes from their capacity for novel imitation. They are not only able to imitate complex actions involving unique combinations of elements but they can also recognize when another individual is imitating them.[22] This ability to imitate novel actions and recognize being imitated suggests that a common form of representation is involved for self and other, which may eventually take the form of whole body representations. Thus, diverse actions of others can be understood as the same as one's own actions. This may be the basis for the ability of chimpanzees and other imitative species to recognize themselves in a mirror, because mirror representation "imitates" their whole body self-image so closely that by varying their behavior before the mirror and "testing the image," they may be able to distinguish the image as a representation of themselves.

Imitation appears to provide a link between self and other that makes possible a form of representation of actions that is the same for self and other even at the level of whole body. It is possible that these representations for chimpanzees are still at level 1 of our model, particularly since there is little evidence that chimpanzees can succeed in role reversal tasks, which we take as an important test of an organism's capacity to conceive of self and other in the same way. But there may be other reasons for this failure. Role reversal tasks that have been tested so far on chimpanzees have involved cooperative tasks and chimpanzees are not very cooperative.[23] So, it may be that they do not attend well to the activity of the other chimpanzee in these tasks and merely attend to their own role. Consequently, when reversal occurs, they need to learn the complementary role.

It may be that while chimpanzees have level 3 forms of representations, their skill in and motivation for using these representations is limited. This hypothesis fits within a larger picture, which suggests that while chimpanzees can imitate others and can imagine the other's epistemic viewpoint, they rarely use this ability compared to humans and it is used mostly in situations that serve self-interest in competitive contexts. Abundant recent research shows that chimpanzee understanding

[21] Moore, Representing intentional relations and acting intentionally in infancy.
[22] Nielsen, The imitative behaviour of children and chimpanzees.
[23] Tomasello and Moll, The gap is social.

of intentional relations of others is almost always limited to competitive rather than cooperative contexts. In the absence of specific training, it is as if they are almost blind to possible cooperative intentions of others. Moreover, they don't try to elicit help from others, or try to achieve joint goals with others. Tomasello and his colleagues suggest that this is due to limited interest in "shared intentionality," the desire to collaborate with others for common goals.[24] This contrasts sharply with human children who engage in shared intentionality during their second year. This notion of shared intentionality has much in common with our notion of shared intentional relations, but rather than focusing on our level 2, it elaborates on processes that occur cooperatively at our level 3. At this level, the activities of self and other are both represented in the same way, as integrated intentional relations of agents who share intentions. At level 2, on the other hand, self and other are represented differently, and only the shared intentional relations are represented in a unified way. Although Tomasello and his colleagues do not make this distinction explicit in their work, they do refer to our account of our notion of shared intentional relations when elaborating their own view.

What we want to focus on here is how face-to-face and joint activity in early infancy is important in distinguishing human from chimpanzee level 3 activities. It appears that chimpanzees do not engage much in face-to-face interaction and may not engage in any joint or shared activity involving other objects. The few examples of shared activity involving objects, such as tools, are brief, and show little sustained activity either by the adult or the infant. This contrasts sharply with human infant–adult interactions represented in level 2 of our model as shared intentional relations, which provide the foundation for later advances in collaboration. A chimpanzee infant may learn to use a tool by observing its mother use a tool or sometimes by the mother's making the tool available to the infant. This is nothing like the rich joint activity found in adult–infant human joint engagements, which involve a large number of socially constituted games and other activities, where roles can change and actions are coordinated with each other. In the case of humans, this shared activity involves shared intentional relations and later shared intentionality, and makes possible future cooperation, collaboration, and cultural learning.

If this interpretation is right, it appears that chimpanzees can understand self and other as embodied agents of actions, but that rather than view self and other with this level 3 concept most of the time, they rarely use it. Usually, they represent self and other in distinct modes, which is

---

[24] Tomasello *et al.*, Understanding and sharing intentions; Tomasello and Moll, The gap is social.

at level 1 of our model. In terms of the Strawsonian theory of person, the lack of interpersonal relations of a cooperative nature in joint actions may limit their ability to represent intentional relations of self and other using a single uniform concept. If shared intentional relations ground human understanding of ourselves and others as persons, then the limited bridge between self and other that we see in level 3 chimpanzee behavior may not be enough. In sum, chimpanzees do not have a concept of embodied agent that they can apply equally to self and other across a variety of intentional relations and this may be due to a rather limited degree of early joint activities between infant and adult, which stems from their fundamentally competitive orientation toward each other. There is reason to think that bonobos, our other closest ape relative, are more affiliative in nature and more capable of entering into shared intentional activities in cooperative tasks.[25] Cetaceans are also more cooperative and on several measures seem to show a more advanced understanding of self and other as equivalent, intentional agents than either of these great apes.[26] But, we will not go further into these comparisons here. Instead, we will now discuss more generally the role of cooperation.

Reciprocal altruism and the evolution of the human concept of person

How did our human conception of person evolve out of earlier primate concepts? We think that the simple answer to this question is reciprocal altruism, a behavior explained by the evolutionary biologist Robert Trivers.[27] If there were not some long-term functional expectation of equal treatment with respect to costs and benefits of cooperation and mutual aid, such activity, and the psychological mechanisms upon which they depend, would not occur. Thus, it was the need to engage in joint activities and mutual aid that extended over time with the same partners, where self and other are treated equally with respect to costs and benefits, which made the concept of person necessary. However, it is important to distinguish between reciprocal altruism in terms of its evolutionary function, which moves altruism beyond the realm of kinship and inclusive fitness to include non-relatives, from the psychological mechanisms

---

[25] Hare, From hominoid to hominid mind.
[26] Marino *et al.*, Cetaceans have complex brains for complex cognition; A. Pack and L. M. Herman, Dolphin social cognition and joint attention: Our current understanding. *Aquatic Mammals* **32** (2006) 443–460.
[27] R. L. Trivers, The evolution of reciprocal altruism. *Quarterly Review of Biology* **46** (1971) 35–57.

142   *John Barresi, Chris Moore, and Raymond Martin*

that create and maintain this ultimate function. There have been significant theoretical and empirical advances since Trivers published his theory, many of which interpret reciprocal altruism as a simple "tit-for-tat" exchange of favors between unrelated individuals, then propose advances beyond this simple mechanism.[28] However, it seems that most of these advances fall within the general domain of Trivers' initial comprehensive vision of function and mechanisms, and we will treat them as such here. For instance, the notion of altruistic punishment of defectors was contained in Trivers' idea of "moralistic aggression." Although group selection as a potential source of within-group altruism was not anticipated, Trivers' notion of indirect, normatively based, reciprocity within groups is a ground that makes group selection possible.

We believe that the conditions that gave a selective advantage to increasing levels of within-group cooperation among non-kin and to more complex forms of reciprocal altruism within the hominid line provided the evolutionary basis for our human concepts of person and self. Essential for these human concepts of self and person are the capacities both to *represent* and to *weigh* the points of view of self and other equally. In cooperative relationships, where joint intentional activities are involved and one must take into account another person's point of view and weigh it equally or almost equally to one's own, the ability to represent and weigh intentional relations of self and other equivalently becomes important.

According to Trivers' theory, costs versus benefits for self and other must be calculated and weighed with respect to action in a manner that will maintain equity across conditions and through time. This applies both to joint activities where benefits might be distributed equally or proportionally based on individual costs, as well as to situations that can warrant individual acts of altruism for another. For both joint collaborative activities and altruistic favors, maintaining equity requires a common metric to calculate costs and benefits across individuals, and not only from one's own point of view. Otherwise, one might be able to calculate and weigh the costs and benefits for oneself for various actions in the present, and possibly into the future, without being able to calculate, or weigh, the costs or benefits for others. In these circumstances, each individual might pursue what seems evidently in their own self interest, while missing out on opportunities for cooperation over time and exchange of

---

[28] R. Axelrod and W. D. Hamilton, The evolution of cooperation. *Science* **211** (1981) 1,390–1,396; H. Gintis, S. Bowles, R. Boyd, and E. Fehr, Explaining altruistic behavior in humans. *Evolution and Human Behavior* **24** (2003) 153–172; M. A. Nowak, Five rules for the evolution of cooperation. *Science* **314** (2006) 1,560–1,563.

favors that would result in greater, long-term benefits both for self and others.

In Trivers' original presentation of the theory, the ability of individuals to calculate and weigh costs and benefits across self and other in a common metric appears to be assumed rather than explained. This would not be a problem, so long as costs and benefits of exchange were immediately advantageous to both sides. While a theory of mind and concept of person that applies equally to self and other would not be required in such cases, it does appear to be necessary for reciprocal altruism in humans. In our case, the use of a common metric requires such a theory in order to judge not only how costs and benefits appear to ourselves, but also how they appear to others. Moreover the theory must make it possible to estimate relative costs and benefits for agents with purposes that vary in their temporal extension. The use of a theory of this sort is essential in our attempts to maintain equity in relative costs and benefits to self and others in reciprocal altruistic relationships, where the medium of exchange is highly variable and depends on diverse individual purposes. Although we certainly have a bias in our own favor in our calculation of costs and benefits to self and other, and in weighing them in our actions, which Trivers associates with "subtle cheating," such cheating can only work in a context where gross differences in costs and benefits are easily detected, but minor deviations are not. To do this, we need a theory of mind, and associated concept of person, that applies equally well to self and other, both at a time and across time.

Trivers himself realized not long after publishing his theory that it could account for our sense of fairness and justice.[29] He had already postulated in the theory that friendship, sympathy, gratitude, guilt, reparation, trust, moralistic aggression, and other social emotions may have evolved as psychological mechanisms that track cost/benefit ratios in generating and responding to altruistic and non-altruistic acts, but he didn't mention our sense of justice or fairness. However, it seems likely that human moral psychology, particularly our concern with equity, emerged as a result of the evolution of reciprocal altruism in hominid species. This moral psychology requires a concept of person that we can apply equally to self and others, where the perspectives of different individuals, including their motivations and actions, can be interpreted and weighed using a common metric.

[29] R. L. Trivers, *Natural Selection and Social Theory: Selected Papers of Robert L. Trivers. (Evolution and Cognition Series)* (Oxford University Press, 2002) 16–17; Reciprocal altruism 30 years later. In P. M. Kappeler and C. P. van Schaik (eds.) *Cooperation in Primates and Humans: Mechanisms and Evolution* (Berlin: Springer-Verlag, 2006) 67–83; and *Social Evolution* (Menlo Park: Benjamin/Cummings Publishing Company, 1985).

If one compares adult humans to great apes in their capacity for such a concept of person, large differences occur both in their understanding and weighing of representational perspectives of self and others, both at a time and across time. Chimpanzees live mainly in the present, and, although they live in social groups with unrelated individuals, their cooperative activities and affiliative attitudes tend to be kin based. Some reciprocal relations and altruistic acts occur with non-relatives, but most of their activities either ignore non-relatives or are more competitive than cooperative with them. Since their attempts to understand each other tend not to be for purposes involving cooperation toward common goals, opportunities both to share intentional relations with common cooperative goals as well as to represent them are limited. Thus, to the extent that their concept of embodied agent depends on shared activity it must be quite narrow. Even adult–infant and other kin interactions tend to be limited in shared activity, so their concepts of each other's intentional relations in general are likely to be isolated from their concepts of their own activities and more at level 1 of our model in Table 7.1 than at level 3 where individual person concepts first appear. As noted in the previous section, what concepts they have that apply across self and other are likely to be imitation-based rather than through original shared activity, and used primarily in competitive rather than in cooperative contexts.

It is also the case that chimpanzees do not act with regard to a distant future or a distant past. In contrast, humans have a notion of self that is extended in time and they have the capacity to engage in mental time travel.[30] This ability to imagine past and future events from different points of view applies to both self and other, and can also be applied to different representational points of view in the present. These capacities are linked together in humans. Our understanding of false belief in others and changing beliefs in self, requires the same ability for imagining changes in perspective through time. Moreover, this capacity is linked to our ability to act based on future motives that may be in conflict with current motives.[31]

---

[30] C. Moore and K. Lemmon (eds.) *The Self in Time: Developmental Perspectives* (Hillsdale, NJ: Erlbaum, 2001); T. Suddendorf and M. C. Corballis, The evolution of foresight: What is mental time travel, and is it unique to humans? *Behavioral and Brain Sciences* **30** (2007) 299–351.

[31] J. Barresi, Extending self-consciousness into the future. In Moore and Lemmon, *The Self in Time*, 141–161; C. Moore, J. Barresi, and C. Thompson, The cognitive basis of future-oriented prosocial behavior. *Social Development* 7 (1998) 198–218; Moore and Lemmon, *The Self in Time*; C. Thompson, J. Barresi, and C. Moore, The development of future-oriented prudence and altruism in preschool children. *Cognitive Development* **12** (1997) 199–212.

Whereas chimpanzees can act now for goals that will be achieved in the future, they cannot do so by delaying gratification of any current desire. By contrast, a 4-year-old child can delay gratification of a current desire in favor of a desire he knows it will have in the future. The child can also remember past episodes with different motives and knowledge as distinct from those he or she has in the present. Thus, the 4-year-old is capable of representing changes in representational perspective for self over time. And, the child's capacity to do this is linked to a similar capacity to represent diversity in the perspectives of others. Thus, in congruence with the need of a common metric for representing diverse perspectives that is required for reciprocal altruism of a general sort to occur, humans have it at an early age, while chimpanzees – and apparently other animals – never acquire it.

It has been argued that only narrow forms of reciprocation occur in non-human cases because most animals lack the mental capacities necessary to deal with costs and benefits extended across time.[32] But, the evidence also suggests that they do not take into account the different perspectives of self and other, when conceiving of costs and benefits, and weigh them both when making decisions.[33] Thus, recent experimental findings are more congruent with the present proposal that what is unique about human reciprocal altruism is its dependence on a uniform concept of person that can be applied equally to self and other, which involves a common metric for calculating costs and benefits across diverse perspectives, and which extends across time. With this system in place, relatively short-term collaboration as well as long-term relationships involving reciprocal altruism of various kinds become possible and a sense of justice becomes a medium by which to think and act with respect to those relationships. With a notion of justice in place, large groups of individuals that mutually recognize each other as persons will be disposed to act even toward strangers in congruence with what is considered fair treatment among persons within their group or culture. This sense of justice can even reach beyond one's culture to humanity at large.[34]

---

[32] J. R. Stevens and M. D. Hauser, Why be nice? Psychological constraints on the evolution of cooperation. *Trends in Cognitive Sciences* **8** (2004) 60–65.

[33] K. Jensen, B. Hare, J. Call, and M. Tomasello, What's in it for me? Self-regard precludes altruism and spite in chimpanzees. *Proceedings of the Royal Society: B* **273** (2006) 1,013–1,021; J. R. Greenberg, K. Hamann, F. Warneken, and M. Tomasello, Chimpanzee helping in collaborative and noncollaborative contexts. *Animal Behaviour* **80** (2010) 873–880.

[34] J. Barresi, On seeing our selves and others as persons. *New Ideas in Psychology*, in press.

Conclusion

In this chapter, we have looked into the evolutionary origin of our human concept of person and its early development. We have provided a person theory account of the development of human understanding of mental phenomena of self and other. In this account, we stress, with Strawson, that the notion of person is primitive and necessary in order to ascribe mental states with equivalent meaning to self and other. In our evolutionary as well as developmental account, we also follow Strawson in stressing the important role that shared mental states have in acquiring reflective understanding of these states and applying them to individuals. In our account, the fundamental asymmetry between the representations that most organisms use for self and other limits their understanding of mental states. It was the need for mechanisms that would support temporally extended cooperation between non-kin that we claim led to the human notion of person. Without the notion of person and a means for representing mental phenomena of self and other in a common format, opportunities for complex forms of reciprocal altruism between unrelated group members would be impossible. With it, there may be no limit on how far cooperation among humans who are willing and able to recognize each other as persons can reach.

8   Position exchange theory and personhood: moving between positions and perspectives within physical, socio-cultural, and psychological space and time

Jack Martin and Alex Gillespie

During the last two decades of the twentieth century, two kinds of positioning theory emerged in a resurgent psychology of personhood – resurgent in the sense that both of these theories draw inspiration and ideas from earlier pragmatic, cultural-historical, and dialogical approaches.[1] One of these recent approaches, positioning theory (PT), developed by Rom Harré and his colleagues, extends earlier pragmatic and discursive accounts of personhood by emphasizing the ways in which persons are positioned as moral agents within socio-cultural practices through their interactions with others.[2] The other approach, dialogical self theory (DST), developed by Hubert Hermans and his colleagues, drawing inspiration from William James and Mikhail Bakhtin, examines the person as a dynamic landscape of subjective, or "I," positions.[3] More recently, a third kind of positioning theory, position exchange theory (PET), has emerged, based on an extension of the social developmental theorizing of the early American pragmatist, George Herbert Mead.[4]

All three of these theories are concerned with embodied, socio-culturally embedded, and psychologically agentive persons who engage

---

[1] Parts of this paper have been presented at the meetings of the International Society for Theoretical Psychology in June 2011, and the European Congress of Psychology in July 2011.

[2] For example, R. Harré, F. M. Moghaddam, T. P. Cairnie, D. Rothbart, and S. R. Sabat, Recent advances in positioning theory. *Theory and Psychology* 19 (2009) 5–31; and F. M. Moghaddam, R. Harré, and N. Lee (eds.) *Global Conflict Resolution Through Positioning Analysis* (New York: Springer, 2008).

[3] For example, H. Hermans and A. Hermans-Konopka, *Dialogical Self Theory: Positioning and Counter-positioning in a Globalizing Society* (Cambridge University Press, 2010); and H. Hermans and G. Dimaggio, Self, identity, and globalization in times of uncertainty: A dialogical analysis. *Review of General Psychology* 11 (2007) 31–61.

[4] See A. Gillespie, Position exchange: The social development of agency. *New Ideas in Psychology* 30 (2012) 32–46; and J. Martin and A. Gillespie, A neo-Meadian approach to human agency: Relating the social and the psychological in the ontogenesis of perspective-coordinating persons. *Integrative Psychological and Behavioral Science* 44 (2010) 252–272.

in discursive positioning (especially PT) and psychological positioning (especially DST). But, neither PT nor DST examine how this discursive and psychological positioning arises. Only PET explicitly theorizes the evolutionary and developmental primacy of positioning within actual physical and socio-cultural encounters as the basis for the emergence of more abstracted discursive and psychological positioning.

In what follows, we discuss PET's contributions to an understanding of the evolution and development of persons. We begin with a general discussion of positioning within physical and social space. We highlight two especially important aspects of our development as psychological persons: the movement from "event time" to "psychological time," and the spatial–temporal distanciation afforded by this shift. Finally, we examine a few illustrative examples of the lines of research opened up by PET.

Positioning within physical and socio-cultural space as a source of personhood

It now is widely acknowledged that long-standing debates between nature on the one hand and nurture on the other limit appropriate description and explanation of personhood and its contexts or conditions of possibility.[5] Many developmental and evolutionary theorists currently subscribe to some form of interactivism among biological and cultural constituents. However, much less consensus and awareness attend two important facts emphasized by PET and which anchor a viable interactivist account, namely: (1) that it is the holistic interactivity of biological humans within a worldly context that is simultaneously biophysical and socio-cultural that is the prime determinant of our development and evolution; and (2) that the most basic character of this foundational interactivity is the physical positioning, and movement between positions, of biological humans within socio-cultural practices. We will illustrate these facts with an analysis of walking and playing. Our purpose is to show just how deeply physical and social positioning extends into even the most basic activities.

Let us begin with walking. We are not born able to walk, yet walking is one of the most basic ways in which we physically position ourselves within social spaces. A young child incapable of walking must get along in a world of others' knees, without ready access to their faces, and

---

[5] See Martin and Gillespie, A neo-Meadian approach to human agency; and J. P. Spencer, M. S. Blumberg, B. McMurray, S. R. Robinson, L. K. Samuelson, and J. B. Tomblin, Short arms and talking eggs: Why we abide the nativist-empiricist debate. *Child Development Perspectives* 2 (2009) 79–87.

without the ability to move with others through the maze of physical–
social spaces of everyday life. Walking enables the older child to insert
herself within the physical–social spaces of familial interaction in a more
equal manner. This is a manner of positioning that wins the approval
of other family members, and is accompanied by new possibilities for
unassisted coordination with the movements, expressions, gestures, and
manners of these others. The child, now upright, by being able to move
position at will, has taken a major developmental step. As we walk, we
put ourselves in position to witness the gaze of others and to be subject
to their actions and reactions. We differentiate our experiences in ways
that are embodied both interpersonally and temporally. Being here in
this situation is different from being there in that other situation, and
each situation has distinctive subjective and objective aspects. Moreover,
the mobile child is able to move location and explore how being there is
different from being here.

In play, we also exchange and coordinate positions with others. Early
play typically revolves around simple alternations of positions within
interactions in which we give and receive objects through passing, rolling,
and throwing them. Throwing, for example, implies catching and vice
versa, and thus this play entails exchanging not just social positions
(thrower/catcher) but also the respective experiences of throwing and
catching. Later in our development, we enter into more formal, rule-
governed physical–social spaces when we participate in games such as
tag and dodge-ball, eventually graduating to more complex coordinations of positions in team sports such as baseball or cricket. The position
exchanges and coordinations that we experience through such interactive
experience expand our abilities to recollect, anticipate, and differentiate
physical–social positions in ways that enhance our self–other understanding, and enable us to distinguish our own and others' perspectives. At
higher levels of play, coordinated perspective taking involves imaginative
anticipations of what the other will do given *their* physical–social position.
When this occurs, our embodied positioning takes on a psychological
cast that is marked by an increased ability to distance ourselves from our
immediate position. Nonetheless, we continue to be both embodied and
embedded, but now our embodiment combines habituation to practiced
forms of interactivity with the ability to transform familiar situations and
patterns of interaction through consideration of alternative perspectives
that are not anchored in our immediate situations. However, even here,
as we will see, our embodied, situated positioning continues to anchor
our newly minted travels within psychological space and time.

Our intention in this section of the chapter has been to outline and
illustrate the myriad ways in which our lives as persons are built on

a foundation of embodied, embedded positioning within the physical–social spaces and times within which our lives unfold. Although activities like walking and playing often are understood as primarily biological, and there is a recent tendency within the sciences and social sciences to reduce them to our genes and/or some combination of genetic and epigenetic particulates and processes, such reductions are not plausible, and may be misleading and dangerous. Although walking and playing are only possible due to biological potentialities, it is as social activities that they feed forward into the development of intersubjectivity. We believe that any viable approach to personhood must privilege the holistic interactivity of individuals with each other as fundamental.

What is position exchange and why does it matter?

Position exchange is ubiquitous, even if rarely explicitly recognized and theorized, in all human cultural and literary traditions. It is central to the plotting and appeal of classic tales like *The Prince and the Pauper*, a story that involves switching social positions with vastly divergent circumstances and privileges, and to contemporary television series like *In Treatment*, in which a psychoanalyst works with a small number of patients, and then switches to the patient position in his weekly sessions with his own psychoanalyst. In stories, one character often pretends to be another (such as the wolf in *Little Red Riding Hood*). When children play with masks, dressing up, or role play, they are "stepping into" the socio-cultural positions of others. Position exchange also is implicated directly in common metaphors of empathy and interpersonal understanding, such as "walking in another's shoes," "putting oneself in the position of another," and "trying to see things from another's point of view." Stories, beliefs, and experiences of adjusting to differences within and between cultures are literally awash in instances of position exchange. Impasses in human affairs, from domestic disputations to international negotiations, frequently are described in language that fits easily with notions of position exchange.

However, position exchange also plays an important role in much past and present cultural, social, and psychological theorizing about personhood, especially with respect to the seemingly unique psychological abilities of persons to attain self-conscious understanding of their actions, experience, and existence (i.e., selfhood), to integrate their own and others' perspectives and thus participate actively in uniquely human forms of intersubjectivity (i.e., perspective taking and coordination), and to engage in two-way volitional control of their actions and intentional self-determination (i.e., agency). In these areas, PET, as developed by Martin and Gillespie, offers an attractive alternative to more familiar theories.[6] The basic assumption of PET is that many social activities are made up of distinctive, yet complementary, social positions. For example, smiling at another person is an interaction that creates the social positions of smiling and being smiled at (and this latter social position invites a smile in response). Much the same can be said about talking (speaking and listening), directing (leading and following), negotiating (proposing and considering), nurturing (caring for and being cared for), and many other common interactive routines. In all of these and many other interactions, each social position includes a particular action and perceptual perspective, which frequently are associated with a particular social role or set of expectations for what each person will do in each position. These anticipations and guidelines are a consequence of each participant's previous experience (direct and/or indirect) within such exchanges, and include conventional responsibilities. For example, buying a food item entails the social positions of buying and selling, each position constitutes the other position (there is no buyer without a seller), and for each to effectively carry out their role they need to orient to the perspective of the other. PET theorizes how this mutual orientation to the perspective of the other occurs.

Importantly, movement across different social positions allows individuals to experience and understand the different perspectives associated with different social positions (buyer/seller, talking/listening, touching/being touched, helping/making progress with assistance, etc.). Although interactors are not mind readers, they are able to understand perspectives different from but related to those that they currently occupy because they have had (and likely will have again) experience in those different but related perspectives. Thus, as a seller, I comprehend a buyer's interests and reservations concerning quality, price, and so forth because I frequently have been, and will continue to be (at different times) in the position of buyer. In this way, position exchange plays a major role in understanding others, and is directly relevant to the traditional philosophical problem of other minds. What position exchange demonstrates

---

[6] See Martin and Gillespie, A neo-Meadian approach to human agency. Also see, A. Gillespie, G. H. Mead: Theorist of the social act. *Journal for the Theory of Social Behaviour* **35** (2005) 19–39; A. Gillespie, Games and the development of perspective taking. *Human Development* **49** (2006) 87–92; Gillespie, Position exchange; J. Martin, Reinterpreting internalization and agency through G. H. Mead's perspectival realism. *Human Development* **49** (2006) 65–86; J. Martin, Positions, perspectives, and persons. *Human Development* **49** (2006) 93–95; and J. Martin, B. Sokol, and T. Elfers, Taking and coordinating perspectives: From pre-reflective interactivity, through reflective intersubjectivity, to meta-reflective sociality. *Human Development* **51** (2008) 294–317.

is that acts of integrating, coordinating, and understanding different perspectives (i.e., intersubjectivity) are not mental acts at all, or at least they do not begin that way. Rather, they are, from a developmental point of view, social acts having their origins in concrete position exchanges.

However, the social, psychological consequences of physical and social positioning and exchange do more than enable an understanding of others and the broader conventions of societies with respect to various patterns of interaction that unfold routinely within social and cultural contexts. Positioning and changing positions within the sociophysical and socio-cultural times, places, and events that contain our interpersonal interactions also enable our understanding of ourselves as both subjects and objects. In other words, we attain our selfhood through our participation with others within those exchanges of social position that partially constitute our social lives with others. This was George Herbert Mead's great insight, when he pronounced that to know ourselves, we first must become other to our selves and act toward ourselves as others do.[7] By taking the perspectives of others toward ourselves, we are revealed to ourselves as the objects of perspectives that differ from our own first-person perspectives. Our selfhood, a crucial part of our personhood, arises through an integration of our own and others' perspectives. Such integration is due, in no small measure, to our experiences of position exchange. These are exchanges which, as we will see in what follows, initially are socio-physical (i.e., that are embodied and enacted within particular socio-physical contexts), but which eventually acquire socio-cultural and psychological dimensions that are not specifically anchored in the here and now. Nonetheless, even these more abstracted socio-cultural and psychological acquisitions are built upon our physical movements within the social world, movements that furnish the raw materials of our selfhood and psychological agency.

Positioning and coordinating with others during phylogenesis

Social positioning within coordinated interactions with others has been of particular importance in our evolutionary history. To appreciate this fully, it is critical to recognize that we and our ancestors have always been social beings. Our survival as a species consistently has depended on our relations to others. Social animals must coordinate movement and action collectively in order to respond effectively to danger, assist those in need

---

[7] See G. H. Mead, *The Philosophy of the Present*, A. E. Murphy (ed.) (University of Chicago Press, 1932); G. H. Mead, *Mind, Self, and Society from the Standpoint of a Social Behaviorist*, C. W. Morris (ed.) (University of Chicago Press, 1934); and G. H. Mead, *The Philosophy of the Act*, C. W. Morris *et al.* (eds.) (University of Chicago Press, 1938).

(such as children), and communicate about securing food, water, and shelter. An animal that fails to move at the startled reaction of another is not long for this world. A mother who fails to attend the distress cries of her off-spring is of little use in furthering her lineage.

Humans have evolved to orient to each other in ways that facilitate coordinated and intentional interactivity. Activities such as hunting, gathering, and agriculture all are more efficient and productive if shared and coordinated with others. The same is true of activities of nurturing, such as child-care and helping. These and other forms of coordinated, cooperative interactivity are particularly important in a species with a lengthy gestation period, and an even more protracted period of infant vulnerability. Altruism and cooperation are not difficult to explain. They are the interactive, behavioral bases for survival, and those members and groups capable of functional coordination with conspecifics will flourish.[8] It therefore is in social animals and in the social domain that the highest levels of intelligent functioning can be achieved. Computational simulations of evolutionary processes show significant benefits of cooperating, provided that the cooperation is reciprocated.[9] Given that one of the primary functions of any social aggregate is to enable coordinated interactivity for the benefit of both the group and the individuals that comprise it, social animals tend to create contexts that maximize these particular interactions and their benefits.

Coordinated mutual orientation and interactivity enable social practices that culminate in ways of life and artifacts of living that themselves change and expand possibilities of living. In the long term, our activities as individuals and groups transform the world within which we exist and interact. Such transformation eventually brings forth social histories that unfold within the biophysical world, and create socio-physical, socio-cultural, and psychological spaces and times within and across which we move as persons. It is within these spaces and times that we human beings have emerged as self-conscious agents capable of planning and creating.

The human brain is a poor thing on its own, an inarticulate, undifferentiating, metaphorizing beast like any other. But joined to a community of its fellows, it has this remarkable capacity to create a community of mind, acquire symbolizing powers, and vastly expand the range of its own awareness, in proportion to the depth of its enculturation.[10]

[8] G. C. Williams, *Evolution through Group Selection* (Oxford: Blackwell, 1986); and D. S. Wilson and E. Sober, Reintroducing group selection to the human behavioral sciences. *Behavioral and Brain Sciences* 17 (1994) 585–654.

[9] R. Axelrod and W. D. Hamilton, The evolution of cooperation. *Science* 211 (1981) 1,390–1,396.

[10] M. Donald, *A Mind so Rare: The Evolution of Human Consciousness* (New York: Norton, 2001) 326.

Within this social evolutionary framework, PET helps to highlight and explain how different positional and perspectival experiences can be integrated and coordinated to enhance human functioning. In particular, PET can be used to explain the uniquely human forms of self–other differentiation, understanding, consciousness, perspective taking, and imagination that have evolved in consort with the plasticity of our cerebral and central nervous functioning. Position exchange theory hypothesizes that our evolution as persons with uniquely human psychological capabilities was enabled by our gradual creation of, and ongoing movement within and across, socio-physical, socio-cultural, and social, psychological space and time. For hominids and early humans, rudimentary forms of coordinated interactivity in which individuals alternated between different, related positions (e.g., shepherding animals toward others who can corral or kill them, and vice versa; gathering basic building materials for others who use them in construction, and vice versa) were especially important.[11] Gradually emergent capabilities to recollect and anticipate experiences in one position while actually engaged actively in the related position eventually provided socio-physical scaffolding for more advanced forms of socio-cultural and social and psychological functioning, including communication through language.

To illustrate, consider the evolution of self-consciousness as a function, at least in part, of position exchange. As already indicated, for physically vulnerable *Homo sapiens*, the adaptive functioning, and thus survival value, associated with communicative gestures and vocalizations was relatively great. As senders and receivers of such gestures and vocalizations, our ancestors undoubtedly learned to alternate positions of sender–receiver, leader–follower, and informer–informant in a wide variety of everyday life situations, and to embed such exchanges into routines and systems of living together. Of central importance to such a communicative, interactive way of life is the ability to anticipate, based on past experience, what others will do. For example, a warning cry emitted while facing in one direction stimulates movement in other directions by both

[11] A. N. Leontiev, *Problems of the Development of Mind* (Moscow: Progress Publishers, 1981). Leontiev analyzed the role of the beater within the hunt, pointing out that the beater's action of chasing away the prey violates the "natural relation" of trying to catch the prey. He shows how it is only by the beater taking the perspective of the hunters waiting in ambush for the fleeing animal that the beater's action makes sense. As also noted by L. I. Held, Jr., *Quirks of Human Anatomy: An Evo-devo Look at the Human Body* (Cambridge University Press, 2009) 40: "it was hunting that set the stage for the evolution of bigger brains. Meat supplied the metabolic fuel for brain growth and brain maintenance, while cooperative hunting behavior established a selective environment that rewarded even the slightest increments in our ability to plan, socialize, and communicate with others."

the crier and those who hear and witness the cry. In this, and myriad similar ways, the gestures and vocalizations of early humans acquired shared meanings that could be used to facilitate more advanced forms of position exchange involving the use of communicative symbols – position exchanges such as speaker–listener, model–imitator, and instructor-learner.

As an indirect consequence of communicating with others within co-ordinated routines, human beings were gradually able to differentiate themselves from others and eventually to understand and integrate different perspectives. These capabilities of self–other differentiation and perspective taking/coordination formed a requisite social, psychological basis for self-consciousness. As noted by George Herbert Mead, the most basic mechanism for the development of self-consciousness is "the individual's becoming an object to himself by taking the attitudes [perspectives] of other individuals toward himself within an organized setting of social relationships."[12] As interpreted by Martin and Gillespie, as cooperative, coordinated systems of interactivity involving position exchange emerged in our evolutionary and cultural history, aided and abetted by the advent of shared systems of symbolic communication and language, it became possible for individual human beings to act toward themselves as others do – i.e., to imagine, "see," and think about themselves in one social position and perspective (e.g., as objects of others' regard and evaluation) while acting in another social position and perspective (e.g., as subjects engaged in particular actions and projects).[13] Such simultaneous experiencing of self and other perspectives in which individuals are both objects and subjects is an important mechanism for both self–other differentiation and self-consciousness.[14]

Understood in this way, our self-consciousness arises as a by-product of the evolutionary success of our coordinated interactivity with others. As Donald contends, "we are collective creatures, even to the texture of

[12] Mead, *Mind, Self, and Society*, 225.
[13] Martin and Gillespie, A neo-Meadian approach to human agency.
[14] H. Werner and B. Kaplan, The developmental approach to cognition: Its relevance to the psychological interpretation of anthropological and ethnolinguistic data. *American Anthropologist* 58 (1956) 866–880. The movement between, and thus experiencing of, self and other positions and perspectives provides a mechanism which can drive forward what Werner and Kaplan described as the basic processes of human development, namely differentiation and integration. By experiencing different social positions and perspectives the individual's psychological structure "differentiates" and by moving between these social positions and thus perspectives these differentiated elements of experience are "integrated" into an intersubjective whole. Although Werner and Kaplan were mostly concerned with development during ontogenesis, the same can be said about evolution within phylogenesis.

our awareness."[15] In evolutionary terms, our coordinated interactivity with others begins with physical position exchanges and moves toward social and psychological exchanges of perspectives, creating both systems of intersubjectivity through which we coordinate with and understand others, and intrasubjectivity through which we coordinate with and understand ourselves.

Although it is not uncommon to encounter evolutionary theorizing in psychology that assumes that it is our genes that lead us through relevant evolutionary corridors, "the general principle [. . .] is that behavior invents and adaptation via gene changes make the invention more efficient. New form follows new function."[16] In this sense, it is our coordinated interactivity with others that has occasioned the phylogenetic development of human linguistic and psychological capabilities (such as perspective taking and integration, and self-consciousness). Relatively complex, group structures have an adaptive advantage over simple, unstructured groups such as herds. Coordinated, complex group interactivity that maximizes this cultural advantage favors enhanced intelligence, planning, memory, and refined emotions, all of which assist more advanced forms of coordination. Eventually, these initially learned psychological capabilities, through well-known evolutionary processes, have been supported by changes to our biological substratum, such as larger brains, especially larger neocortexes, with great plasticity in functioning.[17] In short, it is our socially acquired abilities to orient, interact, and coordinate in groups that have clear survival advantages.[18] With these gradually acquired capabilities, our ancestors created contexts of life that proved sufficiently enduring to allow evolutionary processes such as natural selection eventually to provide a biological basis for our enhanced forms of sociality.

[15] Donald, *A Mind so Rare*, 326.
[16] W. H. Calvin, *A Brief History of the Mind* (New York: Oxford University Press, 2004) 159.
[17] See M. Donald, *Origins of the Modern Mind: Three Stages of the Evolution of Culture and Cognition* (Cambridge, MA: Harvard University Press, 1991); E. Jablonka and M. J. Lamb, *Evolution in Four Dimensions* (Cambridge, MA: MIT Press, 2005); Williams, *Evolution through Group Selection*; and Wilson and Sober, Reintroducing group selection.
[18] Intersubjectivity and perspective taking may not only arise out of cooperation, but also out of manipulation and deception. In evolutionary theory this is often called the Machiavellian hypothesis – based on the book by R. Byrne and A. Whiten (eds.) *Machiavellian Intelligence: Social Expertise and the Evolution of Intellect in Monkeys, Apes, and Humans* (Oxford University Press, 1989), which argues that human intelligence evolved out of manipulation. But, for our argument, this is unproblematic. Deception and manipulation are as intersubjective as cooperation, and position exchange can play just as large a part.

At the neurophysiological level, Walter Freeman has adopted a pragmatic approach that supports the uniquely human forms of experiential
remembering, anticipation, orientation to others, coordination, and distanciation that we have discussed.[19] Freeman understands the brain as
a system that molds itself in direct interaction with the worldly experiences of persons, functioning in a holistic manner to direct its activity
into the world. Freeman emphasizes, in contrast to cognitivist and mate-
rialist approaches to neurophysiology, that we do not react to the world
so much as we act into the world in ways that incorporate our past
worldly interactivities into our future actions. Meaning results from an
experiential history of acting within the world that produces changes to
our cerebral and central nervous systems that predispose us to orient to
relevant aspects of the world in preparation for intentional acting. For
Freeman, "human intentionality is not optimally productive and effective until it has been acculturated through a long educational process,
by which the capacity emerges for cooperative social action based on a
high degree of shared perception and understanding."[20] At both basic
and more advanced levels, human persons are thus uniquely equipped
biologically to act intentionally into the world together and alone, and to
learn from the consequences of their activity and interactivity.

Freeman's emphasis on the social, interactive basis of our neurophysiological anticipations (based on past experiences with others) has been
supported by Lewis, Schore, and others.[21] Schore, for example, observes
that the orbitofrontal cortex seems to push the rest of the brain to a state
of readiness through preconscious expectations based on the reactions of
others from past experiences. Lewis goes further to suggest that both the
orbitofrontal cortex and a second attentional system, the anterior cingu-
lated cortex (with connections to the supplementary motor area and the
limbic system) are associated with action readiness and subjective experience with respect to social situations and encounters. Thus, there is
neurophysiological support for the close linkage between our worldly
interactivity and our evolved capabilities to coordinate with others
and social contexts that we have emphasized as both consequences and

---

[19] W. J. Freeman, *How Brains Make Up their Minds* (London: Phoenix, 2000).
[20] Freeman, *How Brains Make Up their Minds*, 211.
[21] M. D. Lewis, The dialogical brain: Contributions of emotional neurobiology to understanding the dialogical self. *Theory and Psychology* 12 (2002) 175–190; A. N. Schore,
Affect Regulation and the Origin of the Self: The Neurobiology of Emotional Development
(Hillsdale, NJ: Erlbaum, 1994); and A. N. Schore, Early organization of the nonlinear
right brain and development of a predisposition to psychiatric disorders. *Development
and Psychopathology* 9 (1997) 595–631; J. Cromby, Between constructionism and neuroscience: The societal co-constitution of embodied subjectivity. *Theory and Psychology*
14 (2004) 797–821.

enablers of those psychological capabilities that define us as persons. The basic processes of position exchange and perspective integration that we have described above probably played an important evolutionary role, especially with respect to our psychological capabilities as persons with self-consciousness and self-understanding able to coordinate with and integrate the perspectives and actions of others with those of our own.[22]

Positioning and coordinating with others during ontogenesis

As important as position exchange likely was with respect to our evolution as persons, it is during ontogenesis that position exchange and its consequences for the development of self-understanding, intersubjectivity (involving an integration of our own and others' perspectives), and agency (involving a distancing from the control of immediate situations) are most directly discernible. In what follows, we describe a recent attempt we made to theorize a developmental progression of this kind.[23]

In early infancy, the baby experiences tactile position exchanges (touching and being touched, touching objects of differing degrees of resistance and manipulative possibility) and position exchanges involving perceptual recovery (e.g., "losing" and re-locating mother's breast or crib toys). Perceptions of others' responses to what they react to as the infant's signals for attention, nurturance, and interest also assist the infant to experience sensory connections between others' movements and her own activities.

Gradually, the child participates, with increasingly less assistance, in a wide variety of simple sequences of coordinated interactivity that involve occupying different social positions (e.g., giving and receiving toys such as balls, alternating between leading and following in exchanges of facial expressions, and simple imitative actions like peek-a-boo, hiding and seeking, and so forth). Soon, she is able to remember and anticipate being in one position while actually occupying the other, related position – for example, anticipating a switch from initiator to follower and vice-versa. We understand such developments as very early, pre-reflective, situation-bound forms of perspective taking. Within PET, perspective taking and integration are more abstracted forms of position exchange that move from a sociophysical to social-psychological and psychological planes of interactivity.

As the developing child begins to use language, she is able to hear herself more or less as others hear her (i.e., another form of position

---

[22] Also see J. Barresi, On seeing our selves and others as persons. *New Ideas in Psychology* **30** (2012) 120–130.

[23] Martin and Gillespie, A neo-Meadian approach to human agency.

amazon.com

SDX9LfWxGk

Purchase Order #: 02242015
Your order of February 24, 2015 (Order ID 114-2850148-0994625)

Qty.	Item	Item Price	Total
1	How Infants Know Minds Reddy, Vasudevi --- Paperback (** P-8-A883A036 **) 0674046072	$21.47	$21.47
1	African American Psychology: From Africa to America Belgrave, Faye Z. (Zollicoffer) --- Paperback (** P-8-A732A234 **) 1412999545	$88.60	$88.60
1	The Impact of Attachment (Norton Series on Interpersonal Neurobiology) Hart, Susan --- Hardcover (** P-8-A904A195 **) 0393706621	$34.91	$34.91
1	Evolution and Human Sexual Behavior Gray, Peter B. --- Hardcover (** P-5-A009B684 **) 0674072731	$35.96	$35.96
1	Friendships in Childhood and Adolescence (Guilford Series on Social and Emotional Development) Bagwell PhD, Catherine L. --- Paperback (** P-8-A993A759 **) 1462509606	$28.82	$28.82
1	Deep Secrets: Boys' Friendships and the Crisis of Connection Way, Niobe --- Paperback (** P-8-A308C559 **) 0674072421	$14.45	$14.45

exchange), and to act in accordance with her own pronouncements, much as others do. With language providing the necessary significant symbols, cues, and prompts, the developing child is able to separate action possibilities from actual social positions, and to talk, think, and imagine perspectives other than those suggested by her immediate surroundings and location within them. Different social roles, and their various linguistic and relational constituents, are now enacted with others in role-play and pretend games, permitting greater degrees of self–other differentiation, coordination, planning, and evaluation. Informally structured positional play is eclipsed by more formally structured participation in games with multiple, coordinated roles and perspectives.

With greater mastery of language and its symbolic resources, such as indexicality and narrative form, the child is able to participate in forms of intersubjectivity that yield more abstracted, psychological forms of perspective taking and coordination. For example, immersion in real and fictional narratives through a wide variety of cultural media (books, films, internet) provides imaginative means of moving even further beyond present interactions and contexts, enabling the deliberate creation and envisioning of alternative possibilities in the face of problems and obstacles. With the aid of these supplements to direct interactivity and intersubjectivity, an increasingly abstracted set of perspectives associated with diverse traditions and ways of life may be examined for possible ways of proceeding in joint, communal endeavors. Immersion in such multi-perspectival matrices further creates and legitimates an important temporal shift in the experience of the developing person, from "event time" to "psychological time." This is a shift that has gradually attended the developmental progression we have described thus far. But, the kind of multi-perspectivity described here also enables an integrated consideration of perspectives and possibilities experienced in the past, together with those experienced in the present, and in anticipation of those imagined in the future. Such temporal flexibility enables an "accordion-like" ability to compress and expand elements drawn from different temporal experiences and imaginings, within which past, present, and future are selectively melded to yield sensations, perceptions, and ideas relevant to life projects and interests.

Examples of the transformative potential of position exchange

Thus far, we have discussed the relevance of position exchange theory for understanding the evolution and development of persons. In this penultimate section, we consider three additional examples of the relevance

of position exchange to interpersonal problem solving, social development, social cohesion, and socio-cultural engagement. We begin with a
brief discussion of experimental research that examines the effects of position exchange on collective problem solving, then consider an analysis of
position exchange in children's role playing, before moving on to examine approaches to team athletics that make extensive use of ideas and
practices of position exchange.

Gillespie and Cornish and Gillespie and Richardson report a series
of experiments to test the effects of position exchange within a joint
task involving intersubjective coordination.[24] The task in question
was a "communication conflict situation," in which participants either
exchanged or did not exchange the social positions of "director" and
"follower." Directors were provided with a map on which a particular
route was highlighted, and asked to verbally guide the followers (who
were given a blank map) through the marked route, with the stipulation
that directors and followers could not look at each other's maps. After a
few trials during which directors and followers switched or did not switch
positions, a conflict situation was introduced by providing the director
and follower with slightly discrepant maps that they assumed were identical. Results of several such experiments indicate a dramatic difference
between the ability of position switching director/follower dyads, compared to non-switching dyads, to resolve the conflict task by coming to
the conclusion that a successful resolution was impossible because the
maps were different. For example, in the most recent experiment, only
one out of twenty non-exchange dyads solved the conflict task, compared
to seventeen of twenty position exchange dyads.

Transcriptions of the conversations among directors and followers,
when analyzed further by Gillespie and Cornish, revealed that in the position exchange condition, followers were more persistent in describing the
difficulties they were experiencing, and directors were much more likely
to consider and not dismiss the follower's perspective. In short, when
participants had experienced both the typically dominant socio-cultural
position and role of the director, as well as the typically subordinate socio-
cultural position of the follower, they were better able to integrate the
actual perspectives experienced while in both positions/roles – an intersubjective integration that facilitated more effective social coordination
and problem solving.

---

[24] A. Gillespie and F. Cornish, What can be said? Identity as a constraint on knowledge
production. *Papers on Social Representations* **19** (5) (2010) 1–13; and A. Gillespie and
B. Richardson, Exchanging social positions: Enhancing perspective taking within a
cooperative problem solving task. *European Journal of Social Psychology* **40** (2011) 1–9.

As a second example of how position exchange functions to advance the perspective integration and coordination of persons and developing persons, consider the implications of position exchange for understanding children's role playing games. Gillespie notes that such games tend to cease once a child begins to participate in real-life equivalents of the roles previously played, and asks if young children use role play as a form of position exchange in exploratory preparation for real-life role enactment.[25] More specifically, he asks why playing with dolls, especially baby dolls, is so widely spread across historical time and socio-cultural contexts. In considering this question, Gillespie notes that before doll playing begins, young children have been cared for by others in ways that they now reverse as they enact positions of care giving in their doll play. The doll takes the place of the child, while the child enacts the position and role of the care-giver. By putting the doll baby to bed, bathing and feeding it, changing its diapers, taking it to school, correcting it, and comforting it, the child must take and integrate the positions and perspectives of both the baby and the care-giver. Within these role-play sequences, the child moves back and forth between the position of the baby and that of the care-giver, supported by the social–material prop of the doll. This repeated movement between positions allows the child to distanciate from, and understand more clearly and completely, her own actions and experiences as a child, at the same time as it allows the child to participate, at least to some extent, in the perspectives and roles of a care-giver. Research stimulated by such applications of PET to this and other common childhood activities might be directed at questions concerning the extent to which doll play is associated with greater identification with and understanding of care-givers, and with greater self-understanding and self-regulation on the parts of children themselves.

A final example is drawn from the field of team athletics. George Herbert Mead, one of the earliest advocates of perspective exchange with respect to social, psychological development, frequently used the American game of baseball to illustrate and exemplify his texts.

[I]n a game where a number of individuals are involved, then the child taking one role must be ready to take the role of everyone else. If he gets in a ball nine [baseball team] he must have the responses of each position involved in his own position. He must know what everyone else is going to do in order to carry out his own play. He has to take all of these roles. They do not all have to be present in consciousness at the same time, but at some moments he has to have three or four individuals present in his own attitude [perspective], such as the one who is going to throw the ball, the one who is going to catch it, and so on. These responses

25 Gillespie, Position exchange.

must be, in some degree, present in his own make-up. In the game, then, there is a set of responses of such others so organized that the attitude [perspective] of one calls out the appropriate attitudes [perspectives] of the other[s].[26]

Mead referred to the organization of the responses of others within the individual as the generalized other. Individuals with a richly elaborated generalized other should be better able to coordinate their actions in relation to their group. In this regard, it is potentially instructive to note that a recently developed approach to the popular international game of football or soccer, known as total football, makes direct and prescriptive use of many of the ideas central to PET.

In total football, any player other than the keeper (whose position exchanges are more restrictively located in and around the goal area) can take over the position and role of any other player in a team. If a player moves out of a particular position, another moves into the vacated position, and the team as a whole shifts and adjusts flexibly as play continues. In effect, this means that no player is fixed in a particular position or role, and can move across attacking, defending, and mid-field positions, as others on the team adjust. The tactical success of total football depends on the adaptability of each player within the team to quickly and efficiently switch positions as the on-field situation demands. Total football was developed originally by trainer/coach Rinus Michels and the Dutch football club, Ajax, from 1969 to 1974, a period in which Ajax achieved several championship titles.

Inspired by the example of Ajax, the first author and a coaching partner adopted a similar strategy while coaching their daughters' baseball team during the 1990s. Unlike other teams with whom they competed, this team adopted a strategy of having all players learn to play a number of different positions during practices, and actually playing a number of different positions during different segments of games. During several years and seasons of play, across different age levels, the result of enacting this strategy was the same – a slow, uneven start to each season with several early losses, followed by a steady improvement, and eventual team success in play-offs and championship contests. As a particular season of play went by, the players gradually became increasingly proficient at understanding the nuances of play that defined each position, observing and anticipating the actions and reactions of their team-mates and making cohesive adjustments to back up their team-mates during play, a social cohesion that carried over to their lives outside of baseball.

---

[26] Mead, *Mind, Self, and Society*, 151.

Conclusions: position exchange and personhood

Position exchange theory understands our embodied, situated participation within routine sequences of social exchange as a developmental
motor of our abilities to understand ourselves and others, to distance ourselves from our immediate contexts, and to take and coordinate different
perspectives. Such understanding, distanciation, and integration of perspectives enable several additional hallmarks of personhood, including
intersubjectivity and moral and rational agency. Our claim is not that
position exchange is the only process active in the evolution, development, and continuing transformation of persons. However, we do want
to emphasize the likelihood that position exchange, grounded within our
physical, social world of interactivity, provides an important and effective,
enactive pathway for the emergence of more psychologically sophisticated
features and capabilities of persons (such as selfhood and agency) that
typically have been explained in more mentalistic ways – ways that eschew
social and physical processes in favor of theorizing other minds, internal-
izing and representing information drawn from our social and personal
experiences, and so forth. Even here, we have no wish to deny any such
human mental processes and capabilities. Rather, we aim to show that
these and related psychological accomplishments are evolutionary and
developmental achievements, not starting points. They are part of what
requires explanation, not explanations.

If we are correct, both social scientists and social reformers should
consider position exchange as a basic mechanism for introducing change
and transformation in their efforts to comprehend and/or transform persons and their social interactions. Position exchange is a key element
in our graduation from basic, enactive forms of interactivity with others within the biophysical and socio-cultural world to less situationally
and temporally fettered social, psychological forms of intersubjectivity
and imagination capable of supporting personal and communal agency.
More succinctly, position exchange is a basic process that we employ
to bootstrap those advanced psychological capabilities that define us as
persons.

If we can achieve greater understanding of processes and mechanisms
of position exchange and coordination, we potentially might be able to
enhance our recognition of, and obligations in relation to, different forms
of personhood as enacted and practiced in different parts of our contemporary world. For whatever our differences in the ways we understand
and interpret ourselves and others, and in the values, virtues, and ends
we have come to cherish and promote, we all are positioned within our
socio-physical, socio-cultural, and social-psychological ways of living,

with at least two things in common. We are creatures who, through our positioned interactivity in the world, have created coordinated ways of living together, and we care about what we have created. In the words of Kwame Appiah, whatever our differences, as persons, we can recognize "that each other person is engaged in the ethical project of making a life," and on this basis, we can see each other as persons with rights and responsibilities, just like ourselves, that demand understanding and respect, whatever our agreements and disagreements.[27] Such recognition does not prevent us from engaging with others who have developed ways of life different from our own, but rather, signals that such engagement is possible and potentially fruitful with respect to informing us and them of their and our personhood. It is for this reason that systems that prevent us from positioning ourselves with others through engagement in shared social practices and projects – systems of apartheid, rigid and hierarchical class structures, and inequitable privilege – are so obviously wrong. Such systems truncate our personhood by depriving us of opportunities, no matter how difficult and hard-won they might prove to be, for positioning ourselves within potentially informative and ameliorative engagements and participations with those from whom we differ.

[27] K. A. Appiah, *Experiments in Ethics* (Harvard University Press, 2008) 203.

9   The emergent ontology of persons

Mark H. Bickhard

Persons are developmental social emergents. In this chapter, I will present a model of that emergent ontology. The model requires that ontological emergence in general is possible, and that normative emergence in particular is a metaphysical reality. That is, persons are part of the natural world, but this cannot be accounted for within a "naturalism" that excludes emergence and normative emergence.

I argue elsewhere that normativity can be integrated within the world as a natural realm of emergence if we adopt a process metaphysical framework, and, furthermore, that there are deep reasons, independent reasons, for shifting from the substance and entity metaphysics that has dominated western thought for millennia to a process metaphysics. A shift to a process metaphysics is forced by both conceptual and scientific reasons, and a process metaphysics makes possible a natural, non-eliminative, metaphysical emergence, including that of normative emergence. These arguments have been developed elsewhere, and the resulting framework will be assumed here.[1]

Central to this discussion is the normative emergence of agency. Biological creatures are agents, and this is so in the full normative sense in which agentive interactions with an environment can be successful or unsuccessful, relative to the agentive organism itself.[2] A model of agency as a special form of open system interaction provides a full biological ground for agency, and transcends some of the deep problems involved in attempting to model agency in terms of, for example, reasoned computations on symbolic representations, eventuating in some special event

---

[1] See, for example, M. H. Bickhard, Emergence. In P. B. Andersen, C. Emmeche, N. O. Finnemann, P. V. Christiansen (eds.) *Downward Causation* (Aarhus, Denmark: University of Aarhus Press, 2000) 322–348; and M. H. Bickhard, The interactivist model. *Synthese* **166** (3) (2009) 547–591.

[2] This model is developed in several places, including Bickhard, The interactivist model; M. H. Bickhard, Interactivism. In J. Symons and P. Calvo (eds.) *The Routledge Companion to Philosophy of Psychology* (London: Routledge 2009) 346–359; R. J. Campbell, A process-based model for an interactive ontology. *Synthese* **166** (3) (2009) 453–477; and C. A. Hooker, Interaction and bio-cognitive order. *Synthese* **166** (3) (2009) 513–546.

that initiates a causal chain extending into the environment. Every single aspect of this standard framework is false and untenable.[3] Interactive agency will, in this discussion, be the framework within which representation, language, social ontology, and, especially, persons as special kinds of emergent social agents, will be developed. It is the framework within which persons are understood as full normative ontologies within the natural world.

Agency and social ontology

Persons are agents, special socially adapted and socially co-constitutive agents. The developmental emergence of such person-agents occurs in each individual. This is unlike, for example, social insects in which there is arguably a social ontological emergence at the level of the nest or hive, but there is no emergence at the level of the individual insect. The emergence of persons, then, occurs as individuals develop the agencies required in order to participate in, and thereby help constitute, the cultural and social realities within which that development occurs. A first step toward accounting for this is to model complex agency; a second is to model the emergence of social ontologies; and a third is to model the dynamics of developmental processes that create such emergent persons.

Toward complex agency

The selections of which interactions to engage in by simple biological agents, such as a bacterium, are themselves relatively simple. The bacterium that will swim so long as it is headed up a sugar gradient, but tumble if it finds itself headed down a sugar gradient, selects between swimming and tumbling, but the "selection" is primarily a triggering function.

A more complex agent, such as, perhaps, a frog, faces multiple possible interactions at given moments, and must select among those multiple possibilities. It could, for example, flick its tongue to the right in order to eat a fly, or to the left to eat a different fly, or down for a worm. Such selection requires a functional indication of what interactions are currently possible among which the selection(s) can take place, and some sort of sensitivity to the environment in order to set up those functional indications of possibilities.

---

[3] These critiques are presented in, for example, Bickhard, The interactivist model; Bickhard, Interactivism; M. H. Bickhard, Some consequences (and enablings) of process metaphysics. *Axiomathes* **21** (2011) 3–32.

Such branching interaction potentialities are also conditional: setting up an indication of an interaction possibility requires that some appropriate condition has been detected, or differentiated, in the environment. Some differentiation that, at least much of the time, happens to differentiate a fly should have occurred prior to setting up the tongue flicking and eating indication. Such conditional readinesses to set up indications may or may not be engaged: there may or may not be a fly at some given location.

But the combination of the possibilities of *branching* indications of interaction possibility and *conditionalized* indications of interaction possibility generate the potential for interconnected webs, perhaps vast and complex webs, of indications of interaction possibilities. It is within such possibly vast webs that complex agents select and guide their interactions. I call such webs the agent's knowledge of its current interactive situation – or *situation knowledge*.

Situation knowledge is situation specific. It is ultimately conditionalized on the current situation of the agent. Even "distant" possibilities, such as opening one's refrigerator to get a drink, are situated in one's current location, such that, for example, you might have to walk to your car and drive home in order for that possibility to become proximate.

Situations are constantly changing, and so also must situation knowledge. There must be a constant updating, maintenance, and filling out of the possibilities in situation knowledge. I call this dynamic flow of updating and maintaining situation knowledge *apperception*.[4]

In simple agents, the conditionalized set-ups of interaction possibilities, and the triggering among them, may be largely or entirely innate – there is no apperception. For complex situation knowledge in complex agents, these apperceptive processes must themselves be learned – there is nothing innate about knowing how to open refrigerators and obtaining a drink.

In passive models of agentic relationships to the environment, such as signet rings pressing their form into wax (transduction), or a scratching into the wax over time (induction), it is enticing to model learning as similarly a matter of the world pressing itself into the mind (induction writ large). If knowledge consists of knowing how to successfully interact with the world, however – if knowledge consists of the ability to apperceive successfully – then there is no temptation to model the mind as passive with respect to learning.

Learning, thus, must be a matter of construction – the mind must be an active generator. Moreover, unless such constructions are prescient, possible ways of apperceiving must be tried out and selected for their

---

[4] Bickhard, The interactivist model.

success or failure. An action or interaction based model of knowledge requires a constructivism, a *variation and selection constructivism*. It forces an *evolutionary epistemology*.[5]

Furthermore, if new constructions can potentially make use of earlier constructions, perhaps using them as units or as frameworks for inducing variations, then such recursivity in construction yields various kinds of historicities in learning constructions. Such historistic dependencies in constructions – both constraints and enablings – form the subject matter of *development*.[6]

We now have the outlines of a model of the development of agency: it is an evolutionary epistemological constructive process generating further agentive capabilities, and, thereby, generating the development of the agent. Complex agents encounter a special kind of situation when encountering each other that forms the framework for the emergence of social ontology, and the concomitant emergence of social agency.

Social ontology: two or more complex agents

An agent must differentiate its environment in order to appropriately apperceive it – in order to set up appropriate situation knowledge. Kinds of interaction that are engaged in primarily for the purpose of modulating apperception, especially those that involve physiologically specialized systems, are called *perceptual*. Perception, then, is interaction of a specialized kind – interaction to modulate apperception.

Modulation of apperception succeeds, when it does, because situations are massively redundant. Differentiating interactions can support large-scale updatings and modulations of situation knowledge. A visual scan of a rock, for example, (or a refrigerator) provides enough information to be able to anticipate many possible interactions that the rock might afford.[7]

[5] See D. T. Campbell, Evolutionary epistemology. In P. A. Schilpp (ed.) *The Philosophy of Karl Popper* (LaSalle, IL: Open Court, 1974) 413–463; and D. T. Campbell, Levels of organization, downward causation, and the selection-theory approach to evolutionary epistemology. In G. Greenberg and E. Tobach (eds.) *Theories of the Evolution of Knowing* (Hillsdale, NJ: Lawrence Erlbaum Associates, 1990) 1–17.

[6] Discussions of development from this perspective can be found in R. L. Campbell and M. H. Bickhard, Types of constraints on development: An interactivist approach. *Developmental Review* 12 (3) (1992) 311–338; and M. H. Bickhard, Developmental normativity and normative development. In L. Smith and J. Voneche (eds.) *Norms in Human Development* (Cambridge University Press, 2006) 57–76.

[7] Perception as input processing exerts a powerful intuitive pull, but is ultimately untenable. See Bickhard, The interactivist model; and M. H. Bickhard and D. M. Richie, *On the Nature of Representation: A Case Study of James Gibson's Theory of Perception* (New York: Praeger Publishers, 1983).

There is a special class of situations, however, in which there is a reflexive indeterminacy of how they should be apperceptively characterized. These are situations in which a complex agent is in the interactive presence of one or more other complex agents – social situations.

Part of the difficulty in apperceiving another (complex) agent is that much of the interactive potentiality that they afford inheres in their internal processes and conditions, and these are not directly perceptually available. There is, however, a deeper reason for difficulty.

In order for an agent to characterize a situation involving another agent, they must not only apperceive that other agent, but that the other agent is also apperceiving his or her environment, which includes the first agent. So, to apperceive a situation involving you, I must apperceive, among other things, your apperceptions of me, including my apperceptions of you . . . and so on in an unbounded potential regress.

In most circumstances (e.g., not involving deceit), there is a mutual interest in resolving this indeterminate reciprocity in apperceiving the situation, and, in this sense, the problem posed is a version of a *coordination problem* – a problem in which more than one mutually satisfactory solution exists, but in which arriving at any one of the acceptable possibilities requires some sort of appropriately joint activity on the part of the participants: joint complementary apperceptive characterizations and resultant activity, in this case.[8]

Solutions to coordination problems serve as a model of *convention*.[9] In this case, such a solution constitutes a coordinative characterization of the situation, and is, thus, called a *situation convention* – a convention about what kind of situation the participants are participants in.[10]

Situation conventions are emergent in the complementary relations among the participants' apperceptively constructed situation knowledge. In virtue of those relations among their respective situation knowledge organizations, the participants not only *participate* in the situation convention, they *co-constitute* that situation convention in their participations.

Note that the situation characterized in a situation convention is largely constituted by the complementary apperceptions of that situation; it is the complementary factual relationships between (among) the various agents' situation knowledge that constitutes the situation convention

---

[8] T. C. Schelling, *The Strategy of Conflict* (New York: Oxford University Press, 1963).

[9] This model is a revision of D. K. Lewis, *Convention* (Cambridge, MA: Harvard University Press, 1969).

[10] Situation conventions are discussed in, for example, M. H. Bickhard, *Cognition, Convention, and Communication* (New York: Praeger Publishers, 1980); and Bickhard, The interactivist model.

being characterized. So, situation conventions constitute the ontological facts that situation conventions are about.

One special class of situation conventions is those that are invoked via some generally accessible signal or procedure or situation, such as insignia of rank, calling a meeting to order, automobiles passing each other on the right and so on. The power of such signals or procedures to elicit a convention is itself a matter of convention, but the broad accessibility of such means of invocation establishes the conventions as *types* that are potentially available over populations and times. These are called *institutionalized conventions*.

In contrast, the conventions involved in the mutual understandings of sentences in mid-utterance are likely never to have occurred before nor to occur again: these are non-repeated situation conventions – *linguistic situation conventions* in this case.[11]

The ontologies of persons

All biological entities are agents at least minimally: they are constituted by interactive processes that are normative in the sense of contributing to the continuing existence of the process.[12] Differing kinds of agents arise in differing forms of such self-maintaining processes, relative to the environments in which self-maintenance is functionally successful.[13] Persons, so I argue, are special kinds of agents that arise in and are constituted in interactions with social and cultural processes. These interactions include, in particular, interactions with other social persons. Persons and their interactions, therefore, thereby co-constitute the emergence base for those social and cultural realities. This creates an interesting situation in which socio-cultural processes create, via development, the persons who constitute the emergence base for those socio-cultural processes.

That is, social processes emerge in the conventions among social agents, and those agents capable of participating in and thereby constituting social processes emerge in the *development* of individual biological

---

[11] Bickhard, *Cognition, Convention, and Communication*.

[12] Normativity as related to the continuing existence of a process has been at the center of this model since its inception. See M. H. Bickhard, A model of developmental and psychological processes. PhD dissertation, University of Chicago (1973), published as M. H. Bickhard, A model of developmental and psychological processes. *Genetic Psychology Monographs* **102** (1980) 61–116. Bickhard, *Cognition, Convention, and Communication*; M. H. Bickhard, Representational content in humans and machines. *Journal of Experimental and Theoretical Artificial Intelligence* **5** (1993) 285–333; and Bickhard, The interactivist model.

[13] Bickhard, The interactivist model.

agents as they become social agents. This is an individual level emergence, and this emergence of individual persons occurs with respect to the society and culture within which the development occurs. As mentioned, such individual level emergence of social agents differs drastically from, for example, social insects, for which there is arguably a social emergence at the level of the nest or hive, but no developmental emergence at the level of the individual insects. Human infants are special kinds of biological creatures, open to and adapted to such socio-cultural developmental emergence.[14]

In this model, agents are constituted in their interactive dynamics; such dynamics constitute their ontology. They are not independent entities that might happen to engage in action, but organizations of self-maintenance process that are constituted in that process, and that cease to exist if those interactions cease – they *are* those (self-maintaining) interactions.

This is in strong contrast to, for example, a computational model of agency, in which the computational system may engage its environment, but for which there is no ontological necessity to do so. Computational systems are not constituted by their computational interactions.

Agents, then, are constituted in their interactive dynamics, and human infants that develop in social and cultural environments develop as special kinds of agents that participate in those environments. Those environments are themselves emergent environments, emergent in the social and institutional conventions and conventionalized processes that constitute them. Agents that develop to become participants, thus constitutive participants, in those environments are themselves, therefore, emergent kinds of agents – social agents: *persons*.

Language and social ontology

Social ontology is emergent in conventions and the processes involving and constituting them. There is a special class of conventions that forms a central aspect of these ontologies: language. Institutionalized conventions are constituted in the availability of conventionalized tools, such as insignia of rank, for invoking those conventions. Some such convention-invoking tools can recursively modify each other, such as when the convention of a play changes the significance of the convention of a marriage ceremony, or when the conventional consequences of "good" modify those of "thief." In a play, an otherwise perfectly correct marriage

---

[14] P. L. Berger and T. Luckmann, *The Social Construction of Reality* (New York: Doubleday, 1966).

172   *Mark H. Bickhard*

ceremony does not have the same social consequences as it would if performed in a correct legal setting. In the case of the adjective "good," we may construe a construction such as "good person" as differentiating the intersection of good things and persons, but such an intersective strategy does not work for, for example, "good thief." In such cases, "good" picks out – modifies – some salient characteristics of "thief" rather than intersecting with that category. Note that such modifications also account for cases, like "good person," that look intersective.

When the possibilities of such recursive modifications become productive – when the potentialities of such recursive constructions become unbounded – then the conventionalized tools that can participate in those invocating constructions constitute a *language*.[15] Language, in this model, is a socioculturally conventionalized tool system for constructing utterances with conventionalized effects on situation conventions. That is, language is a socioculturally available tool system for constructing, changing, and maintaining situation conventions.

In this model, language is a tool system for the dynamics of social interaction. This differs on a metaphysically deep level from standard conceptions in which words denote things or properties – the framework that has dominated language studies for millennia.[16] I argue elsewhere that (1) standard approaches to modeling language are at root incoherent; and (2) a fully interactive-apperceptive model of language (there are a number of partial convergences with such a model in the literature, but none takes the operative perspective to account for all of language) accounts both for standard paradigmatic "denotational" language phenomena as well as multiple aspects of language that are anomalous or inexplicable on standard accounts.[17]

Situation conventions are constituted in the complementary relationships among the participants' characterizations of the situation. Those characterizations, in turn, are constituted as anticipations of ranges of potential further interaction. With the emergence of language, many of those further interaction potentialities will themselves be potentialities of further conversation, of further "languaging." The potentialities that constitute human social realities, thus, are in major ways potentialities of

[15] Bickhard, *Cognition, Convention, and Communication*; M. H. Bickhard, Language as an interaction system. *New Ideas in Psychology* 25 (2) (2007) 171–187; and Bickhard, The interactivist model.

[16] Bickhard, *Cognition, Convention, and Communication*; Bickhard, Language as an interaction system; and Bickhard, The interactivist model.

[17] For discussion, see Bickhard, *Cognition, Convention, and Communication*; Bickhard, Language as an Interaction System; Bickhard, The interactivist model; and M. H. Bickhard, *The Whole Person: Toward a Naturalism of Persons – Contributions to an Ontological Psychology* (in preparation).

language. So, language is not only a tool system for interacting with social realities – the potentialities of language constitute many of those social realities that utterances interact with. Language, thus, both operates on and constitutes social realities. Language potentialities, consequently, are also central to the ontologies of social persons.[18]

Developmental emergence

How does the developmental emergence of ontologically social persons occur? What is the nature of the relevant dynamics? I will outline a model of one central aspect of this development – an aspect involving agentive *presuppositions* (language development *per se* will not be addressed here).[19]

Consider first an infant learning to interact with a toy wooden block. There are many visual scans, manipulations, dropping, chewing, and other interactions that are possible with the block. The infant learns (via individual-level evolutionary-epistemological variations and selections) not only how to engage in such interactions, but also that any of them indicates the possibilities of any of the others: the web of interactive possibilities is internally completely reachable – any such possibility is reachable from any of the others. Furthermore, the infant learns that such internally reachable organizations of situation knowledge are invariant under an important class of transformations: the block can be thrown, put in the toy box, left on the floor and the entire internally reachable web can be re-accessed by returning to the place where the block was left (unless someone has cleaned up in the meantime!). Organizations of internally reachable, relatively invariant, subpatterns of interactive potentialities become an important type of apperceptive possibility in constructing situation knowledge.

Social interactions constitute a different kind of pattern of interaction possibilities. Central to such differences is the contingency pattern of the interactions. Playing peek-a-boo, for example, involves contingent interactions on the part of both infant and adult. These contingencies are in one sense similar to those for the toy block: engaging in one visual scan indicates that a particular manipulation of the block will bring into view

---

[18] M. H. Bickhard, The social ontology of persons. In J. I. M. Carpendale and U. Müller (eds.) *Social Interaction and the Development of Knowledge* (Mahwah, NJ: Erlbaum, 2004) 111–132; M. H. Bickhard, Are you social? The ontological and developmental emergence of the person. In U. Müller, J. I. M. Carpendale, N. Budwig, and B. Sokol (eds.) *Social Life and Social Knowledge* (New York: Taylor and Francis, 2008) 17–42; and M. H. Bickhard, A process ontology for persons and their development. *New Ideas in Psychology* **30** (2012) 107–119.
[19] See Bickhard, *The Whole Person.*

another visual scan possibility. But a major difference between the two kinds of interaction patterns is that the current condition of the block is visually recoverable at many points (so long as the block is not hidden), while the current "state" of the social interaction is not. A currently ongoing conventionalized social interaction is in a current condition that is dependent on the immediately prior history of the engagement in that interaction. That current condition is constituted in the complementary anticipations of what will or could follow from this point in the unfolding of the interaction. That is, the current condition is constituted in the relationships among the participants' characterizations of the situation that constitute it as a situation convention – and those relationships are not directly perceptually accessible. One of the special abilities of human beings is that of being able to keep track of such hidden trajectories of situational flow and change.[20]

Presuppositions and roles

Anticipatory situation knowledge of social practices involves various positions within those forms of practice that constitute "locations" for other contingent agents – occupiers of the relevant *roles* in the practices.[21] Learning to engage in such a practice requires not only learning how to engage in one's own – one's roles – contingent interactions, but also learning to anticipate the contingent interactions of the other(s).

Such anticipations of further possible interactions involve presuppositions about the environments and environmental conditions: some environments will support such anticipations and some will not. Engaging in these anticipated kinds of interaction, or even simply having an anticipation of how things would go if they were engaged in, presupposes that the relevant supporting conditions hold. This is so for the toy block: if the initial visual scan is with a hologram, then the supporting conditions for manipulations will not hold. And it is so for social practices: if the other agent does not manifest the "correct" contingent interactions, if the convention constituting the practice does not hold, then the anticipations of how the practice will go will be false.

These presuppositions are implicit, not something explicitly represented, but they constitute a realm of properties of fundamental importance. Elsewhere I argue, for example, that the truth or falsity of such

---

[20] Bickhard, *The Whole Person*.
[21] For this point, see Berger and Luckmann, *The Social Construction of Reality*; and Bickhard, *The Whole Person*.

presuppositions constitutes the realm of emergence of primitive representational normativity.[22] Here the focus is on the kind of knowledge involved in being able to apperceive patterns with such presuppositions, particularly those of social practices.

The anticipations involved in being able to engage in a social practice, such as peek-a-boo, are anticipations of the contingent responses of the other that successfully continue the conventional interaction. They constitute, therefore, anticipations of the role that the other plays in that kind of interaction. This will be the case whether or not the infant or child (or adult) is able to actually engage in that *other* role in the practice, though being able to take that other role clearly involves more explicitly developed patterns of interaction on the part of the infant or child. The other role(s) in the practice, in turn, involve anticipations of the infant's or child's contingent activities. This is "just" the filling out of the point that situation conventions are solutions to the coordination problem of characterizing the other's characterizations of self, including one's own characterization of the other, and so on.

This structure of reciprocal interactive anticipations is what enters the child into the social world, and the development of the ability to engage in practices with such reciprocal interactive anticipations is the emergence of social agency. These abilities are learned and developed via constructive processes that "seek" success in interaction, just like abilities to interact with toy wooden blocks. But social interactions are special in that (1) they can be of enormous complexity; (2) they are inherently unfolding in time, and not easily recoverable at a given moment if that historicity has been missed or mis-apperceived; and (3) they are conventionalized sedimentations of social and culture historistic processes that have undergone their own evolution in the history of the culture and societies involved.[23] They require keeping track of the temporal flow of the unfolding of the conventionalized interaction. As these institutionalized forms of interaction become more and more complex, temporally extended and with greater ranges of possible splitting of interaction trajectories, they require greater and greater abilities to be able to engage in them. Language, of course, enables and introduces enormous complexities. Human beings belong to a species that has evolved to be adapted, thus adaptive, to such "hidden" historistic complexities.

---

[22] Bickhard, *Cognition, Convention, and Communication*; Bickhard, The interactivist model; and Bickhard, Interactivism.
[23] See Bickhard, *The Whole Person*; Berger and Luckmann, *The Social Construction of Reality*; and N. K. Humphrey, The social function of intellect. In P. P. G. Bateson and R. A. Hinde (eds.) *Growing Points in Ethology* (London: Cambridge University Press, 1976) 303–317.

The social self

As the infant and child develop abilities to engage in social practices, including specific communicational interactions that may not be fully institutionalized in the broader society (though they might be institutionalized for the pair of the infant and care-giver), they *ipso facto* develop more and more complex implicit presuppositions concerning the presuppositions of others about their own roles and manners of engaging in those roles. This can become even more explicit if other roles in the patterns or forms of interaction – the practices – are at times *explicitly* taken up by the infant or child. It is this development of both implicit and explicit knowledge of societies' presuppositions concerning one's own participation in social realities that constitutes a central aspect of the "position exchange" process in social development.[24] Social development, in this manner, intrinsically involves the development of at least implicit, and increasingly explicit, understandings of others' views of one's own position, and others' expectations concerning one's own manners of carrying out those positions.

Developing as a social person, thus, intrinsically involves developing at least an implicit sense of how one's self is taken by others. It intrinsically involves coming to have a self, and to have an implicit understanding of that self – implicit in the abilities to interact with situations involving the presuppositions of others about one's self.[25]

Normativities of social ontology

There are numerous social normativities that are emergent in the ontology of social processes, and I will here outline a few of them. First, insofar as social conventions are solutions to coordination problems, the normativity of participants' interest in arriving at one of the fixed point solutions – arriving at a convention – is a fundamental normativity, an instrumental normativity, in the nature of coordination problems. But social normativities go much deeper than that.[26]

---

[24] J. Martin and A. Gillespie, Chapter 8, this volume.

[25] With the advent of the ability to engage in reflective thought, at about age 3.5 to 4, these implicit senses of self can become unfolded into explicit self representations. For the age 3.5 to 4 transition, see J. W. P. Allen and M. H. Bickhard, Transcending the nativist-empiricist debate: methodological and conceptual issues regarding infant development. *Cognitive Development* (in press); and M. H. Bickhard, Commentary on the age 4 transition. *Human Development* 35 (1992) 182–192. For the model of unfolding, see Bickhard, The social ontology of persons; and Bickhard, Are you social?

[26] Some have argued that the Lewis model of convention cannot account for any deeper normativities, e.g., M. Gilbert, *On Social Facts* (Princeton University Press, 1989). This

The normativities that I will focus on here are those that arise from the fact that participating in social processes intrinsically involves presenting oneself as a legitimate, competent, reliable social agent with sufficient integrity to be able to be counted upon to carry out the forms of interaction at issue – as trustworthy. Furthermore, it involves being accepted as such by others.

These self presentations are implicit early in development, but may become at least partly explicit later. In some cases, there may even be an explicit deceit in such self presentations, and/or acceptances.

Participating in social processes, thus, involves presenting oneself as a co-constitutive member of that society, and having those presentations accepted. There is a strong stake involved in these presentations and acceptances: they are necessary to functioning as a social being, and, thus, ultimately to existing as a social being, as a social person. Without such acceptance, the social ontology of a person is denied. I would suggest that herein lies the power of such practices as shunning and exile.

Presentations of self as a social agent, and their acceptances, are rarely explicit, though they may be – as when someone presents him or herself as a legitimate performer of a marriage ceremony. The basic form for self-presentations, however, is presumptive: an agent begins interacting in such a way as to presume some conventional frame for the interaction, including for their position in that frame. So long as others proceed within the presumed frame, they have implicitly accepted not only the conventional form, but also the person as having a particular position in that form, and, thus, the person as a social agent in general.

With reflection on such processes, presentations and acceptances can become explicit. The individual can also develop values concerning various person-properties, such as integrity, reliability, competence, legitimacy, and so on. At times, such values may explicitly contradict the presuppositions of lower-level, presumptive interactions, such as will be the case for crucial interactions of a spy: as a spy, or con-man, I may undertake presumptive interactions regarding social agent properties that I intend to be accepted, but to be false.

There is a still deeper stake involved: insofar as a social person has developed as being constituted as a social agent in this society and culture, the ontology of that person is constructed on massive presuppositions of being and being accepted as such a social agent. It is such

may or may not be correct, but the model presented in the text differs in crucial ways from Lewis', and arguably does account for deeper normativities (M. H. Bickhard, Social ontology as convention. *Topoi* **27** (1–2) (2008) 139–149).

presuppositions that may become explicit in higher order values.[27] But, if those presuppositions of one's basic ontology come to be challenged, or, worse, refuted or denied, then that constitutes a challenge, or worse, to (the presuppositions of) that person's very existence as a social being. That is, a person's existence as a social being presupposes their general legitimacy and acceptance as a socio-cultural agent. A refusal on the part of others to accept that legitimacy can constitute a challenge to their being as a person.[28]

There is no deeper ground for existence as a social being than such presuppositions as are involved in engaging as a social being, so these constitute a necessary aspect of the ontology of social persons. Social persons, then, can have a fundamental existential stake in those presupposed characteristics. And, insofar as they become explicit, they constitute the core of a person's sense of self, and of whatever they value about their self.

Social ontology and ethics

The normativities involved in the social ontology of persons extend into considerations of ethics, and I will outline one of those central implications: insofar as the ontology of personhood is intrinsically social, then functioning or developing in ways that distort or stunt that social ontology is a violation of one's own ontology, a distortion or stunting of one's own potential as a person.

This notion of potential violations of one's own intrinsic ontology has echoes of Aristotle's notion of the "function" of human beings, and of ethics as involving full realization of that function.[29] And this framework similarly has strong convergences with notions of ethics based on virtue and character.[30] The ontologically social-person framework differs, however, in that fulfillment of the potentialities of a social ontology is not a function or purpose. Rather, violations of that ontology are intrinsically in error with respect to that ontology: the ontology is inherently normative, with some forms of the development of personhood inherently more in accord with the ontology of persons than other possible forms of development. There need be no further purpose on top of that ontology;

---

[27] Bickhard, Developmental normativity.

[28] Importantly, internal doubts about such legitimacy – doubts about one's being as a social, sexual, trustworthy, interesting (and so on) person – can frame many kinds of neurotic psychopathology.

[29] R. Barney, Aristotle's argument for a human function. *Oxford Studies in Ancient Philosophy* 34 (2008) 293–322; and S. Darwall, *Virtue Ethics* (Oxford: Blackwell, 2003).

[30] Bickhard, Some consequences of process metaphysics.

the ontology is already, intrinsically, normative. "Reason" is one aspect of this ontology, but it does not constitute the function or purpose of social being.

There are two differentiable aspects of this point concerning distortions of social being. One is that some ways of being are *more fulfilling* than others, as fulfillments of social ontological possibilities: in particular, ways of being that are open to the fundamental interactive social ontology of persons are intrinsically more fulfilling than ways of being that deny or distort the possibilities of that social ontology. And another is that some ways of being *preclude* others: becoming a person who enjoys torturing others precludes becoming a person who can fully appreciate closeness with others. So, the possible errors are not just in terms of current modes of functioning, but in terms of modes and directions of development as well.

But current modes of being *are* current modes of developing: development occurs as a historistic aspect of the processes of being. So ethical choices involve not only choices of actions and interactions, but also of directions of development, and of kinds of developing.[31] Ethics is concerned not only with *ways* of being and becoming persons, but also with the *manner* of becoming persons – development never ceases.

Conclusion

Persons are emergent natural processes in the natural world. They are emergent as biological agents in general, and social agents in particular. They are not biological computers that gather social data and that happen to compute actions. Interacting with their environments is constitutive of the ontology of persons, both as biological beings and as social beings. Interaction is internally related, not externally related, to the nature of persons.[32]

Social realities are themselves emergent in the forms of interaction among persons, and persons, thus, constitute the emergence base for social ontology. Persons develop within each individual, and constitute an individual level emergence of the kind of agent that can participate in, and thereby co-constitute, the society(ies) and culture(s) in which the person has developed. Persons, then, are emergent relative to their biological bodies; they are an entrance into the social realms around them.

---

[31] Bickhard, Some consequences of process metaphysics.
[32] Bickhard, The interactivist model.

The social ontology of persons is intrinsically normative, in multiple ways. These normativities involve a person's stake in being the social-ontological person that they have become, and extend to considerations of ethics as a fulfillment of the possibilities of such social ontologies – or of intrinsic errors with respect to those ontologies.

10 Theorizing personhood for the world in transition and change: reflections from a transformative activist stance on human development

Anna Stetsenko

The goal of this chapter is to contribute to recent scholarship emerging in the last ten to fifteen years that is pushing for a radical revision of our models of personhood – the sets of ideas about what constitutes humanness, how people come to be the way they are, and what makes each person unique.[1] The traditional models of this kind that are still prevalent in contemporary psychology and education (and in many neighboring disciplines), largely inherited from the early twentieth century, are still mired in outdated notions of human development and its foundational principles, relying on construals of human beings as isolated, self-sufficient individuals who develop essentially in a vacuum.[2] These prevalent models portray persons as either governed by genetically predetermined programs inherited from the evolutionary past as distant as Pleistocene (in evolutionary psychology); or as onlooking hosts of internal information processing (in cognitivism); or as automatons mechanically reacting to external stimuli that direct, prod, and coerce behavior (in behaviorism that, under various guises, is still alive and well in psychology); or as organisms full of unconscious drives who seek to discharge energy impulses (in psychodynamic perspectives); or as individuals who blindly follow commands issued by the intracranial play of neurons, while being neither aware nor in control over the biochemistry of their own brains (in a recently popular strand of brain reductionism).

All these models celebrate a certain sort of person who, firstly, is a solitary, autonomous individual not only unrelated and unattached to others but in constant antagonism with them, impelled to avoid and resist social

---

[1] Parts of this chapter have been published in A. Stetsenko, Personhood: An activist project of historical becoming through collaborative pursuits of social transformation. *New Ideas in Psychology* **30** (2012) 144–153.

[2] For an overview, see A. Stetsenko and I. M. Arievitch, The self in cultural-historical activity theory: Reclaiming the unity of social and individual dimensions of human development. *Theory and Psychology* **14** (2004) 475–503.

forces that are somehow separate from and even intrinsically oppressive and alien to a forever fixed (once and for all) human "primordial nature." Secondly, this person is at the whim of powerful forces outside of one's control and even awareness, and thus can hardly expect or be expected to act purposefully and responsibly. Thirdly, the underlying theme (associated with psychology's long allegiance with evolutionary theory) is that individuals are compelled to adapt to what is given in the present, driven to fit in with the world and its established structures in their *status quo*, as a frozen and static reality.

What is common to these views at a deeper, and more hidden, level is a powerful overriding message that we, as individual persons (let alone as communities, because they are not addressed as playing a role in fashioning personhood), *do not matter*, that we cannot make, or even hope to make, a difference in the course of events in our society, our lives, and our world. In this sense, these models are profoundly political and ideological as they assume and assert a certain normative view of human conduct and the role of individuals *vis-à-vis* the social world – as utterly passive and merely adaptive, that is, lacking in agency. It is a deep irony that though supposedly in line with the liberal notion of individualism – where (as the saying goes) "each individual is the captain of his [*sic*] own ship" – many of the leading frameworks addressing personhood in fact do not grant individuals the power of being in charge even of their own life and decisions, let alone of the social structures and processes that they are part of. Notions such as non-deliberate emotion, unconscious habits, inherited instincts, and automaticity of choice and conduct, all devaluating agency, responsibility, and even conscious reasoning, have been put at the forefront in studying human development, especially in the past two decades, reaching a crescendo in the idea that "we are all puppets" or machines under the control of brain chemistry or genetic blueprints.[3] This recent proliferation of views reducing human development (more boldly now than at any other time in recent history) to machine-like, automatic processes is in a conspicuous clash with the proclaimed Enlightenment ideals of individualism central to modern western democracies, unmasking the hypocrisy of these ideals as a form of mythology of liberalism. The core principle of autonomy at the heart of liberalism with its political system and doctrine of human rights centered on securing individual freedom against external forces is based in the notion of person as a rational decision and choice maker, as self-sufficient and self-creating, yet key doctrines in social sciences including

[3] See J. Wright, *The Moral Animal* (New York: Basic Books, 1994).

psychology have converged on views that are anything but consistent with these ideals.

The popularity of these models of personhood is not surprising because theories are known to reflect societies and prevalent ideologies serving them that capture realities of life through the lens of dominant interests. These theories can also be examined from the point of view of what it is they tell us about the world we live in. What the presently dominant models of personhood reveal about our societies is that beneath the thin veneer of liberal ideals lies a very different ideology consistent with socio-economical hierarchies driven by the interests of controlling, disciplining, and regulating public life and individual conduct by making them fit in and comply with the established social structures. The truly reigning ideology appears to be that of a free enterprise in the form of market fundamentalism that permeates even apparently self-reliant models of personhood. This ideology is really about how it is the market with its blind forces, rather than individuals, that is fully in charge. Instead of promoting agency and responsibility, this ideology creates a thin veil of illusion about self-reliant individuals somehow steering their lives in complete detachment from society, while in essence fostering, all the way through, an utter passivity and lack of self-determination in the face of the all powerful forces of the market.

In effect, these traditional models of personhood reflect the harsh reality of contemporary society in which individuals in fact do not have much agency other than, at best, a limited freedom to choose among given consumer market options. Furthermore, these models implicitly affirm, rather than challenge, the values represented by existing power structures even while they claim to be discovering and "objectively" describing human nature and development. There is an ironic coherence about these theories in that they "do exactly as they say," that is, they base themselves on the notion of humans passively adapting to the world as the key notion and, in a striking parallel, they themselves strive to fit in with the existing world in its *status quo*, rather than attempt to make a difference by charting new visions and reflecting on and meeting emerging challenges.

It is hardly surprising that these models of personhood have flour-ished in the 1990s through 2000s, climaxing in a rising tide, indeed a tsunami, of converging and starkly mechanistic and reductivist views. This page in the history of psychology can be seen as closely related to the peculiarities of the socio-political climate of the time, when history has been proclaimed to have purportedly reached its supposedly glorious end embodied in "the final triumph of capitalism" and an unabashed vic-tory of economic and political liberalism (as Fukuyama has notoriously claimed).[4] This "end of history" metaphor conveyed the sense that there was nothing left to imagination and social action by ruling out the need to envision a world that is essentially different from the *status quo* and the possibility to commit ourselves to creating it.

However, in a remarkable twist of events, this peculiar historical period was immediately followed by an unprecedented turmoil and crisis in the world economy and politics that is still unfolding. In light of these drastic events and developments, it is becoming increasingly more difficult to legitimize and find meaningful applications for the outdated models of personhood. With the turbulent and often violent spasms in the world economy continuing to unfold, there is a growing realization that the world is indeed rapidly changing – leaving very little for people to "adapt to," as the *status quo* crumbles, with even its seemingly most indomitable and invincible structures "melting in the air." In this context, it becomes imperative that psychology develops new models and approaches to personhood. The challenge, as I see it, is to shift away from the ideology of adaptation to the world, with its established structures, in its *status quo*, towards integrating the notion of *social change and activism as central, indeed formative constituents of human nature*, into accounts of human development and models of personhood.

A model of personhood of this kind would conceptualize it in ways that capture and do justice to the dynamism and uncertainties of today's world, where the only given is its ceaseless and unpredictable transformations. The socio-cultural situation we are engulfed in requires persons to be active agents in their own lives and their own society, to be conscious and conscientious, responsive and responsible agents in society who are implicated in its dynamics and change, rather than simply "undergoers" of solitary experiences or responders to brain chemistry and unconscious drives and habits. This model would revive the commitment to solidarity and communion (as in Vygotskian and other emancipatory approaches), with its time-honored insight that each human being is intimately linked with collective social practices and social life.[5] Yet it would also assert, *on a new foundation* of a communal view about human development as a collective and collaborative socio-historical process, the centrality of personal agency, commitment, responsibility, and ability to contribute to social transformation. Such a model of personhood would not so much reproduce or describe "what is," but instead, predicate itself on a transformative goal of designing and creating "what is possible" – and thus,

[4] F. Fukuyama, The end of history. *The National Interest* 16 (Summer 1989).
[5] I. Prilleltensky, Values, assumptions, and practices. Assessing the moral implications of psychological discourse and action. *American Psychologist* 52 (1997) 517–535.

address not who we are but who we could be – while taking a clear stand
on what our ends for the world we live in, and therefore for ourselves,
should be. In other words, developing such a model would inevitably be a
critical project of simultaneously political and moral as well as scientific,
nature and import.

To make steps in achieving this goal, I revisit and expand Vygotsky's project of cultural-historical psychology.[6] This is a uniquely activist
(in multiple meanings of this term) framework underpinned by ideals
of social justice and transformation conceived during the time of an
unprecedented social experiment fueled by the revolutionary impulse
to create a better society, all the tragic failings of this experiment
notwithstanding.[7] Premised on the notion about collaborative transformative practice as the core grounding for human development and personhood, this project offers a unique foundation on which to develop a
dialectical framework that brings together the notion of individuals as
fully interdependent (with each other and the world around them) while
also encompassing individual agency and personhood.

In doing so, I join in with recent attempts to develop an alternative to
both the dominant reductionist, individualist accounts on the one hand,
and those post-modernist (e.g., social constructionist) approaches that,
in their reaction to the traditional individualist trends, shift the pendu-
lum all the way to the other extreme and refrain from theorizing personhood and agency at all.[8] A number of these recent frameworks have
made important steps forward in theorizing persons as agents of their
own and social life while navigating between the extremes of naturalism
and social constructivism to develop understandings of individuals as
simultaneously determining and determined by the world. These frameworks offer alternative analytics including relational notions of discourse,
dialogue, meaning-making, interaction, difference, and embodiment

---

[6] For a broad characterization of what is meant by Vygotsky's project, see A. Stetsenko and
I. M. Arievitch, Cultural-historical activity theory: Foundational worldview and major
principles. In J. Martin and S. Kirschner (eds.) *Sociocultural Perspectives in Psychology:
the Contextual Emergence of Mind and Self* (New York: Columbia University Press, 2010)
231–253. For more details, see P. Sawchuk and A. Stetsenko, Sociology for a non-
canonical activity theory: Exploring intersections and complementarities. *Mind, Culture
and Activity* 15 (2008) 339–360.

[7] See A. Stetsenko, Introduction to "tool and sign" by Lev Vygotsky. In R. Rieber and
D. Robbinson (eds.) *Essential Vygotsky* (New York: Kluwer Academic/Plenum, 2004)
499–510; and A. Stetsenko and I. M. Arievitch, Vygotskian collaborative project of
social transformation: History, politics, and practice in knowledge construction. *The
International Journal of Critical Psychology* 12 (2004) 58–80.

[8] For a representative sample of these approaches, see S. R. Kirschner and J. Martin (eds.)
The Sociocultural Turn in Psychology: the Contextual Emergence of Mind and Self (New York:
Columbia University Press, 2010).

drawing on theories, among others, by Merleau-Ponty, Wittgenstein, Mead, and Levinas.[9] One prominent theme has been to treat personhood, and associated psychological processes including mind and agency, as constituted within socio-cultural contexts and practices and based in interactions with others.[10] A related important development has been to reinstate a construal of humans as partially creating themselves on the basis of their own self-interpretations centered around ethics and morality.[11] This would then turn to narrativity in order to account for the ambiguities and complexities of human life.[12] Understanding humans as profoundly relational – dialogical, embedded in socio-cultural context, embodied, interrelated with others, and therefore ethical – is, in my view, the major achievement of this recent theorizing. However, more work is needed to construe models of personhood that meet the challenges of today's rapid dynamism and transformation and that fully integrate the notions of social change and activism as central to human nature and personhood.

In line and agreement with these recent frameworks, I suggest that persons are agentive beings who develop through profound embeddedness in socio-cultural contexts and within inalienable relations to and interactions with others. However, in building upon this construal, my proposal is to dialectically expand relationality through the notion that human development is not only dialogical and relational. In addition to these characteristics, and more originary in the ontological sense, human development is grounded in collaborative, purposeful, and answerable – that is, *activist* – deeds formed and colored by visions of, stands on, and commitments to particular projects of social transformation. This position, termed transformative activist stance (TAS), places an activist stance *vis-à-vis* the world that all human beings exercise (whether they

---

[9] For example, see I. Burkitt, Psychology in the field of being: Merleau-Ponty, ontology, and social constructionism. *Theory and Psychology* 13 (2003) 319–338; R. N. Williams and M. S. Beyers, Personalism, social constructionism and the foundation of the ethical. *Theory and Psychology* 11 (2001) 119–134; J. Martin and J. Sugarman, *The Psychology of Human Possibility and Constraint* (Albany: State University of New York Press, 1999).

[10] See S. R. Kirschner and J. Martin, The sociocultural turn in psychology: An introduction and an invitation. In Kirschner and Martin, *The Sociocultural Turn in Psychology*, 1–30; Stetsenko and Arievitch, The self in cultural-historical activity theory.

[11] Based in philosophical works by Charles Taylor, among others, see C. Taylor, *Sources of the Self: The Making of the Modern Identity* (Cambridge, MA: Harvard University Press, 1989); and C. Taylor, *Philosophical Arguments* (Cambridge, MA: Harvard University Press, 1995). For example, see J. Sugarman, Persons and moral agency. *Theory and Psychology* 15 (2005) 793–811.

[12] For example, see C. Daiute and C. Lightfoot (eds.) *Narrative Analysis: Studying the Development of Individuals in Society* (Thousand Oaks, CA: Sage, 2004).

know it or not) at the core of human nature and development.[13] The central argument is that it is the realization of this activist stance through answerable deeds composing one unified life project – itself made possible only within ongoing collaborative practices and as defined through them – that forms the path to personhood. In this perspective, the ethical dimension appears as foundational to Being and knowing because it is integral to actions through which we become who we are while changing the world in collaborative pursuits of social transformation. From a transformative activist stance, persons are agents not only for whom "things matter" but *who themselves matter* in history, culture, and society and, moreover, who come into Being as unique individuals exactly through their own activism, that is, through and to the extent that they take a stand on matters of social significance and find ways to make a difference in these processes by contributing to them.

Vygotsky's collaborative project of social transformation

Explicitly grounded in Marxist philosophy and profoundly saturated with goals of a radical social transformation, Vygotsky's theory stands out even today in its philosophical depth and conceptual breadth coupled with a clear ideological commitment to social justice that is built into its core premises. A remarkable (but overlooked in contemporary interpretations) feature of this theory is that it is based in an original worldview – a coherent system of ideas about the way humans and the world they live in are – that stands in stark contrast with the worldview on which presently dominant models of personhood, and much of mainstream psychology, operate. This complex worldview, just as an underlying deep oceanic current that shapes all the surface phenomena while remaining hidden beneath, is not easy to discern. It has not been spelled out by Vygotsky in a neatly packaged set of premises – not surprisingly, given the frantic pace of Vygotsky's work under the extreme circumstances of his life (including two revolutions, a world war, and a civil war, as well

---

[13] TAS is elaborated by A. Stetsenko in a series of recent papers; see, among others: A. Stetsenko, From relational ontology to transformative activist stance on development and learning: Expanding Vygotsky's (CHAT) project. *Cultural Studies of Science Education* 3 (2008) 471–491; A. Stetsenko, Standing on the shoulders of giants: A balancing act of dialectically theorizing conceptual understanding on the grounds of Vygotsky's project. In W.-M. Roth and K. Tobin (eds.) *Re/structuring Science Education: ReUniting Psychological and Sociological Perspectives* (New York: Springer, 2010) 53–72; A. Stetsenko, Teaching-learning and development as activist projects of historical Becoming: Expanding Vygotsky's approach to pedagogy. *Pedagogies: An International Journal* 5 (2010) 6–16; A. Stetsenko, Personhood.

as his illness), which made it impossible for him to retrospectively self-reflect on his works and offer comments on their cumulative meaning. This requires that we detect this meaning from the overall flow of his ideas, epistemic principles, and methodologies. I would even venture a hypothesis that Vygotsky himself was not fully aware of how his works were shaping up to form a coherent, worldview-level, corpus of ideas and principles that were of a revolutionary novel import much in tune with the transformative zeitgeist and realities of his time.

It should be noted that given the fluidity of Vygotsky's thought as it emerged in his works and how it was later developed by several genera-tions of his followers in disparate and often conflicting directions, and in light of how any understanding is possible (with this process itself being an activist endeavor, as suggested in the following sections), it goes with-out saying that my interpretation is not an attempt to deliver some kind of a "timeless truth" about what Vygotsky "truly and really had in mind." Claiming and debating faithfulness to the original in ways that religious dogmas are claimed and debated are impossible and fruitless from the position that takes activism as central to human being and knowing and that aims at developing novel models of personhood. Instead, this inter-pretation is consciously an endeavor of an activist type – at stake in it is what can be done on the grounds of Vygotsky's deep insights (in ways we can make sense of them) for solving problems and addressing issues in *our* world today, in *our* present projects and endeavors.

This worldview has not been discussed in contemporary interpreta-tions of Vygotsky because they often focus on fragmented aspects and dimensions of his theory rather than on its overall import and meaning. Most regrettably, Vygotsky's worldview has not been applied to devel-oping models of personhood, with this topic being neglected in much of contemporary Vygotskian scholarship because of its overall tendency to address processes at the social, distributed level to the exclusion of how individual agency is formed by these processes and itself plays a role in forming them.[14]

At one level, Vygotsky's worldview can be described as premised on a fully relational ontology, thus being, in this regard, akin to conceptual systems developed by Dewey, Piaget, and many other thinkers of the early to mid-twentieth century. At the heart of this ontology was the idea of a relational nature of development as a process that connects indi-viduals and their world, undermining the dualism of subject and object

---

[14] For details, see A. Stetsenko, Activity as object-related: Resolving the dichotomy of individual and collective planes of activity. *Mind, Culture, and Activity* **12** (2005) 70–88.

at the core of the mechanistic worldview that gave rise to two extremes represented by mentalistic psychology and brain reductionism (which, as any extremes, bear much similarity in that they eschew human agency from their respective accounts). This type of ontology was worked out by members of Vygotsky's project as a result of absorbing key influential strands of thinking at the start of the twentieth century. These strands included, first, the philosophical system developed by Marx (itself assimilating earlier achievements of Kant and Hegel) with its dialectical premise about reality as a unitary (total, indivisible) process that is constantly and dynamically in motion, transition, change, and development – replacing commonsense notions of things and entities with notions of process and relation. Second, Vygotsky's project integrated understanding of development in Darwin's theory that centered on relations between organisms and their world as the driving force of evolutionary change.[15] According to this understanding, all living forms evolve and develop within processes of continuous relations with their surrounds and with other living forms, rather than as a preordained and fixed inner essence unfolding from some primordial source. Third, it included many insights from literary theory, pedagogy, linguistics, and semiotics that provided a foundation for incorporating processes of sign mediation and symbolization into an account of human development.

Conceptualizing human development based in humans' mode of relationship to the world was one of the great achievements of Vygotsky's psychology (likening it to systems of thought developed by Dewey and Piaget). But it is the *next*, and related, step – providing an original ontological specification for relations that ground human development while introducing the notions of collectivity, culture, and historicity – wherein the novelty and revolutionary import of Vygotsky's project, according to TAS, lies. As Vygotsky stated, "[i]n the process of historical development, the social human changes modes and ways of own behavior, transforms natural pregivens and functions, works out and creates new forms of behavior – the specifically cultural ones."[16] He did not have time however to fully articulate this worldview and to develop its implications for personhood.

---

[15] For details, see A. Stetsenko, Vygotsky and the conceptual revolution in developmental sciences: Towards a unified (non-additive) account of human development. In M. Fleer, M. Hedegaard, J. Tudge, and A. Prout (eds.) *World Year Book of Education. Constructing Childhood: Global–Local Policies and Practices* (London: Routledge, 2009) 125–142.

[16] L. S. Vygotsky, The history of the development of higher mental functions. In R. W. Rieber (ed.) *The Collected Works of L. S. Vygotsky: The History of the Development of Higher Mental Functions*, Vol. 4 (New York and London: Plenum Press, 1997) 1–251 (18).

Transformative activist stance as a worldview

The dramatic shift at the worldview level assumptions that can be surmised from Vygotsky's works (and that had been captured in Marxist theory before him, though not in its application to psychology) is a novel specification of what constitutes the unique relationship that is characteristic of human life. This shift concerns a move away from the notion of adaptation toward what Vygotsky termed "active adaptation" and what could be more precisely termed an *activist collaborative transformation of nature*. In this logic (expanding on Vygotsky's insights), the beginning of a uniquely human life is associated with and marked by a shift from adaptation to a given environment (that governs in the animal world) to an active and even pro-active (that is, goal-directed and purposeful), collaborative transformation of the environment with the help of collectively invented and gradually elaborated, from generation to generation, cultural tools.

That people transform their environment while relying on cultural tools has been a common theme in many Marxist, including Vygotsky-inspired, writings. However, what needs to be explicated and ascertained more forcefully and consistently is the positing of this process as *ontologically foundational* to human development. This entails positing the collaborative transformative practice (that unfolds and gradually expands in time connecting each human being and each generation with all others) as a new relation to the world, precisely *as a new form of life* (*Lebensweise*) unique to humans that in essence has brought about their emergence in evolution and that constitutes *the foundation for their development* in all its expressions, dimensions, and facets. This change signifies the end of strictly biological evolution and marks the "leap to freedom," entailing a new reality of human Becoming where forces of history, culture, and society reign.

According to TAS, humans come to be and come to know – each other, themselves, and the world – while transforming their world whereby they collectively create their own life and their own nature. This process of collaboratively transforming their world, while building on efforts of each other and on achievements of previous generations (embodied in cultural tools including language and expanded by each new generation), can be seen as the primary ontological realm, the "fabric" of human development, including its aspects of knowing, being, and Becoming. This idea can be advanced against the naturalistic understanding "that only nature affects human beings and that only natural conditions determine their historical development," forgetting that "man in turn acts upon nature, changes it, creates new conditions of existence for himself."[17]

The major import of taking collaborative transformative practice (as suggested by TAS) as the ontological foundation of human development is that it is directly *through* and *in* this process – not in addition to it! – that people not only constantly transform and create their environment; they also, simultaneously, create and constantly transform their very life, thus changing themselves in fundamental ways too and, in the process, becoming human and gaining knowledge (about themselves and the world), while also developing as unique individuals, that is, as persons. It is the *simultaneity*, or in even stronger terms, *the unity* of human transformative practice on the one hand, and the process of becoming (and being human) and of knowing oneself and the world – on the other, that is conveyed in TAS. Human beings come to be themselves and come to know their world and themselves *in the process and as the process* of changing their world (while changing together with it), in the midst of this process and as one of its facets, rather than outside of or merely in some sort of a connection with it. Therefore, human activity – material, practical, and always by necessity social, collaborative processes mediated by cultural tools and aimed at transforming the world – can be seen as the basic form of human life that is formative of everything that is human in humans, including their subjectivity and personhood.

Importantly, transformative collaborative practice supersedes adaptation and relationality in human life and development, that is, dialectically absorbs (or negates, in a Hegelian sense), without eliminating, them. The notion of superseding and negating conveys the sense of something being taken over by a new process and integrated into it so that the former processes continue, yet now as transformed within and subordinated to the dynamics of the new and larger reality of social transformation. The hallmark of human collaborative transformative practices is that they do not narrowly conform to existing reality and do not aim to fit in with it. Instead, their goal is to change the world and the persons within it – with both instantaneously created in and through human practices.

These practices continuously and cumulatively evolve through time while being enacted and carried out by human collectivities through *unique activist contributions* by individual participants (the point often neglected in Vygotsky's project especially in its later stages) who always

---

[17] K. Marx and F. Engels, The German ideology. In R. C. Tucker (ed.) *The Marx–Engels Reader*, second edn (New York: W. W. Norton, 1978) 146–200 (156).

act as social subjects.[18] In this dialectical process, there is always an enduring nexus of relations with past and future generations because activities in the present inevitably build on previous conditions and accomplishments of others; they also contribute to unfolding collective practices, thus incurring changes for the future. Moreover, activities in the present are *contingent on the future* because they are goal-directed and purposeful. In expansion of the relational worldview, this conceptualization posits collaborative human practice directed at transforming the world as a radically new ontology of historical Becoming that represents *a unified, and uniquely human, realm*. Processes through which humans collectively change their world are primary and foundational in the sense that all other phenomena of human life are seen as grounded in these transformative collaborative practices, as growing from these practices, constituting their dimensions, serving their goals and never completely breaking away from them. Importantly, no ontological gaps are posited to separate phenomena within this realm, with human mind and personhood, self-regulation, and cognition all seen as representing instantiations (or moments) of human practice. The centrality of collaborative transformative practices for human life and development can be viewed, I suggest, on a par with the centrality of evolution in biology and therefore as a condition *sine qua non* for understanding these processes. It is also within and for these practices that human personhood becomes necessary and possible.

This proposition is in line with the famous statement by Marx that "[t]he philosophers have only *interpreted* the world, in various ways; the point, however, is to *change* it."[19] However, this statement draws attention to and has been interpreted only in its epistemic dimension, as a maxim that humans know the world through changing it. The expansion suggested herein goes beyond the epistemological level to the ontological one by stating that while there is indeed no gap between changing one's world and knowing it, there is also *no gap* between changing one's world and being (becoming) oneself as a unique person, with both simultaneously created in this process of change. There is, in other words, no knowledge and no person that exist prior to and can be separated from a transformative activist engagement with the world (including, importantly, with other people and oneself).

---

[18] For details, see Stetsenko, Activity as object-related; and Sawchuk and Stetsenko, Sociology for a non-canonical activity theory.

[19] K. Marx, Theses on Feuerbach. In Tucker, *The Marx–Engels Reader*, 145.

Personhood: an activist project of a historical becoming-through-doing

The interrelated implications from this transformative ontology of historical Becoming, or the transformative activist stance (TAS), for the notion of personhood are the following. First, TAS overcomes the contemplative stance in that humans are understood as not passively dwelling in the world or observing it from afar, outside of direct and immediate engagement. Instead, humans are understood as being connected with the world precisely through their own activist deeds – through what has been termed "engaged agency" in moral philosophy.[20] Similar to this philosophy, in TAS too the disinterested observers and the self-contained individuals understood as separate units existing prior to and independently of the world are replaced with the notion that persons are constituted by their own enduring, engaged agency and as a nexus of relations. What is added however is that TAS provides a worldview-level rationale for this construal of personhood by means of specifying the core ontological realm in which engaged agency is theorized. In addition, TAS dispenses not only with the notion of a passive human being but simultaneously also with the construal of the world as self-contained and existing prior to and independently from human beings. Therefore, the second implication is that the world itself is understood in its human relevance – as a dynamic uninterrupted flow of activist human deeds stretching through time, as a flow of collaborative practice brought into existence and enacted by collectivities and their participants. Thus understood, the world cannot be described apart from individuals, in isolation from what they actually do and perform in their lives, with human actions and deeds constituting no less than the lived world itself.[21] The term best capturing reality thus understood is *actuality* (in its etymology deriving from "act" in many languages – *Wirk*lichkeit [German], *deijstvi*telnost [Russian]) – a realm where human collaborative activities (praxis) and deeds make up the world that is not discovered but created by humans. Third, because the world is taken in its human relevance – as inhabited and even enacted, or performed, in human practice – it appears as indelibly imbued with meanings and other phenomena of human subjectivity (what was termed "ideality" by Ilyenkov).[22] These phenomena are thus de-mystified as they

---

[20] See Taylor, *Philosophical Arguments*.

[21] See M. M. Bakhtin, *Toward a Philosophy of the Act*, V. Liapunov and M. Holquist (eds.) (Austin: University of Texas Press, 1993).

[22] E. V. Ilyenkov, *The Dialectics of the Abstract and the Concrete in Marx's Capital* (Moscow: Progress, 1982).

are shown only to exist through their role in creating the world through making changes and leaving tangible traces in it (in artefacts of culture, in contributions to how practices are carried out, etc.)

Fourth, although transformative practice is carried out by individuals in and through their unique and irreducibly personal (but never *a*-social) contributions, from their unique positioning in history and society, the collective dimension is taken to be primary in TAS – because each individual contribution is inextricably relational, representing a nexus of inter-relations with other people, and thus with society and history. Therefore, individuals never start from scratch and never completely vanish; instead, they enter and join in with unending social practices as participants who build upon previous accomplishments and also inevitably and forever change the social matrix of these practices (if only in modest ways), leaving their own indelible traces in history through their unique contributions to it. This type of person is starkly different from the traditional solipsistic individual who is merely self-defining, existing in isolation from other people and history.

Fifth, this perspective also implies that people perceive the world only through the prism of its relevance in the overall fabric of *their* life – what things and phenomena in the world stand for in *their* activity and *vis-à-vis their* goals and purposes. That is, the meaning of things is grounded in how they matter to people (cf. the notion of "import").[23] This is not the same as the egotistic instrumentalism of narrow individualism where the end goal is limited to reaching self-serving and self-gratifying goods and payoffs. What is at stake is a broader point about the all-encompassing centrality of activist engagement in and with the world, implicating that there is no way that we can extract ourselves out of this engagement. We can never take a neutral stance of a disinterested observer uninvolved in what is going on. This brings the dimensions of activism, and with it, of the ethical to the very center of the whole human enterprise of Being and Becoming.

The last two implications are well understood in relational ontology and moral philosophy (and downplayed by some neo-Marxists such as Ilyenkov).[24] However, the advantage that TAS brings about is that of simultaneously overcoming both outdated biases – that of seeing the world as composed of static things separate from individuals and that of seeing individuals as solipsistic entities separate from the material world of human practice. That is, this stance bridges the gap between apparently disparate phenomena of seemingly outward, "fixed" social institutions such as, say, the Federal Reserve on the one hand, and the

[23] See Taylor, *Sources of the Self*.   [24] See Stetsenko, Activity as object-related.

apparently "inward" phenomenology of human subjectivity such as thoughts and feelings, on the other, understood as separately existing, static phenomena. Rather, these seemingly "sturdy" social institutions and these purportedly ephemeral mental contents (appearing to be the exact opposites of each other in the old mode of thinking) are revealed to be in fact closely connected as made of the same "cloth" (or fabric). They all represent interrelated moments (more or less fleeting or durable) belonging to *one and the same* realm of human practice enacted by people in their collective pursuits. In other words, the materiality of the world is revealed as endowed with meaning and relevance though always only for someone – for an agent who is actively engaged in the world; and, vice versa, human subjectivity at the same time stands infused with the materiality of always tangible human practice (and its artefacts and products) out of which it emerges and through which it exists. That is, the world is revealed as "a forum of human deeds" which takes the natural world into its orbit, absorbs and transforms it on its own unique grounds – the specifically human realm of collaborative meaningful practice. Therefore, the most critical point is that unlike in moral philosophy and in some neo-Marxist interpretations, the world of facts and that of human experience are bridged through ascertaining the human relevance of material practice alongside and simultaneously with ascertaining the material, practical relevance of human subjectivity and intersubjectivity.

From the perspective of TAS, the ethical can be situated at the core of human development in strikingly obvious and direct ways. This is because human collaborative transformative practice is precisely the type of realm that lends itself naturally (not naturalistically) to formulations in ethical terms. Namely, such a realm implies that the world is constituted by none other than incarnate, answerable (responsive and responsible) – that is, activist – deeds united as one ceaseless process of what Bakhtin termed "ideological Becoming" in pursuit of meaningful changes in the world.[25]

Given their core and defining quality of being directed at and orientated to an activist change, these deeds cannot unfold without being anchored in the notions of what is good or bad, right or wrong and especially(!) what to do next. A being who in order to be needs to act in the *social world that is constantly changing*, and moreover, that is changing *through one's own deeds*, cannot be neutral or uncertain because such acting (unlike reacting or passively dwelling) presupposes knowing which way is up and

---

[25] Bakhtin, *Toward a Philosophy of the Act*. And on Bakhtin's idiosyncratic term "pos-tuplenie," see A. Stetsenko, Being-through-doing: Bakhtin and Vygotsky in dialogue. *Cultural Studies of Science Education* 2 (2007) 25–37.

what direction to go. This type of being-through-activist-deeds requires that we develop a compass about our location in the ongoing flow of transformative collaborative practices – where we are coming from, where we are now, and where we are going. The last part – the direction of our deeds (or life projects) formed by our goals and hopes, our aspirations and visions for the future, by the stand we take *vis-à-vis* the world and the path we chart to achieve certain destination – is in fact critical in TAS.

In particular, the core premise of TAS, also directly pertaining to personhood, is that it is in taking a stand and making a commitment, in charting a life agenda premised on a vision for social change enacted through collaborative transformative practice and one's own contribution to it, that the person comes to be a unique individual with an irreplaceable role in history and society – a *de facto* mission in the world – and thus essentially comes to be. However, this is just one side of the matter; the equally important one is that it is in and through the same process that world itself simultaneously comes into being as it is rendered meaningful, whereby the world and the person become answerable to each other in a mutual and bi-directional, continuous and dialogical alignment and dynamic co-constitution.

All of this implies that human beings – already by virtue of being human – always act from within their life agendas and visions for the future and are thus activists who cannot and should not try to avoid acting as such. Visions and commitments (and attendant emotions, feelings, and passions) are critically embodied in every act, including those of speaking and knowing, seeing and understanding, theorizing and inquiring. To expect or demand that people should be otherwise (for example, merely intellectual, or dispassionate, impartial and "objective") amounts to nothing less than a futile request that they are *de-humanized*, that is, turned into a machine-like exercise of tossing facts and making moves that have no human meaning and as such can neither be understood nor carried out in ways that have lasting, meaningful effects.

That is, what TAS highlights is the activist, forward-looking stance and therefore, the *future, the horizon and the destination* of development and personhood. This dimension has been somewhat under-theorized by cultural-historical theory, where the major focus was on history and thus the past, to the exclusion of questions about how the future, conceived in activist terms as a vision and commitment, plays a role in development.[26] The reason for this, among others, has to do with the unfounded fear of portraying development in teleological terms that, in my point of view,

---

[26] However, see Michael Cole on prolepsis, M. Cole, *Cultural Psychology: A Once and Future Discipline* (Cambridge, MA: Harvard University Press, 1996).

too often equals indecision and abstention from taking responsibility on the researchers' part. Teleology indeed has no place in the biological world, where processes of change (including evolution) do not have a destination and are not driven by preconceived goals. This does not mean, however, that human development and especially the development of personhood is or can be directionless. In shifting away from the narrow confines imposed by the mechanical worldview and, moreover, in making the next step after ascertaining the relational ontology of human development (with its uncommitted stance), TAS takes a clear-cut vision for social change as a prerequisite and foundation for development and personhood, understood in, yet not confined to, relational terms, and outlines the rationale for how this is possible.

The directionality of development as posited in TAS has nothing in common with the traditional teleology, inherited from the nineteenth-century Enlightenment and embedded in the mechanistic worldview. This traditional teleology implies a top-down, normative imposition of some outside endpoints and criteria on human development, as a transcendent controlling purpose, an implicit design superimposed on human activities from outside to guide their development, as if setting it on iron rails. The directionality in TAS – embedded as it is in the worldview based in the flux of collaborative transformative practices enacted through individually unique contributions – is warranted to be fluid and dynamic, rather than static and imposed from outside; instead, it is an inherent feature of development itself, an inalienable emergent dimension of how people do things together while creating their world and themselves.

Therefore, the danger that an activist stance and attendant concepts of goals and commitments, visions and agendas be cast in rigid and static terms, as dogmas immune to debate and criticism, can be avoided. These concepts are situated in and belong to a shifting and moving terrain of transformative ontology with its roots in continuous social engagements and change. That is, persons and their commitments and stands, their life projects and agendas are always in the process of changing and coming about. Persons are never cast in stone; instead, persons' defining quality is who they are becoming – who they can and aspire to be, rather than who they already are. Hence, personhood is perhaps best described with the notion of a *struggle* – a struggle through contestation and in constant dialogue, with others and oneself, to work out and come about with one's life agenda, goals, and ultimately, mission in life. In this light, the danger is not in taking a stance and making a commitment (which is an inalienable part of human nature), but in taking them as finite and unchanging instead of engaging in an open-ended dialogue with others who have their own disparate visions and commitments. In other words, the danger is in elevating one's own agenda and commitment as the pre-established and immutable frame not amenable to change, instead of exposing and revealing them to oneself and others, bringing them to light and critically interrogating them all while negotiating points of agreements and conflicts with others.

Given the key premises of TAS, it differs from the relational ontology grounded either in immediate experiences (in hermeneutics and phenomenology), or narrativity (in self-interpretative and discursive accounts) or embodiment and difference (in recent interpretations based in Merleau-Ponty and Levinas). The difference is that positing transformative collaborative practice enacted through activist deeds at the core of human development suggests that development and personhood are active and even *activist projects* of historical Becoming aimed at contributing to common human history. In relational ontology, a person is embedded in the social world and is a special kind of agent for whom things have characteristically human significance – for whom things matter.[27] From the activist transformative stance outlined herein, however, persons are agents not only for whom things matter but *who themselves matter in history, culture and society* and, moreover, who come into Being as unique individuals exactly through and to the extent that they matter in these processes by making a contribution to them.

In closing, it is important to once again remember that personhood is not conceived in TAS as anything related to an isolated, singular, solipsistic individual. In TAS, just as in cultural-historical theory and other deeply relational approaches, personhood and agency can be realized only in and through membership in communities, by drawing on their resources and while developing *a common vision* of social transformation. An activist stance is only possible within solidaristic relations that are inextricably connected with and co-emergent with personhood, as warranted by the transformative ontology of *collaborative* practice and the relational nature of subjectivity. In this sense, each and every person is a "*we*" – a collective subject formed in society and history and, at the same time, forming them and co-emergent with them. In this sense, personhood as a notion might ring hollow, especially amid the vulnerabilities of international turmoil and collapse that demand collective actions. Perhaps it can even be conceded that personhood, in a way, is an illusion; yet it is a necessary one – as a kind of concept that is needed for communities and individuals to take a stand in order to bring about social change.

While acknowledging limitations of this concept, and instead of dispensing with it, the better option is to legitimize it as non-individualist,

[27] See Sugarman, Persons and moral agency.

while dispensing with the strict dichotomy between collective and individual levels in human development, as TAS suggests. What it offers instead is one process (in need of a new term, perhaps "collectividual," to convey the amalgamation of social and individual in one unified realm) of people always acting together in pursuit of their common goals, bound by communal bonds and filaments, yet individually unique. In this dialectical approach, there is no need to get rid of the individual and of personhood because *there is no such thing as a solitary person* performing anything in disconnection from other people, outside of history and the social fabric of life.

Along these lines, the challenge is to consider each individual human being as an ensemble of social relations (as Marx famously stated), who is first formed within and out of these relations and then comes to embody, carry out, and expand them through one's own life and deeds.[28] What this deceptively simple point implies is that each individual human being always matters in some way or some sense – that is, represents the totality of human history (in all its vicissitudes though in a particular time and place, and under a particular perspective), carries it on, contributes to it and ultimately bears responsibility for its future. To be able to see history and society embodied and expressed in, and even created through, the deeds of persons regardless of how powerless, insignificant, and fragile they may appear to others or even to themselves, is a truly formidable task in a contemporary world in crisis and in need of profound social changes.

On a final note, the answers to the dilemma of personhood lie not in seeking to understand it in some sort of a speculative and contemplative way, for example while wondering whether this construct and phenomenon is real or illusionary. Instead, if we see our construals and theorizing not as descriptions of what is but as an activist project of what must or could be, then this dilemma itself disappears. In this case, our concepts can be guided by efforts and commitments to what we take to be a direction worth pursuing – itself shaped by understanding the nature of the present crisis, its roots, and what contribution can and needs to be made to resolving it. This is the key question simultaneously for each person and for psychology striving to make a difference and thus ultimately to matter in the world.

---

[28] Marx, Theses on Feuerbach.

Part IV

Narrative perspectives

11 Identity and narrative as root metaphors of personhood

Amia Lieblich and Ruthellen Josselson

Narrative and identity are concepts that contain the paradoxes of personhood: they encompass the problem of continuity and change over the life course and the phenomena of meaning-making. Both "fuzzy" and fluid in their definitions, they denote but do not limit the ways in which people make sense of their experiences and locate themselves in society and in time.

The concepts of narration and identity are used in many ways and carry a variety of meanings in current psychological literature. Narration refers to the act of producing a story, either oral or written. The relevant narration for the study of identity is narration about the self, personal accounts, life stories, or autobiographical narratives. Most psychologists use the terms narrative and story as synonyms.[1] Some equate the term narrative with any verbal utterance, talk, or text, while others limit the use of the term to verbal products that conform to a list of formal criteria. For the sake of clarity in the present chapter, we use the terms self narrative or life story for a specific genre of discourse, centered around the narrator and his or her life – not including chronicles, reports, arguments, question and answer exchanges etc.[2] What distinguishes narrative from other forms of discourse is, according to Riessman, its "sequence and consequence."[3] A number of events are selected, organized, connected, and evaluated in a story which has a beginning and an end, carrying some meaning or a lesson for a particular audience.

The kind of story or narrative which may be utilized for the study of personhood concerns accounts of events or experiences in the narrator's life. Rather than reflection or accurate representation of the reality of

---

[1] See T. R. Sarbin (ed.) *Narrative Psychology: The Storied Nature of Human Conduct* (New York: Praeger, 1986).

[2] D. Polkinghorne, Narrative configuration in qualitative analysis. *International Journal of Qualitative Studies in Education* 8 (1995) 5–23.

[3] C. K. Reissman, Narrative analysis. In M. S. Lewis-Beck, A. Bryman, and T. Futing Liao (eds.) *The SAGE Encyclopedia of Social Science Research Methods* (Thousand Oaks, CA: Sage, 2004) 705–709.

one's past or present life, we consider these narratives or stories as constructions created, formulated, and assembled from fragments of one's experience, thoughts, and feelings at a certain moment in time. They may or may not have "historical truth," but from the scholars' perspective they always have "narrative truth."[4] In other words, how facts, ideas, events, or experiences are selected, assembled, and formulated into a story may teach us something about the narrator's truth and his/her identity. On the other hand, a life story always reflects the culture in which it is situated, and the context in which it was produced (e.g., if in the setting of a work interview or in telling about the past at a family gathering). The four realms of life story, identity, context, and culture interact and influence each other in a number of ways, as we will see below.

The stories we tell about ourselves and our personal experiences grow in complexity and detail as we move through childhood into adolescent and young adult years.[5] According to developmental research, it is not until adolescence that people are able and motivated to conceive of their life as a full-fledged, integrative narrative of the self.[6] From then on, people produce and reproduce their life stories in a number of circumstances which require or motivate them to do so. The balance of past, present, and future events in one's life story changes as life goes on.

Beyond these more-or-less agreed upon ideas, there is a vast variety and spread of their applications in scholarly investigations. Using the same terms, some researchers who study narration and personhood refer to an entire life history.[7] Others, meanwhile, utilize selected accounts of particular episodes, such as examples of a high point, low point, turning point and/or earliest memory in one's life.[8] Some scholars attend to the linguistic aspects of the produced narrative.[9] Others talk about the

[4] D. P. Spence, *Narrative Truth and Historical Truth* (New York: W. W. Norton, 1982); Sarbin, *Narrative Psychology*.

[5] R. Fivush and C. A. Haden (eds.) *Autobiographical Memory and the Construction of a Narrative Self* (Mahwah, NJ: Erlbaum, 2003).

[6] T. Habermas and S. Bluck, Getting a life: The emergence of the life story in adolescence. *Psychological Bulletin* 126 (2000) 748–769.

[7] For example, E. G. Mishler, *Storylines: Craftartists' Narratives of Identity* (Cambridge, MA: Harvard University Press, 1999); or R. Atkinson, The life story interview as a bridge in narrative inquiry. In J. D. Clandinin (ed.) *Handbook of Narrative Inquiry* (Thousand Oaks: Sage, 2007) 224–245.

[8] D. P. McAdams, *Power, Intimacy and the Life Story: Personological Inquiries into Identity* (New York: The Guilford Press, 1985).

[9] W. Labov, Speech actions and reactions in personal narratives. In D. Tannen (ed.) *Analyzing Discourse: Text and Talk* (Washington, DC: Georgetown University Press, 1982) 219–247; W. Labov and J. Waletzky, Narrative analysis: Oral versions of personal experience. In J. Helm (ed.) *Essays on the Verbal and Visual Arts* (Seattle, WA: American Ethnological Society, 1967) 12–44; and C. Linde, *Life Stories: The Creation of Coherence* (New York: Oxford University Press, 1993).

need to interpret silence or the "unsayable."[10] Reading, analysis, and interpretation of narratives may take place in reference to the content or the form of the narrative, in a holistic or a categorical manner.[11]

The concept of identity

The concept of identity is rich with a variety of significant definitions. Essentially, identity provides an answer to the questions "Who am I?," "In what sense am I the same person yesterday, today, and tomorrow?," "What makes me unique, namely different from others?," "What do I stand for in my world?," and "To what do I devote my life?" In other words, identity depicts the image or concept one has about oneself; it evokes a list of characteristics and attributes, values, and motives which the individual person uses to draw a picture of himself or herself, distinct from (or related to) others, with a past that foreshadows the present and a planned-for future. Identity, then, is foundational to a sense of personhood.

Historically, identity also meant the opposite of change, stressing continuity, constancy or stability as a central aspect of one's personhood. In the earlier period of modern psychology, the concept of the self or self-identity was sought as a means to understand the "basic substance or substratum that remains the same and confers individuality on a person."[12] It was the aim of scholarship in the field to explore and discover this underlying substance. This notion has undergone a dramatic shift with the introduction of the concept of dynamic identity, narrative identity, or identity-as-a-process, as we will discuss below.

If identity is one's answer to the question: "What is it that gives me my sense of being a particular person who is different from all others?" then it concerns an internal dialogue, whereby the person tries to answer the question first of all to himself or herself. However, it is also part of one's interpersonal negotiations and social relations, namely the image one projects for his or her family, friends, and society in general. Finally,

---

[10] A. G. Rogers, The unsayable, Lacanian psychoanalysis, and the art of narrative interviewing. In J. D. Clandinin (ed.) Handbook of Narrative Inquiry (Thousand Oaks: Sage, 2007) 99–119.

[11] A. Lieblich, R. Tuval-Mashiach, and T. Zilber, Narrative Research: Reading, Analysis and Interpretation (Thousand Oaks, CA: Sage, 1998); and R. Tuval-Mashiach, "Where is the story going?" Narrative forms and identity construction in the life stories of Israeli men and women. In D. P. McAdams, R. Josselson, and A. Lieblich (eds.) Identity and Story: Creating Self in Narrative (Washington, DC: American Psychological Association, 2006) 249–268.

[12] D. Polkinghorne, Narrative Knowing and the Human Sciences (New York: State University of New York Press, 1988) 147.

identity also concerns the internalization of others' perceptions of the self as part of one's self-image. Thus, in classical studies inspired by Carl Rogers' personality theory, individuals were asked to describe how they see their actual selves, their desired selves, and their social selves (how they assumed others perceived them).[13] The configuration of all these three realms together consists of the concept of one's personhood or identity.

According to Polkinghorne, the continuity of identity and its substantive nature could be postulated as a result of the identity of the body and/or the identity of memory.[14] If my body is the same one over time, and my personhood resides in it, then its continuity is assured. However, with the realization that the body is not static but undergoes constant physiological changes, this continuity is undermined, unless we limit our arguments to the individual, particular genetic configuration. As to the other source for continuity, namely the unique set of memories that the individual carries along his or her life development, there is a growing sense of mistrust of personal memory, with a gradual realization of the plasticity of one's memory due to a great number of influences and circumstances.[15]

Linking narrative and identity

Being an entirely subjective and internal phenomenon, psychologists have been puzzled about the adequate tools to study identity, or to provide an operational definition for it. The scientific model of academic, objective psychology was committed to the notions that only physical objects in time and space or their inter-relationships could be adequately studied, and that only experimental designs should be utilized in this inquiry. In this framework, attempts in the human disciplines to deal with the concepts of personhood or self through tools of measurement were highly problematic.

With the disappointment in the outcomes of such academic work for the exploration of significant human concerns, interest in more philosophical and subjective approaches has re-emerged in the field of academic psychology. Within this movement, during the last three decades, researchers have realized that first-person narratives are an effective means for capturing the elusive concept of identity and for gaining an understanding about how the self evolved over time. Following Bruner's

[13] See R. C. Wylie, *The Self Concept* (Lincoln: University of Nebraska, 1974).
[14] Polkinghorne, *Narrative Knowing and the Human Sciences.*
[15] See, for example, E. Loftus, *Memory* (New York: Addison-Wesley, 1980).

leadership (to be elaborated below), we accept that through the study of self-narrative process, scholarship can secure useful information and come to a desired understanding of the self or one's identity as a meaning-maker with a place in society, culture, and history.[16] Moreover, narrative psychologists claim that the mere act of telling the story about one's life and experiences is the major process whereby the individual forms or constructs his or her identity. Thus, this understanding of identity in the context of self narration (often titled "narrative identity") paints identity as an ever-evolving, dynamic (rather than a substantive, stable, static) entity – or, succinctly formulated, identity is a process rather than a thing. Narrative identity research investigates how individuals make use of narratives to create and sustain a sense of unity or coherence in their personhood through diverse experiences and social locations across the lifespan.[17]

Developmental research indicates that it is not until adolescence or young adulthood that individuals are able and motivated to provide a narrative of their development and experience throughout their lives.[18] This timing corresponds neatly with the emergence of identity according to Erikson.[19]

Human life stories have many common facets, which provide a matrix to be filled by personally remembered experiences or events and their emplotment. Moreover, one may conceptualize these facets as perspectives for reading and studying life stories for research purposes.[20] Following the reasoning presented above, these facets can be further conceived as components of one's evolving identity.

A major facet in one's self-narrative regards *the body*, and its development through the life cycle. This facet is most prominent in stories about aging or about illness, which received much attention in recent years (e.g., Frank, 1995).[21] Most life stories can be sorted along the facet of *individual traits or characteristics* manifested in them, such as high achievement needs versus affiliation needs;[22] the modality of agency

---

[16] M. Freeman, *Rewriting the Self: History, Memory, Narrative* (London: Routledge, 1993).

[17] J. A. Singer, Narrative identity and meaning making across the adult lifespan: An introduction. *Journal of Personality* 72 (3) (2004) 437–460.

[18] Habermas and Bluck, Getting a life.

[19] E. H. Erikson, *Childhood and Society*, second edn (New York: Norton, 1963).

[20] See J. D. Baddeley and J. A. Singer, Charting the life story's path: Narrative identity across the life span. In J. D. Clandinin (ed.) *Handbook of Narrative Inquiry* (Thousand Oaks: Sage, 2007) 177–202.

[21] B. C. Myerhoff, *Number our Days* (New York: Simon and Schuster, 1978).

[22] See for example Lieblich *et al.*, *Narrative Research*.

versus communion;[23] or the integrative tendency for redemption versus contamination.[24] The facet of *human relations* is another dimension of narrative and identity, and stories may be examined from the perspective of the significant characters that are depicted in one's life story, and their reflection on the person's identity.[25] Another facet concerns *social reality*, and recounts the narrator's roles or scripts in his or her particular social-cultural setting. Class and gender have been documented to produce consistent differences in the form and content of life stories.[26] *Cultural environment or historical time* provide another significant facet for reading and interpretation of autobiographical stories.[27] Thus, the individual life story of Nisa was selected by the anthropologist Shostak, and the story of Esperanza by the anthropologist Behar, as means to introduce these women's culture to the western readership.[28,29] Less prominent may be facets which provide an evaluative dimension to one's life story, e.g., the place of *religion or spiritual concerns*, and values which the person seems to adopt as guidelines for life.[30]

The development of the concepts of identity and narrative within psychology

While there is a certain disagreement about the definitions of "narrative" and "identity" in psychology, scholars tend to agree that the use of them, and especially of the term "narrative," has grown tremendously. In a recent review, Riessman and Speedy put forward the claim that the terms narrative and story have reached a level of popularity few would

[23] D. Bakan, *The Duality of Human Existence: Isolation and Communion in Western Man* (Boston: Beacon Press, 1966); and D. P. McAdams, *The Person: An Integrated Introduction to Personality Psychology*, third edn (Fort Worth: Harcourt College Publishers, 2001).

[24] D. P. McAdams and P. J. Bowman, Narrating life's turning points: Redemption and contamination. In D. P. McAdams, R. Josselson, and A. Lieblich (eds.) *Turns in the Road: Narrative Studies of Lives in Transition* (Washington DC: American Psychological Association, 2001) 3–34.

[25] R. Josselson, *The Space Between Us: Exploring the Dimensions of Human Relationships* (San Francisco: Jossey-Bass, 1992); and McAdams, *Power, Intimacy and the Life Story*.

[26] G. C. Heilbrun, *Writing a Woman's Life* (New York: Norton, 1988); and M. C. Bateson, *Composing a Life* (New York: Plume, 1990).

[27] A. MacIntyre, *After Virtue: A Study in Moral Theory* (Notre Dame, IN: Indiana University Press, 1981).

[28] M. Shostak, *Nisa: The Life and Words of a !Kung Woman* (Cambridge, MA: Harvard University Press, 1981).

[29] R. Behar, *Translated Woman: Crossing the Border with Esperanza's Story* (Boston: Beacon Press, 1993).

[30] MacIntyre, *After Virtue*.

have predicted twenty years ago.[31] This historical development has been termed the "narrative revolution,"[32] "narrative turn," or "the interpretive turn" in the social sciences, and it carries the double idea that narratives are central in our human experience of and actions in the world, and that narratives are also the key to the understanding of identity and personhood.[33]

We can go back to William James for the idea that personal identity is constructed by the individual. He believed that the development of a personal identity is an outcome of an ongoing effort to synthesize many different ideas about oneself into a single, coherent self concept. The complete self concept combines three kinds of identity, all integrated into one. These are the material self, which involves one's body as well as all material aspects of one's life, such as family, home, and property; the social self, which contains one's values and social norms as well as significant individuals or groups in the individual environment and their own perceptions of the individual; and the spiritual self, which is the awareness of religious beliefs and one's own evaluation *vis-à-vis* such systems.[34]

Yet, the primary contributor to the study of identity is Erik Erikson. In *Childhood and Society* and *Identity, Youth and Crisis*, he conceptualized what identity might be and what place it might have in the life cycle.[35] In his psychobiographies, *Young Man Luther* and *Gandhi's Truth*, he painted the manifestations of and struggles with identity that a person may encounter in the course of a life.[36] Erikson described the construction of a coherent and purposeful self concept, which he called identity, as a psycho-social process (and frequently turned to case examples and narrative to demonstrate his meanings). Young people in modern societies are faced with the psychological challenge of constructing a self that provides their lives with unity, purpose, and meaning. They are challenged with the dual questions: "Who am I?" and "How do I fit into my

[31] C. K. Reissman and J. Speedy, Narrative inquiry in the psychotherapy professions: A critical review. In D. J. Clandinin (ed.) *Handbook of Narrative Inquiry: Mapping a Methodology* (Thousand Oaks, CA: Sage, 2007) 426–456.

[32] Lieblich *et al.*, *Narrative Research*.

[33] J. Brockmeier and D. Carbaugh (eds.) *Narrative and Identity: Studies in Autobiography, Self and Culture* (Amsterdam: John Benjamins Publishing Company, 2001); and J. D. Clandinin (ed.) *Handbook of Narrative Inquiry* (Thousand Oaks: Sage, 2007).

[34] W. James, *Psychology* (Greenwich, CT: Fawcett, 1892/1963).

[35] Erikson, *Childhood and Society*; E. H. Erikson, *Identity, Youth and Crisis* (New York: Norton, 1968).

[36] E. H. Erikson, *Young Man Luther: A Study in Psychoanalysis and History* (New York: W. W. Norton and Company, 1993); E. H. Erikson, *Gandhi's Truth: On the Origins of Militant Nonviolence* (New York: W. W. Norton and Company, 1993).

society as an adult?" Identity is at the juncture of biological, psychological, and social dimensions of the individual, and all three dimensions are necessary for understanding it. Thus, the individual's identity serves to integrate and organize many different things.

According to Erikson, a comprehensive and meaningful understanding of an individual's personality is achieved by studying how people move through crises which are typical of eight distinct stages of the human life cycle from birth to death. The concept of identity is framed within this developmental scheme. Forming identity, according to Erikson, is the major developmental task of late adolescence or early adulthood – the fifth stage of the life cycle. Since western industrial culture is highly complex and offers the individual many possible roles, value systems, or life styles, adolescents "try them on" to see which ones fit best – what vocation, which ideology, which group membership, sexual orientation etc. Part of the trying on of possible roles or identity elements is undertaken for the benefit of others, who then serve as a mirror in which the adolescent can see himself or herself. As adolescents strike a succession of postures in trying various positions, they eventually find their most suitable set of roles, beliefs, and life expectations, which will create a foundation for their personhood. Industrial societies, in Erikson's view, co-create this process by making available a "moratorium" period, a period in which exploration and experimentation are encouraged. Identity emerges as the young person declares, in one way or another, fidelity and commitment that s/he will abide by and will expect to be held to by the social surround. The next tasks of adulthood, in the Eriksonian framework, are built on the assumption that the young adult has acquired an identity firm enough to shoulder the next tasks of intimacy and generativity.

Erikson's conceptual presentation of identity has been highly influential in the areas of psychology, sociology, and education. Developing further the ideas of Erikson, Jim Marcia focused on the concepts of crisis and commitment to identity elements in the transition from a childhood identity (ascribed by the child's family, school, and environment) to the individuated adult identity.[37] He argued that in order to forge an identity, adolescents must experience some crisis in ideas derived from their given identity as sons or daughters to their families, educated in a given milieu. They consider a variety of options of occupation and ideology, some present in their background, and some new and even rebellious. As a result of these deliberations and experimentations, young adults, according to Marcia, must make commitments about what person to become

---

[37] J. E. Marcia, Development and validation of ego-identity status. *Journal of Personality and Social Psychology* 3 (5) (1966) 551–558.

and what to believe. These commitments consist of the core of the newly wrought adult identity. Consequently, Marcia distinguished between four "identity statuses" or types, based on the presence or absence of crisis and commitment in occupational and ideological (religious or political) areas, and provided guidelines for their assessment by his life interview method.[38] From narratives about decision-making and decisions, Marcia delineated a four-group typology of "identity statuses" that has since spawned hundreds of research studies in identity formation.

Narrative identity

While Marcia used narrative means to assess identity, other scholars were working to theorize the relationship of narration and identity. Ted Sarbin and Jerome Bruner, both in the 1980s, pioneered the claims that we lead our lives as stories, and that our identity is constructed both by stories we tell ourselves and tell others about ourselves, and by the master cultural narratives that consciously or unconsciously serve as models for our individual stories.[39]

Bruner proposed a distinction between two cognitive human modes: *paradigmatic* cognitive functioning is based on logic, numbers, and formulas, and relies on verification of well-formed propositions about how things are; *narrative* cognitive functioning manifests itself in stories, is subjective and directed to how things might be or might have been.[40] This idea about narrative modes of knowing has become the basic premise of the area of narrative psychology.

Relating his ideas to constructivist theory, Bruner argued that all stories represent some kind of brain processing of events which the person has experienced, rather than of reality *per se*. Life stories are selected out of the multitude of events we experience. What is chosen or omitted from our autobiographies is of immense significance to understanding our identity. Life stories include our intentions, emotions, and motivations. They imitate life and therefore are highly influenced by life as lived. However, stories deviate from the real; they are different from events *qua* events because they are always interpreted. Our stories construct

---

[38] See also E. Bourne, The state of research on ego identity: A review and appraisal. *Journal of Youth and Adolescence* 7 (1978) 223–251.

[39] S. Rimmon-Kenan, The story of "I": Illness and narrative identity. *Narrative* 10 (1) (2002) 9–27.

[40] J. Bruner, *Actual Minds, Possible Worlds* (Cambridge, MA: Harvard University Press, 1986); J. Bruner, *Acts of Meaning* (Cambridge, MA: Harvard University Press, 1990); and J. Bruner, The narrative construction of reality. *Critical Inquiry* 18 (1) (1991) 1–21; and J. Bruner, *Making Stories: Law, Literature, Life* (New York: Farrar, Straus and Giroux, 2002).

reality and experience. In other words, the link between story and life is bi-directional. The mere act of telling, and therefore language and linguistic behavior, produce personal experience. We become the stories that we tell each other or ourselves. As we change our stories, we change our memory and identity, and in so doing, we transform our lives.

Following Russian theorists about the nature of stories, Bruner claimed that every story has a theme, a form, and a style.[41] In the composition of a story, the ordinary has to be made special or unique. This ensures that one's identity, too, will be unique and different from all others. Uniqueness of a person can be obtained in form or style of narration, not necessarily in the contents of the story.

Life stories contain the "fabula," namely a lesson the story teaches the reader or the listener. This lesson may be considered the life-motive of the individual's identity. The dramatic effect of a story is achieved by "trouble" or crisis – some break in the direction of events and their initial flow that poses a challenge for the protagonist. The person's constructed relationship to this crisis determines whether the story will be a tragedy or comedy, or other genre of literary form. Modern stories, like the novel, create tension between the hero's reality and his or her inner world. This duality provides the drive for the progress of the story. Identity, too, is therefore partly internal and partly external, with possible tension between these two components.

In his most recent book, *Making Stories: Law, Literature, Life*, Bruner analyzes the psychological meaning of literature in our culture.[42] In this work, he returned to Aristotle's "Poetics" as the classical source for studying stories. A sequence of events is turned into a story, according to Bruner's reading of Aristotle, with a sudden reversal of circumstances, or "peripeteia."[43] Stories usually begin in some "normal" state of affairs in which something is taken for granted, and something then upsets the expected course of events and thus creates the dramatic effect of the narrative. A story, then, is about a plight and the road undertaken as a result of it, about coping with imbalance or surprise. In claiming this, Bruner is deeply influenced by Kenneth Burke.[44] He expresses this basic idea in many different ways, e.g., "It is our narrative gift that gives us the power to make sense of things when they don't";[45] "It is a way to domesticate human error and surprise";[46] or "Narrative in all its forms is a dialectic between what was expected and what came to pass. For there

[41] Bruner, The narrative construction of reality.
[42] Bruner, *Making Stories*.   [43] Bruner, *Making Stories*, 5.
[44] K. Burke, *A Grammar of Motives* (New York: Prentice-Hall, 1945).
[45] Bruner, *Making Stories*, 28.   [46] Bruner, *Making Stories*, 31.

to be a story, something unforeseen must happen."[47] The characters of the story are free agents, who cope with or come to terms in their way with the breach in the expected state of affairs.

Stories always have a message, although it is often concealed and open to various interpretations. The reader, even while aware that he or she reads fiction, constructs reality in accordance with the story. "Fiction creates realities so compelling that they shape our experience not only of the worlds the fiction portrays but of the real world."[48]

These created realities, however, also reflect the culture of the author or the narrator. The deep link of story-identity and culture is highly characteristic of Bruner's contribution. There is a strong connection between the culture in which the person is embedded and his or her stories. In starting a story from what was expected – and later interrupted – the teller uses cultural norms and conventions, such as are prevalent in cultural myths and folktales. Both culture and story, according to Bruner, are about the tension between the expected life and what is humanly possible. Sharing common stories creates a community and promotes cultural cohesion.

All stories must have a narrator or an author, and a listener or a reader. A final feature of stories is their coda, often a moral point of view, a retrospective evaluation of what it all might mean.

In his attempt to explicate the self, Bruner starts with the question of whether there is some essential self inside the individual. Bruner's post-modern argument is that there is no such thing as an essential self or identity, something which resides inside us and waits for us to tell about "it." Rather, we constantly construct and reconstruct our selves by telling our life stories. These self stories, which are performed or uttered repeatedly in different contexts, accumulate over time and often pattern themselves in familiar genres. New events and characters which happen in our life require frequent re-writing of these self narratives. "Self making is a narrative art" says Bruner.[49] It is doubly influenced from the "inside" – by one's subjectivity, one's memories, beliefs, feelings, and motivations, and from the "outside" by cultural norms and by the expectations of others in our social world. In combining all these effects, narrators create a fluid and flexible story which establishes their uniqueness. The mere act of self telling demonstrates that "the self is also other."[50] Finally, Bruner tackles the problem whether selfhood requires more than a reasonably good story, a story whose episodes

---

[47] Bruner, *Making Stories*, 15.   [48] Bruner, *Making Stories*, 9.
[49] Bruner, *Making Stories*, 65.   [50] Bruner, *Making Stories*, 66.

hang well together, and frame the problem as "another chicken-and-egg puzzle."[51]

It is apparent that Bruner's way of constructing identity as fluid and developing throughout life is quite different from Erikson's or Marcia's presentation of the stable, coherent identity as a personal achievement of the adolescent. From Bruner's perspective, a stable identity would be just one possible narrative construction.

Sarbin, Polkinghorne, McAdams and others

Ted Sarbin's edited book, *Narrative Psychology*, which appeared in the US in 1986, is another important formative event in directing attention to the intersection of narrative and identity. He offers the idea of "the narrative as a root metaphor for psychology" and suggests a revival of interest in experience and a holistic approach to psychology through a focus on story making, story telling, and story comprehension as sources of insights about human motives and actions.[52] A "root metaphor" – a term developed by Pepper – means an organizing principle, or a succinct clue to understand the world.[53] In other words, it is a basic concept "that constrains the kinds of philosophical or scientific models to be applied either to the task of observing and classifying or to the task of interpreting and explaining. The categories of analysis and the sorts of questions asked are similarly constrained by the choice of the root metaphor."[54] Furthermore, Sarbin proposed that self concepts take the form of stories. This idea is particularly taken up by Scheibe (in the same volume) who argues that identity *is* narrative, and emphasizes the importance of social and historical contexts for the construction of life stories. "Human identities are considered to be evolving constructions," says Scheibe, and they often develop like hero narratives.[55]

Don Polkinghorne developed and elaborated the ideas explicated above.[56] His claim for the link between identity and narrative is clear and direct – "we achieve our personal identities and self concept through the use of the narrative configuration, and make our existence into a whole by understanding it as an expression of a single unfolding and developing story."[57] Polkinghorne emphasized the dynamic aspect of the

---

[51] Bruner, *Making Stories*, 73.   [52] Sarbin, *Narrative Psychology*, 3–19.
[53] S. Pepper, *World Hypotheses* (Berkeley: University of California Press, 1942).
[54] Sarbin, *Narrative Psychology*, 4.
[55] K. E. Scheibe, Self narratives and adventure. In T. R. Sarbin (ed.) *Narrative Psychology: The Storied Nature of Human Conduct* (New York: Praeger, 1986) 129–151, 131.
[56] Polkinghorne, *Narrative Knowing and the Human Sciences*.
[57] Polkinghorne, *Narrative Knowing and the Human Sciences*, 150.

self-as-a-story. Since we are in the middle of the plots of our lives, we have no clear idea about how they will evolve and end. We have to revise our story constantly, reshuffle the memories of the past and perform new selection of events and characters, in accordance with new current experiences or life development, and with the changing expectations regarding our future. Thus, identity is constructed as a dynamic entity, as a process rather than a substance.

With the use of hermeneutics and its research tools, post-modern scholars explore how people compose their stories or dramas. They seek to understand identity as an expression, in the same manner that we try to understand the meaning of an uttered sentence or a paragraph. "The self is a concept defined as the expressive process of human existence, whose form is narrativity."[58]

Ideas about the unity and uniqueness of an individual self or identity have not disappeared, however, in this transition from "thing" to "process." Rather, we are called to study the process of narration itself as a means to create the unity and uniqueness of identity.

Another point made clearly by Polkinghorne relates to the coherence of life stories. How do we form our special autobiographical story and what does it convey? People create their life story out of the events and actions that they participated in or undertook in their lives and the meanings attributed to these memories, in such a manner that discrete events are connected into an integrated, coherent plot, leading to the present reality as experienced by the narrator.

As a coherent story, the experience of the person is organized along a time dimension. Therefore, one might claim that identity is that temporal order of human existence which begins at birth, has as its middle all kinds of episodes, life stages, or development, and ends with the present moment or with death. The plot of the story connects the various events and characters into a coherent whole. Every single episode or character in the story finds its meaning through its place or contribution to the narrative as a whole. It is important to note that the narrative of one's life is not a list or a chronicle of events and personalities, but a chain of happenings manifesting some values or directions which characterize the individual narrator in his time and culture. One's identity can therefore be conceived as the meaning of this life story or autobiography.

Dan McAdams theorized this position in the arena of personality psychology. McAdams argued that identity as explicated by Erikson should be seen as first and foremost an integrative life story that a person begins

---

[58] Polkinghorne, *Narrative Knowing and the Human Sciences*, 151.

to develop in late adolescence, and goes on revising throughout life.[59] "Identity is a life story – an internalized and evolving narrative of the self."[60] The evolving identity narrative binds together many different aspects, events, and characters, as well as past, present, and future of one's experienced life. This integrated story, which provides answers to the questions "who am I" and "how I came to be" – confers upon a life unity, purpose, and meaning. Like Bruner and others, McAdams argues that a person's life story, namely his or her identity, is a psychosocial construction, determined by culture. Life stories reflect gender and class division and power positions that prevail in society at a certain historical time in which the individual is embedded.[61]

In his integrative textbook about personality, McAdams collected six different views, from different academic fields, about the relations between stories and human lives, summarizing the theories of Frye, Elsbree, Sartre, MacIntyre, Elkind, and Hankiss to demonstrate that the tie between narration and identity has been in existence (if not popularity) in the academic discourse of a variety of fields since the middle of the twentieth century.[62] Psychology was, perhaps, slower to recognize the research possibilities of this conceptual linkage.

McAdams' theoretical work on narrative and identity was accompanied by a vast array of empirical work. For example, he studied the themes of agency and communion in life stories – and therefore in the narrators' identity. Agency and communion are modes of human existence previously proposed by Bakan.[63] In their narrative application, McAdams and his co-researchers defined the theme of agency as manifestations of self mastery, status/victory, achievement/responsibility or empowerment in

[59] D. P. McAdams, Biography, narrative, and lives: An introduction. *Journal of Personality* **56** (1) (1988), 1–18; D. P. McAdams, *The Stories We Live By: Personal Myths and the Making of the Self* (New York: William Morrow, 1993); D. P. McAdams, The case for unity in the (post)modern self: A modest proposal. In R. Ashmore and L. Jussim (eds.) *Self and Identity: Fundamental Issues* (New York: Oxford University Press, 1997) 46–78; and McAdams, *The Person*.

[60] McAdams, *The Person*, 643.

[61] C. Franz and A. Stewart (eds.) *Women Creating Lives: Identities, Resilience and Resistance* (Boulder, CO: Westview Press, 1994); and G. C. Rosenwald and R. L. Ochberg (eds.) *Storied Lives: The Cultural Politics of Self-understanding* (New Haven, CT: Yale University Press, 1992).

[62] McAdams, *The Person*, 644; N. Frye, *Anatomy of Criticism* (Princeton University Press, 1957); L. Elsbree, *The Rituals of Life: Patterns in Narrative* (Port Washington, NY: Kennikat Press, 1982); J.-P. Sartre, *Essays in Existentialism* (Secaucus, NJ: The Citadel Press, 1964); A. Hankiss, On the mythological rearranging of one's life history. In D. Bertaux (ed.) *Biography and Society: The Life History Approach in the Social Sciences* (Beverly Hills, CA: Sage, 1981) 203–209.

[63] Bakan, *The Duality of Human Existence*.

a personal self story. The theme of communion was defined as expressions of love/friendship, dialogue, caring/help, and unity/togetherness.[64] In another group of empirical studies, McAdams studied stories characterized by redemption versus contamination sequences – another profound distinction which is relevant to both narration and identity.[65] A redemption sequence according to McAdams is a sequence of telling emotionally positive or good outcomes which result from negative or bad beginnings. By contrast, contamination sequences describe the reverse, namely stories in which a positive experience is spoiled or contaminated by its emotional negative outcome. These narrative patterns were found to be characteristic of certain individuals, and related to a number of the narrators' personality traits.

An important event in the history of the field of narration and identity is the conference on this topic which took place in the International Research Center for Cultural Studies in Vienna, in December, 1995. Scholars from psychology, philosophy, social sciences, literary theory, classics, psychiatry, communication, and film theory came together to explore the significance of narrative "as an expressive embodiment of our experience, as a mode of communication, and as a form for understanding the world and ultimately ourselves."[66] The edited papers presented in the conference were collected into a volume by Brockmeier and Carbaugh, and consist of an excellent source for the elaboration of issues discussed in the present chapter.[67] In their introduction, the editors argue that while the questions of narrative and identity have a long history in human scholarship, only recently were these terms systematically connected to each other. This is not surprising, since the fields of literature and psychology differ fundamentally in their approaches to human knowing. The editors agree with Albright's famous quote from 1996 that "Literature is a wilderness, psychology is a garden."[68] In other words, while literature is fascinated by human differences, by wild nature – psychology attempts to be systematic and generalize about universal rules. This is exactly the gap which the conference and the volume attempted to narrow by bringing together the humanities and social science perspectives on the questions of narrative and identity. As Freeman puts it succinctly in his summary, life imitates art, namely story, but on

---

[64] McAdams, *The Person*, 649.
[65] McAdams and Bowman, Narrating life's turning points.
[66] Brockmeier and Carbaugh, *Narrative and Identity*, 1.
[67] Brockmeier and Carbaugh, *Narrative and Identity*.
[68] D. Albright, Literature and psychological models of the self. In N. Neisser and R. Fivush (eds.) *The Remembering Self: Construction and Accuracy in the Self-narrative* (Cambridge University Press, 1996) 19.

the other hand art grows out of life.[69] He calls scholars to include the poetic dimension as a cognitive function highly relevant to the study of personhood, of experience, and of autobiography.

The papers collected in the volume embrace current narrative theory as well as psychological empirical studies. Language, discourse, and narrative, according to the authors, enrich the traditional psychological study of self or identity. Brockmeier addresses the retrospective teleology in autobiography and argues that life stories connect beginnings to endings and almost always provide narratives of development.[70] In autobiographical narratives, the factors of chance, arbitrariness, and uncertainties in life are minimized, and a sense of agency prevails. This pattern of coherence almost always takes place, according to Brockmeier, whenever we are narrating history – whether collective or individual. Consequently, our identity as well is mainly distinguished by its coherence and consistency.

In Freeman's concluding comments of the volume, he formulated the post-modern position as follows: "There is no history apart from the narrative event in which it is told; and in a distinct sense, there is no past outside of the present and the questions it poses regarding the meaning of one's life."[71]

The narrative study of lives

Between 1993 and 2007, we (Josselson and Lieblich, and between 2001 and 2007 together with Dan McAdams) published a series of eleven volumes titled *The Narrative Study of Lives*, dedicated to interdisciplinary work on life stories, identity, culture, and development in a variety of settings.[72] In one of these volumes, titled *Identity and Story*, we gathered

---

[69] M. Freeman, From substance to story: Narrative identity and the reconstruction of the self. In J. Brockmeier and D. Carbaugh (eds.) *Narrative and Identity: Studies in Autobiography, Self and Culture* (Amsterdam: John Benjamins Publishing Company, 2001) 283–298.

[70] J. Brockmeier, From the end to the beginning: Retrospective teleology in autobiography. In J. Brockmeier and D. Carbaugh (eds.) *Narrative and Identity: Studies in Autobiography, Self and Culture* (Amsterdam: John Benjamins Publishing Company, 2001) 247–280.

[71] Freeman, From substance to story, 286.

[72] See R. Josselson and A. Lieblich (eds.) *The Narrative Study of Lives, Vol. 1* (Thousand Oaks, CA: Sage, 1993); A. Lieblich and R. Josselson (eds.) *Exploring Identity and Gender. The Narrative Study of Lives, Vol. 2* (Thousand Oaks, CA: Sage, 1994); R. Josselson and A. Lieblich (eds.) *Interpreting Experience: The Narrative Study of Lives, Vol. 3* (Thousand Oaks, CA: Sage, 1995); R. Josselson (ed.) *Ethics and Process in the Narrative Study of Lives. The Narrative Study of Lives, Vol. 4* (Thousand Oaks, CA: Sage, 1996); A. Lieblich and R. Josselson (eds.) *The Narrative Study of Lives, Vol. 5* (Thousand Oaks, CA: Sage, 1997); R. Josselson and A. Lieblich (eds.) *Making Meaning of Narratives. The*

the work of an interdisciplinary and international group of scholars whose work addressed what we saw as the most important and difficult issues in the study of narrative identity. Three central dilemmas were the focus: the issue of unity versus multiplicity, the tension of person *vis-à-vis* society, and the question of stability and growth.

Regarding the issue of unity and multiplicity, we argue that Erikson saw identity as serving an integrative function in human lives in that it provides the adolescent (and later, the adult) with some measure of unity and purpose. In the process of identity formation, life which otherwise might be experienced as fragmented and diffuse is constructed as a more or less coherent whole. Our work, and that of the other scholars mentioned in this paper, indicates that life stories are the means or process which attempt (and often succeed) in bringing aspects of the person together into a unifying and purpose-giving identity. We recognize that recent scholarship also underscores the extent to which life stories express multiple aspects of the self.[73] Like a multi-vocal, polyphonic novel, life stories and identity are also fragmented, multi-layered, and may include a variety of discordant parts.[74] Perhaps there is no complete coherence and integration among these parts, but rather, the most we may expect is an ongoing dialogue among them. Opposition within narrative identity is a normal phenomenon of post-modern personalities. People tend to construct their stories in a fashion which is partly conforming to their cultural scripts, and partly in opposition to them. Unity and purpose in life stories and identity are probably more complex than we wished them to be, when psychology itself was a relatively systematic field of study.[75] More complex theories are required, such as for example proposed by Gregg, who demonstrates in his narrative analysis how multiple images of the self are related to each other in terms of their

Narrative Study of Lives, Vol. 6 (Thousand Oaks, CA: Sage, 1999); D. P. McAdams, R. Josselson, and A. Lieblich (eds.) *Turns in the Road: Narrative Studies of Lives in Transition* (Washington, DC: American Psychological Association, 2001), 3–34; and R. Josselson, A. Lieblich, and D. P. McAdams (eds.) *Up Close and Personal: The Teaching and Learning of Narrative Research* (Washington, DC: American Psychological Association, 2003); A. Lieblich, D. P. McAdams, and R. Josselson (eds.) *Healing Plots: The Narrative Basis of Psychotherapy* (Washington, DC: American Psychological Association, 2004); McAdams et al., *Identity and Story*; and R. Josselson, A. Lieblich, and D. P. McAdams (eds.) *The Meaning of Others: Narrative Studies of Relationships* (Washington, DC: American Psychological Association, 2007).

[73] K. J. Gergen, *The Saturated Self: Dilemmas of Identity in Contemporary Life* (New York: Basic Books, 1991).

[74] H. J. M. Hermans, Voicing the self: From information processing to dialogical interchange. *Psychological Bulletin* 119 (1) (1996) 31–50.

[75] D. Albright, Literature and psychological models of the self.

oppositionality.[76] Currently, researchers are talking about the dialectical nature of narrative identity, searching for "multiplicity in unity, unity in multiplicity."[77]

A second issue highlighted in this collection of papers was the relationship of identity to society. While it is evident that Erikson placed identity at the crossroads of the individual and society, for many scholars who followed him in the field, identity was defined and explored as an internal personal achievement. The influence of context, culture, and society on this process, the importance of the audience and the purpose of telling, were often neglected or put in the background of the main focus of the study. More recent work has emphasized the social construction of life narratives and therefore, identity.[78] From an anthropological-cultural perspective, research and theory emphasized that history and culture shape the stories people tell about their lives, and different societies privilege various kinds of stories. Several papers in this volume deal with the manner in which individual agency interacts with social or historical context to produce the outcome we name identity. For example, Cohler and Hammack present their study about life stories of gay men of three different generations and demonstrate in a powerful fashion how the narrative construction of sexual identity is influenced by the dramatic change in social norms regarding gay life style and identity, which we have experienced since the second world war.[79] What people absorb from social discourse, from reading and conversations about the subject, deeply affects the way they construct their gay identity. "The very act of telling or writing the identity story is thus itself a social practice."[80]

Finally, our volume refers to the issue of stability versus growth, which has always been an important dilemma for psychologists who studied human personality and identity. Is personality stable over time? Can human temperament be characterized as showing life-long continuity and stability? Do we carry a constant identity over time? While Erikson did talk about the dynamic and changing aspect of the individual's identity,

---

[76] G. S. Gregg, The raw and the bland: A structural model of narrative identity. In D. P. McAdams, R. Josselson, and A. Lieblich (eds.) *Identity and Story: Creating Self in Narrative* (Washington, DC: American Psychological Association, 2006) 63–88.

[77] See D. P. McAdams and R. L. Logan, Creative work, love and the dialectic in selected life stories of academics. In D. P. McAdams, R. Josselson, and A. Lieblich (eds.) *Identity and Story: Creating Self in Narrative* (Washington, DC: American Psychological Association, 2006) 89–108, 6.

[78] See Rosenwald and Ochberg, *Storied Lives*; and A. Thorne, Personal memory telling and personality development. *Personality and Social Psychology Review* 4 (2000) 45–56.

[79] B. J. Cohler and P. L. Hammack, Making a gay identity: Story and the construction of a coherent self. In D. P. McAdams, R. Josselson, and A. Lieblich (eds.) *Identity and Story: Creating Self in Narrative* (Washington, DC: American Psychological Association, 2006) 151–172.

[80] Cohler and Hammack, Making a gay identity, 154.

the general impression adopted by many scholars from Erikson's work was that the adolescent "achieves" identity, and then it remains as his or her self image for life. Minor fluctuations in identity are probably normal, but can it be conceived as undergoing major changes throughout one's life? How shall we recognize each other if we allow for extreme changes in identity from one moment to the next?

When it comes to life stories, we also expect them to have a stable core. However, as explained above, the concept of identity-as-story is more dynamic and flexible than conceptual formulations which existed before. It is normal for a person to produce different versions of his or her autobiography, but there is an expectation that some basic facts will remain constant. Life stories tell us what remained the same over time and also what changed and developed.[81] Jennifer Pals, for example, examines how narrators express both continuity and change in their narrative accounts of negative life scenes.[82]

A recent paper by Kraus provides a broad and updated perspective on the interface of narration and identity.[83] According to Kraus, psychological identity theories employ narratology in order to understand fundamental changes in the construction of self or identity within postmodern cultures. The social process of individuation in late modernity or post-modernity resulted in fragmentation, diffusion, and lack of coherence of personal identity.[84] Individuals are not expected to obtain their stable identity as their personal life project, and the construction of identity does not guarantee its coherence, because collective identities are not provided by society ready-made. "Identity development thus becomes a story without closure, constantly open to change."[85] Actually, it was Lévi-Strauss, according to Kraus, who commented that self-experience is always fragmented, and modern cultures did not provide individuals with models of coherence to adopt.[86] The problem of unity does not reside only in the realm of the private, individual experience, but rather in a culture or society as a whole.

Like his forerunners, Kraus endorses a model of identity construction which might deal with identity as a process, preserving its

---

[81] Habermas and Bluck, Getting a life.

[82] J. Pals, Narrative identity processing of difficult life experiences: Pathways of personality development and possible self-transformation in adulthood. *Journal of Personality* 74 (2006) 1,079–1,110.

[83] W. Kraus, The narrative negotiation of identity and belonging. *Narrative Inquiry* 16 (1) (2006) 103–111.

[84] P. Wagner, *A Sociology of Modernity: Liberty and Discipline* (London: Routledge, 1994); U. Beck, A. Giddens, and S. Lash, *Reflexive Modernization: Politics, Tradition and Aesthetics in the Modern Social Order* (Cambridge, UK: Polity Press, 1994).

[85] Kraus, The narrative negotiation of identity and belonging, 104.

[86] C. Lévi-Strauss (ed.) *L'Identité* (Paris: Presses Universitaires de France, 1977) 9–12.

multi-voicedness. Narratives which are multi-faceted are therefore the starting point for a current identity theory.

This claim is embedded, according to Kraus, in the wider intellectual trends of deconstructionism and post-structuralism. In narratology, the deconstructive point of view aimed to highlight the active role of the reader or listener as co-constructors of the narrative's meaning.[87] The post-structuralist perspective endorsed narratives as highly complex, heterogeneous, and multi-voiced. Thus, the traditional view of narrative as always manifesting explicit or implicit unity and coherence was challenged by the post-structuralists, who considered this idea as a mere reduction of the profound complexity of human language, thinking, and discourse. Their aim was to deconstruct the apparent closure of life narratives and self-experience. In a similar vein, according to Kraus, post-modern identity theory opposes the classical concepts of identity or self as stable and unified, which could be constructed as a narrative with closure and coherence. Identity must be understood as a process, a performance in which the telling, the listener, and the context are of utmost significance for the consequent life narrative.

Kraus also credits the tremendous influence of Mikhail Bakhtin on the field of narrative and identity.[88] Bakhtin's theory about polyphony and heteroglossia in story, discourse, and language became an important vehicle for the expression of these new ideas about identity and narrative in the social sciences. His concepts regarding the diversity of voices and meanings found their way into current theories of the self.[89]

In summary, the concept of narrative and narration has revived the psychological study of self and identity in recent years and rejuvenated the personological tradition begun by Gordon Allport, Robert White, Henry Murray, and Silvan Tomkins. There is a great deal of theoretical agreement among scholars who study this intersection and there has been a massive outpouring of empirical research as well as conceptual debate about the various ways in which narratives construct identity and how identity influences narrative forms. There seems now to be little dissension from the ideas that identity (in its complex forms, beyond a list of social identifiers) can only be understood narratively or that personal narratives are woven by the threads of identity that constitute personhood.

[87] M. Currie, *Postmodern Narrative Theory* (New York: St. Martin's Press, 1998).
[88] M. Bakhtin, *The Dialogic Imagination* (Austin: University of Texas Press, 1975).
[89] For example, H. J. M. Hermans, The dialogical self: Toward a theory of personal and cultural positioning. *Culture and Psychology* 7 (3) (2001) 243–281.

12 Storied persons: the double triad of narrative identity

Mark Freeman

This chapter aspires to be a work of synthesis and reconciliation, one in which the fundamental ingredients of narrative identity are brought together into a comprehensive image.[1] This image might be conceptualized in terms of two interrelated triads, the first of which is largely concerned with time, the second with relatedness to the Other, by which I refer to those sources of "inspiration," outside the perimeter of the ego, integral to the fashioning of identity. Drawing on the work of Paul Ricoeur in addressing the first triad, *spheres of temporality*, I suggest that narrative identity emerges in and through the interplay of past, present, and future in the form of remembering, acting, and imagining. Drawing on the work of Martin Buber, Emmanuel Levinas, and Charles Taylor in addressing the second triad, *spheres of otherness*, I suggest that this temporal interplay is itself interwoven with our relation to other people, to the non-human world, and to those moral and ethical "goods" that serve to orient and direct the course of human lives. By thinking about these two triadic spheres together, my aim is to arrive at a picture of narrative identity appropriate to the complexities entailed in its formation. With this summative description in mind, I shall proceed as follows.

First, I will say a few words about my own understanding of narrative identity – more specifically, why the idea of identity (as I understand it and wish to speak about it) *requires* narrative. Second, I will turn to the three spheres of temporality, dealing with past, present, and future respectively. These correspond to three quite different perspectives on the figuring of narrative identity – so different, in fact, that they might seem irreconcilable. Bearing this in mind, I will try to see if some sort of reconciliation is possible without flattening out the differences at hand. Third, I will turn to the second, less well explored, triad, spheres of otherness. Here, I am more explicitly concerned with the *relational* dimension of narrative identity, my guiding presumption being that the different

[1] Portions of this paper were presented at a conference on Narrative and Identity: Questions of Perspective (Humboldt-Universität, Berlin, 2009).

spheres of relation in which we are engaged – the sphere of others, of the non-human world and of moral and ethical "goods" – are constitutive of our own individuality and uniqueness as persons. As I have suggested elsewhere, whatever role I might play in fashioning the story of my life, "I" am not its ultimate origin.[2] It might therefore be said that, while the *proximal* source of one's story is the self, the *distal* source is the Other. Indeed, taking this idea one step farther, it might plausibly be said that the Other is the distal source of identity itself. I shall say more about this in due time. Fourth, and finally – and by turning to the life of someone I know quite well – I am going to try to link these two spheres together, in the hope of putting together a model of narrative identity and its formation. I must confess that this is a reach for me; generally speaking, I am not the model-building type. But as I have tried to come to terms with the sheer complexity of the process at hand, and as I have tried to dimensionalize it – to specify the different dimensions or levels operative – it has in fact led me to want to "build" something, in which the pieces somehow manage to fit together. Whether this build-ing is structurally sound only time will tell.

As I shall also try to show in this last section of the chapter, the idea of narrative identity and the idea of personhood are intimately related to one another. To be a person is to have a story – or at least a sense of one. For those fortunate enough to have fully functioning brains and minds, this story is filled with particulars, episodes, linked together, however tenuously and changeably, through reflection. For those, on the other hand, whose brains and minds are not quite so fully functional – as in dementia, for instance – this story will likely change: in place of discrete episodes there may emerge a kind of obscure tundra of pastness, and in place of reflection there may emerge only the vaguest intimations of how this pastness constitutes *me*, this specific person. At an extreme, these vestiges of narrative identity may disappear entirely. Until that time, however, there may still remain in view an image – if not of *this* person, with this particular story, then of *a* person, who once had one. There may be a wish to return to this state of being, but also the recognition that it is too late, that the days of full, storied personhood have passed. The situation is a tragic and complicated one, indeed. My hope is to make some headway in thinking it through in the pages to follow.

---

[2] For example, M. Freeman, Narrative and relation: The place of the Other in the story of the self. In R. Josselson, A. Lieblich, and D. McAdams (eds.) *The Meaning of Others: Narrative Studies of Relationships* (Washington, DC: APA Books, 2007) 11–19; and M. Freeman, *Hindsight: The Promise and Peril of Looking Backward* (New York: Oxford University Press, 2010).

The idea of narrative identity

Before launching into the idea of narrative identity, it may be useful
to provide a brief outline of why there emerged a "narrative turn" in
the first place. There is of course one very basic reason for this turn:
in order to learn about persons, it makes good sense to explore their
lives; and narrative is, arguably, the most appropriate vehicle for doing
so. But there are actually deeper, more intellectually significant, reasons
for turning to narrative as well.[3] First, and perhaps most controver-
sially, there are psychodynamic reasons for turning to narrative. As Paul
Ricoeur was to argue sometime ago, following the lead of Freud, the
idea and ideal of self-knowledge via conscious reflection was no longer
tenable.[4] Phenomenology thus had to give way to hermeneutics, reflection to interpretation: "There is no direct apprehension of the self by the
self, no internal apperception or appropriation of the self's desire to exist
through the short-cut of consciousness but only through the long road of
the interpretation of signs."[5] Along these lines, the Cartesian *cogito* was,
for Ricoeur, a "wounded *cogito*, which posits but does not possess itself,
which understands its originary truth only in and by the confession of
the inadequation, the illusion, and the lie of existing consciousness."[6]
And the only path to this originary truth was precisely through its
history.

It wasn't long after pursuing this psychodynamically inspired
hermeneutical work that Ricoeur would dive headlong into the problem of historical understanding and knowledge.[7] At the heart of this
exploration was an ostensibly simple, but extremely significant, idea –
namely, that the meaning and significance of any given event or experience was inevitably *deferred* (to a greater or lesser extent) until some
later time. In part, this was because there could be aspects of experience
that one either could not or would not see at the time of occurrence. In
addition, however, there was the fact that a given event or experience had

[3] See M. Freeman, Why narrative? Hermeneutics, historical understanding, and the sig-
nificance of stories. *Journal of Narrative and Life History* 7 (1997) 169–176. See also
J. Brockmeier, From the beginning to the end: Retrospective teleology in autobiography.
In J. Brockmeier and D. Carbaugh (eds.) *Narrative and Identity: Studies in Autobiography,
Self, and Culture* (Amsterdam and Philadelphia: John Benjamins, 2001) 246–280.
[4] The central text here is P. Ricoeur's monumental *Freud and Philosophy: An Essay on
Interpretation* (New Haven, CT: Yale University Press, 1970). Also important is his
collection of essays entitled *The Conflict of Interpretations* (Evanston, IL: Northwestern
University Press, 1974).
[5] Ricoeur, *Conflict of Interpretations*, 170.   [6] Ricoeur, *Conflict of Interpretations*, 173.
[7] See, for instance, P. Ricoeur, *Hermeneutics and the Human Sciences* (Cambridge University
Press, 1981).

to await subsequent experience in order for its meaning and significance to be discerned.

Alongside the covert workings of the unconscious, therefore, was the fact that, in a distinct sense, one frequently doesn't know what's going on when it's going on but can only gain a sense of things later, looking backward over the terrain of the past. Ricoeur thus comes to speak of the positive and productive function of what he calls "distanciation," while Gadamer, similarly, speaks of the positive value of "temporal distance," the main idea being that there exists a certain advantage in looking backward, at the movement of events, from afar – that is, from the distant perch of the present.[8] Indeed, it is precisely this measure of distance that allows for the possibility of historical objectivity. This objectivity, however, is not to be equated with recovering the past "as it was." Rather, it is an objectivity, of a sort, achieved in and through the hermeneutical process. What we see here, in any case, is an emerging rationale for the process of self-understanding being not only *interpretive* but *retrospective*. For Ricoeur, taking these ideas one step further, there would also emerge the idea that narrative was the key figure in the process: events and experiences were to be seen as "episodes," and in order for understanding to occur, there had to be a synoptic process of "seeing-together," that is, seeing these episodes, in their interrelationship, as parts of an evolving whole.[9] Self-understanding, therefore, was irrevocably *narrative* in nature. Moreover, there was no separating self *identity* from the narrative process. With this too brief sketch of the narrative turn in mind, let me now try to sketch out my own perspective on narrative identity.

Even though I am sometimes considered a "big story" narrative theorist – that is, someone who generally looks to large tellings of lives (memoirs, autobiographies, and so on) as an inroad into issues of self and identity – I have also tried to argue in much of my work that the narrative process is part and parcel of ongoing life itself, including the small stories (as Michael Bamberg has called them) that comprise it.[10] This is not to say that the narrativity involved in ongoing life itself is the same as

[8] Ricoeur, *Hermeneutics and the Human Sciences*, see especially the chapter entitled: The hermeneutical function of distanciation. See H.-G. Gadamer, *Truth and Method* (New York: Crossroad, 1982), especially 258–267.

[9] See especially P. Ricoeur's seminal essay Narrative time. In W. J. T. Mitchell (ed.) *On Narrative* (University of Chicago Press, 1981) 165–186.

[10] See M. Freeman, Life "on holiday"? *Narrative Inquiry* 16 (2006) 131–138; M. Freeman, Stories, big and small: Toward a synthesis. *Theory and Psychology* 21 (2011) 114–121; M. Bamberg, Stories: big or small – why do we care? *Narrative Inquiry* 16 (2006) 139–147; M. Bamberg, Narration and its contribution to self and identity. *Theory and Psychology* 21 (2011) 3–24; A. Georgakopoulou, Thinking big with small stories in narrative and identity analysis. *Narrative Inquiry* 16 (2006) 129–137.

what is found in those larger stories that are told "after the fact," looking backward; life is not – or not quite – literature. All that's being said is that there is a measure of *continuity* between these two narrative sites.

Ricoeur puts the matter well in a 1991 piece called "Life in quest of narrative."[11] Among the key ideas he explores in this piece is the notion of *emplotment* as a "synthesis of heterogeneous elements."[12] From this mode of narrative analysis, "we can retain three features: the mediation performed by the plot between the multiple incidents and unified story; the primacy of concordance over discordance; and, finally, the competition between succession and configuration."[13] In an important sense, what Ricoeur is addressing in this piece is in fact the idea of *identity* – conceived not just in terms of strict "sameness" but *continuity in difference*, which is to say, between the multiple events that comprise the narrative and the configurational work of emplotment.

Ricoeur goes on to speak in the piece of the "pre-narrative" dimension of life and of "life as a story in its nascent state . . . an *activity and a passion in search of a narrative*." Hence his decision "to grant to experience as such a virtual narrativity which stems, not from the projection of literature onto life, but which constitutes a genuine demand for narrative."[14] "Without leaving the sphere of everyday experience," he asks, "are we not inclined to see in a given chain of episodes in our own life something like *stories that have not yet been told*, stories that demand to be told, stories that offer points of anchorage for the narrative?"[15]

From Ricoeur's perspective, we are "entangled" in stories; narrating is a secondary process "grafted" onto this entanglement. "Recounting, following, understanding stories is then simply the continuation of these unspoken stories."[16] And so, he continues,

Our life, when then embraced in a single glance, appears to us as the field of a constructive activity, borrowed from narrative understanding, by which we attempt to discover and not simply to impose from outside the *narrative identity which constitutes us*. I am stressing the expression "narrative identity" for what we call subjectivity is neither an incoherent series of events nor an immutable substantiality, impervious to evolution. This is precisely the sort of identity which narrative composition alone can create through its dynamism.[17]

It should be noted that in some of Ricoeur's other work, including *Oneself as Another*, he seems to posit a bigger distinction between life and

[11] P. Ricoeur, Life in quest of narrative. In D. Wood (ed.) *On Paul Ricoeur: Narrative and Interpretation* (London: Routledge, 1991) 20–33.
[12] Ricoeur, Life in quest of narrative, 21.   [13] Ricoeur, Life in quest of narrative, 22.
[14] Ricoeur, Life in quest of narrative, 29.   [15] Ricoeur, Life in quest of narrative, 30.
[16] Ricoeur, Life in quest of narrative, 30.   [17] Ricoeur, Life in quest of narrative, 32.

narrative and, by implication, a different way of thinking about narrative identity.[18] Of "the notion of the narrative unity of a life," for instance, he suggests that "it must be seen as an unstable mixture of fabulation and actual experience. It is precisely because of the elusive character of real life that we need the help of fiction to organize life retrospectively, after the fact, prepared to take as provisional and open to revision any figure of emplotment from fiction or from history."[19] Here, in other words, he seems to suggest that the "narrative composition" that is involved in the fashioning of identity is in fact an "imposition" of sorts, with "fiction" serving as a kind of prosthetic device, designed to provide a measure of order amidst the flux. David Carr, among others, has taken Ricoeur to task for moving in this direction, seeing in this move a somewhat impoverished view of both life, which comes to be viewed as essentially formless, and narrative, which comes to be viewed as a kind of existential defense mechanism for warding off our own dis-orderliness and dis-unity.[20]

As for where I stand on the issue, I am inclined to say the following. On the one hand, I remain, along with the first Ricoeur, very much a continuity theorist: even though life is not quite narrative, it is close enough, I would hold, to posit continuity between the two and, in turn, to see narrative identity as being tied to this continuity and hence discovered rather than being imposed from without. On the other hand, I have come more and more to see some of the profound differences between the not-quite narrativity of ongoing life and the after-the-fact narrativity of what I have come to call *narrative reflection*, issuing from the work of hindsight.[21] Along with the second Ricoeur, therefore, I am fully prepared to speak of the "elusive character of real life" – life "in the moment," in the "now" – and also to sign on to the idea of the retrospective "organization" of this elusive character in and through narrative. What I am not prepared to do is see this process of retrospective reconfiguration as one of defensive fictionalization. It *can* be that, to be sure; there can be "positive illusions," self-aggrandizing myths, even, in some instances, outright lies.[22] But there can also be authentic insights and truths, of a sort that are *only* available in retrospect. In highlighting a dimension of *dis*symmetry

---

[18] P. Ricoeur, *Oneself as Another* (University of Chicago Press, 1992).

[19] Ricoeur, *Oneself as Another*, 162.

[20] See D. Carr, *Time, Narrative, and History* (Bloomington, IN: Indiana University Press, 1986).

[21] Freeman, *Hindsight*.

[22] See, e.g., S. Taylor, *Positive Illusions: Creative Self-deception and the Healthy Mind* (New York: Basic Books, 1991); M. S. Gazzaniga, *The Mind's Past* (Berkeley, CA: University of California Press, 1998); D. L. Schacter, *The Seven Sins of Memory (How the Mind Forgets and Remembers)* (Boston, MA: Houghton Mifflin, 2001).

between life and narrative, I do so, therefore, not to offer the frequently made distinction between the supposedly formless reality of the former and the fictionality of the latter but, on some level, the exact opposite: owing to the essential openness (the not-quiteness or not-yetness) of ongoing life, narrative emerges as a vehicle precisely for putting one's life – and oneself – in perspective. As for the implications of this view for the idea of narrative identity, let me move on to the first triad, dealing with the three spheres of temporality.

Triad one: spheres of temporality

In much of my work, most of which deals with memory, I have tended to focus on the first of these spheres – the past – and my emphasis has tended to be hermeneutical in its basic orientation. But through the work of Michael Bamberg, Jens Brockmeier, and others, I have come around to seeing both the performative aspect of identity-making – what is being *done* in and through the act of narrating – and also the more "local" aspect of identity-making – that is, what it is that transpires, in the present, in the context of everyday *acting* in the world.[23] This basic orientation has found its way into certain strands of literary theory too. In Paul John Eakin's recent book *Living Autobiographically: How We Create Identity in Narrative*, he notes that his thinking about narrative identity has undergone some significant changes over the years.[24] "When I first became interested in autobiographies thirty years ago," he explains, "I thought of such narratives simply as convenient containers for our life stories... Now, decades later," however, "I see [them] as only the most visible, tangible evidence of the much larger phenomenon [at hand], the construction of identity that talking about ourselves and our lives performs in the world." Note the key words: *construction, talking, performs.* "I believe that our life stories are not only *about* us," Eakin adds, "but in an inescapable and profound way *are* us, at least insofar as we are players in the narrative identity system that structures social arrangements."[25] From an essentially cognitive approach, rooted in autobiographies and the like, therefore, he has moved on to one that is more "social and

---

[23] See Bamberg, Narration and its contribution; also, M. Bamberg, Positioning between structure and performance. *Journal of Narrative and Life History* 7 (1997) 335–342. For a quite different perspective, see J. Brockmeier, Autobiographical time. *Narrative Inquiry* 10 (2000) 51–73.

[24] P. J. Eakin, *Living Autobiographically: How We Create Identity in Narrative* (Ithaca, NY: Cornell University Press, 2008).

[25] Eakin, *Living Autobiographically*, ix–x.

cultural," rooted more in the quotidian conditions of the present than the more distant concerns of the storied past.

In any case, and with this "new wave" of thinking about narrative identity in mind, I want to pose two basic questions: First, how might we begin to think about the relationship between these two perspectives on narrative identity? Is one more important, more formative or fundamental, than the other? Second, how does the *future* enter the picture? That *remembering* and *acting* are key aspects of the formation of narrative identity seems self-evident. But what about *imagining*, projecting oneself into the future, or possible future? Let me see if I can begin to answer these questions by saying a bit more about the three spheres of temporality and how they might enter into the fashioning of narrative identity.

What I want to say, first, is that *acting*, in the *present*, is indeed an important, and somewhat neglected, aspect of the fashioning of narrative identity. Here, I am thinking especially of what Ricoeur had referred to as those "heterogeneous elements," found in the movement of life itself, that are in some sense "pre-narrative" or "quasi-narrative." Along with Anthony Paul Kerby, I acknowledge that "we are not self-consciously narrating ourselves all the time," but that nevertheless, "we are always already caught up in narratives," such that "the implicit narrative structure of life is taken up and augmented in our explicit narratives."[26] From this perspective, in other words, "life" is understood to be "inherently of a narrative structure," one "that we make explicit when we reflect upon our past and our possible future."[27] What I would in turn suggest here – cautiously – is that alongside the pre-narrative or quasi-narrative quality of ongoing experience is its quality of being "pre-identity" as well. Just as we can speak of "life" as what Ricoeur had called "an *activity and a passion in search of a narrative*," so too can we speak of the person whose life it is as a character in search of an identity. This is in no way to diminish the import of ongoing, local experience for the fashioning of narrative identity. Nor is it to claim that such experience is completely devoid of reflection, of configurational meaning-making. In an important sense, this first sphere of temporality is indeed *primary*. But this pre-narrative, pre-identity constructive doing is of a different order than that which takes place in the retrospective, reflective work of narrative. In addressing this *secondary* process of narrating, what we are considering is more of a synthetic and synoptic taking-stock; and insofar as it is oriented to the question of who I am, "through it all," it is that much more explicitly tied to identity.

<hr/>

[26] A. P. Kerby, *Narrative and the Self* (Bloomington, IN: Indiana University Press, 1991).
[27] Kerby, *Narrative and the Self*, 40.

As I argue in my book *Hindsight*, subtitled *The Promise and Peril of Looking Backward*, narrative reflection, the process of looking backward over the terrain of the personal past, frequently takes the form of "correcting," one might say, the "shortsightedness" of the immediate moment, thereby allowing us to see what we either could not, or would not, see earlier on.[28] It is right here, I suggest, that the third sphere of temporality, oriented toward the future, comes into play, in the *tertiary* process of imagining: in seeing my own shortsightedness from the distant perch of the present moment, looking backward, I have already begun to move beyond it. And even though I may not yet know with any certainty where exactly this movement will take me, I have already begun to face the difficult ethical and moral challenge of moving forward, to a better place. In reconstructing the past I thus reconstruct the future as well, re-imagining the developmental *teloi* or ends of my life.[29] In the process of doing so I also re-imagine my very identity.

It is perhaps with this sort of transformation in mind that Ricoeur has insisted on thinking about personal identity beyond the category of *idem*, "sameness," insisting on the dialectic of *idem* and *ipse*, sameness and selfhood.[30] We are emphatically *not* the same, either from moment to moment or across larger swaths of time. But nor are we utterly different and disparate. By turning to the idea of narrative identity, as we have been exploring it thus far, we have in hand a vehicle for crafting a middle path between the two. As suggested already, however, there is more at work in the fashioning of narrative identity than temporality. Or, put another way, there is more at work in temporality, as we just considered it, than time alone. For, in speaking of somehow redressing the shortsightedness of the past and present and thereby opening up the possibility of a better way in the future, we have already entered what I am here calling "spheres of otherness." Let me turn to them.

Triad two: spheres of otherness

In speaking of spheres of otherness, I am speaking of those particular aspects of relation that Martin Buber, in particular, underscores in

---

[28] Freeman, *Hindsight*.
[29] See, e.g., M. Freeman, History, narrative, and life-span developmental knowledge. *Human Development* **27** (1984) 1–19; also M. Freeman and R. Robinson, The development within: An alternative approach to the study of lives. *New Ideas in Psychology* **8** (1990) 53–72.
[30] Ricoeur, *Oneself as Another*.

considering the "I/Thou" relationship.[31] For Buber, there are, again, three such fundamental spheres. "Man's threefold living relation," he writes, "is, first, his relation to the world and to things, second, his relation to men [and women] – both to individuals and to the many – third, his relation to the mystery of being – which is dimly apparent through all this but infinitely transcends it – which the philosopher calls the Absolute and the believer calls God, and which cannot in fact be eliminated from the situation even by a man who rejects both designations."[32] The last point is a particularly interesting and provocative one: even the atheist, Buber implies, must be oriented in some way to the Absolute in order for there to exist the possibility of meaning. The main idea, in any case, concerns the centrality of the relation to the *other*-than-self in the fashioning of personal identity. Indeed, he writes, "The genuineness and adequacy of the self cannot stand the test in self-commerce, but only in communication with the whole of otherness."[33]

Notice in this context that Buber does *not* speak about the relation to oneself. "Besides man's threefold living relation," he acknowledges, "there is one other, that to one's own self. This relation, however, unlike the others, cannot be regarded as one that is real as such, since the necessary presupposition of a real duality is lacking. Hence it cannot in reality be raised to the level of an essential living relation."[34] I am not sure whether to follow Buber in this exclusion. Here, I am thinking of the very real consequences of the I/me relationship – including, especially, the fact that I can effect very real changes in myself as a function of how I relate to my past. At the same time, strictly speaking, "I" cannot inspire myself, precisely because inspiration must derive from without, from something other than me. The "dialogue" that transpires between "I" and "me" can thus never be quite as substantial as that which takes place with objects outside of me. Hence Buber's assertion that "The question of what man is" – and the question of who *I* am, as this particular person – "cannot be answered by a consideration of existence or of self-being as such, but only by a consideration of the essential connection of the human person and his relations with all being" – as it unfolds, we can add, through narrative.[35] It is along these lines that I earlier suggested that while the *proximal* source of one's story is the self, the *distal* source is the Other. Taking this idea one step farther, it might also be said that the

---

[31] M. Buber's best known work is *I and Thou* (New York: Charles Scribner's and Sons, 1970). Also noteworthy, and in many ways more fully developed, is his *Between Man and Man* (New York: Charles Scribner's and Sons, 1965).

[32] Buber, *Between Man and Man*, 177.   [33] Buber, *Between Man and Man*, 178.

[34] Buber, *Between Man and Man*, 180.   [35] Buber, *Between Man and Man*, 180.

Other – manifested in Buber's three spheres – is the distal source of personal identity itself.

Now, if Emmanuel Levinas is right, the primary and most fundamental sphere of otherness is that of other people, the basic idea being that one's identity – both as *a* human being and as *this* human being – has as its main source of inspiration the "face" of the other person, to whom and for whom we are responsible.[36] Levinas, it should be emphasized, is not just offering a variant of Cooley's "looking glass" self or Mead's notion of the self as a "social structure." Rather, he is underscoring the *ethical* dimension of identity: "In the alterity of the face, the for-the-other commands the *I*."[37] So it is that he wants to speak of "responsibility as the essential, primary and fundamental structure of subjectivity."[38] The idea is a strange and surprising one. But I have come to find it compelling too. To take but one simple example: it was difficult in some ways to come to the conference on which this chapter is based. As I had written at the time, "Yesterday was Thanksgiving, and I left behind my wife and two daughters, who shared the Thanksgiving meal with my 86-year-old mother, who suffers from dementia, at her assisted living residence. Sunday is my wife's birthday." (And so forth and so on.) "Who I am," I continued, "is intimately tied to all of them – not only in that they are a part of me but that they call forth the deepest dimensions of my care and concern." Identity here is "ex-centric," we might say, outward-moving, drawn forth by the Other.

As Levinas puts the matter in an important essay entitled "Substitution," "The ego is not merely a being endowed with certain so-called moral qualities, qualities which it would bear as attributes." Rather, it is always in the process "of being emptied of its being, of being turned inside out."[39] There is much more that might be said about Levinas' claims in this context. For present purposes, I shall simply reiterate the idea that our relatedness to others – particularly those with whom we share a history and a story – is, for him, the sphere of spheres, and is in this sense the primordial source of identity.[40]

---

[36] See, e.g., E. Levinas, *Ethics and Infinity* (Pittsburgh, PA: Duquesne University Press, 1985); also, *Outside the Subject* (Palo Alto, CA: Stanford University Press, 1994).

[37] E. Levinas, *Alterity and Transcendence* (New York: Columbia University Press, 1999) 103.

[38] Levinas, *Ethics and Infinity*, 95.

[39] E. Levinas, Substitution. In A. T. Peperzak, S. Critchley, and R. Bernasconi (eds.) *Emmanuel Levinas: Basic Philosophical Writings* (Bloomington, IN: Indiana University Press, 1996) 80–95.

[40] The situation is actually a bit more complicated than I have just made it out to be. On the one hand, the face of the Other is primary for Levinas. As he writes in *Alterity and Transcendence*, "It demands me, requires me, summons me." But there is more

In regard to the second sphere of otherness, which Buber referred to as our relation to the world and to things, we might turn to some of Iris Murdoch's work.[41] For Murdoch, it is not only other people who inspire us and give form and meaning to identity but also the vast variety of non-human "objects" – works of art, for instance – that at once "take us out of ourselves" (she uses the word "unselfing" to describe this process) and, at the same time, return us *to* ourselves, on a deeper plane. "In enjoying great art," in particular, "we experience a clarification and concentration and perfection of our own consciousness. Emotion and intellect are unified into a limited whole. In this sense art also *creates* its client," binding the heterogeneous elements of our experience.[42] We might also think of the variety of life projects to which we are committed – the next article or book, for instance – and how these too are constitutive of identity, such that we become "wrapped up" in them. Indeed, much of "who I am" has been constituted and conditioned by working through a number of projects of just this sort, including this very one; and in the wake of each of them, "I" will have changed in some way. The main point to be emphasized here, in any case, is that the particular Other to which we are related is in no way limited to the human realm. Pragmatically speaking, in fact, the Other might be said to consist of any and all objects outside ourselves – people, projects, nature, art, God – that "inspire" us and thereby draw us beyond our own borders.

This brings us, finally, to Buber's third sphere of otherness, which he referred to as our relation to the mystery of being. Just in case this sounds a bit too ethereal (or theological), let me turn to Charles Taylor, who is somewhat more earthbound about these matters (at least when he's speaking as a philosopher) and whose work may also help provide a bridge of sorts between the three spheres of temporality and the three spheres of otherness. According to Taylor, the moment I pause to reflect on my life, I do so against the backdrop of the question of goodness. His discussion of "frameworks" in *Sources of the Self* is particularly useful in this context.[43] "To articulate a framework," he writes, "is to explicate what makes sense of our moral responses."[44] It is a structure of hierarchically ordered commitments, an identification of one's priorities, and doing without

to this demand than meets the eye. Indeed, "Should we not call this demand or this interpellation or this summons to responsibility the word of God?" (p. 27).

[41] See especially I. Murdoch, *The Sovereignty of Good* (London: Routledge, 1970); and *Metaphysics as a Guide to Morals* (London: Penguin, 1993).

[42] Murdoch, *Metaphysics*, 8.

[43] C. Taylor, *Sources of the Self: The Making of the Modern Identity* (Cambridge, MA: Harvard University Press, 1989).

[44] Taylor, *Sources of the Self*, 26.

them, he insists, "is utterly impossible for us."[45] More to the point still, "we cannot do without some orientation to the good."[46] Indeed, "we are only selves insofar as we move in a certain space of questions, as we seek and find an orientation to the good."[47] This is precisely where narrative enters the picture: "(T)his sense of the good," Taylor argues, "has to be woven into my life as an unfolding story." What's more, "as I project my life forward and endorse the existing direction or give it a new one, I project a future story, not just a state of the momentary future but a bent for my whole life to come."[48]

As Taylor goes on to suggest in *The Ethics of Authenticity*, there is a tendency within modernity to emphasize "being true to oneself" in thinking about personal identity.[49] What Taylor wants to show, however, is that thinking about authenticity in this self-enclosed way, without regard to the demands of our ties to others or to demands "emanating from something more or other than human desires or aspirations," is self-defeating and, ultimately, meaningless.[50] Things take on importance against a background, a horizon, of intelligibility. "Even the sense that the significance of my life comes from its being chosen ... depends on the understanding that *independent of my will* there is something noble, courageous, and hence significant in giving shape to my own life." Authenticity, therefore, he insists, "is not the enemy of demands that emanate from beyond the self; it supposes such demands."[51] That is to say, it supposes that these demands issue from what is *other*-than-self, from spheres of influence and inspiration that draw the self forward and fuel the ongoing process of fashioning and refashioning one's identity.

Among the various goods to which we may be oriented, there exist what Taylor calls "hypergoods" – that is, "goods which not only are incomparably more important than others but provide the standpoint from which these must be weighed, judged, decided about."[52] I am not sure how far to go with this idea, whether it is Buber's religiously tinged form or Taylor's (manifestly) more secularized version. There is no doubt that for some – those, for instance, who see themselves as being "called upon" to live out their lives in some prescribed way – such hypergoods are indeed operative in their identity. But whether these hypergoods are *required* in the fashioning of narrative identity seems more questionable. At this juncture, therefore, I want to ask: What *is* required in the fashioning of narrative identity? What are its minimal requirements?

45 Taylor, *Sources of the Self*, 27.   46 Taylor, *Sources of the Self*, 33.
47 Taylor, *Sources of the Self*, 34.   48 Taylor, *Sources of the Self*, 48.
49 C. Taylor, *The Ethics of Authenticity* (Cambridge, MA: Harvard University Press, 1991).
50 Taylor, *The Ethics of Authenticity*, 35.   51 Taylor, *The Ethics of Authenticity*, 41.
52 Taylor, *Sources of the Self*, 63.

An existential excursus: dementia, identity, and personhood

As "luck" would have it, I may be able to answer these questions by turning to the case of my mother, whom I introduced earlier, an 88-year-old woman with dementia, chronic obstructive pulmonary disease (COPD), and a number of other maladies.[53] The reason I am doing so is that her situation, as it has transpired in the seven or so years since her diagnosis, has taught me a great deal about memory, identity, and, not least, the nature of personhood. There are times when she seems to have no sense of identity at all. It often happens upon her waking from a nap and finding everything around her utterly unfamiliar. It is difficult to fathom what her world is like at these times. Occasionally, I wake up in the middle of the night, in a hotel room for instance, and have no idea where I am or how I got there. But after a few weird moments, I can remember and go back to sleep. However, this is exactly what my mother cannot do. It's not at all like being in a new place – that can be interesting and exciting. Instead, she has said, it's like being in "another world."

For a time, the result was panic and a desperate attempt to find me, her only remaining touchstone. (I live just a mile or two away from her, and for that reason, among others, there is a special connection.) This is telling in its own right: I am referring to the fact that my mother's very sense of "location," in a recognizable world, has come to depend in part on me. I could help return her to the world and to her*self*, such as it was, at least for a while. It was a good thing I arrived when I did, she told me one day a while back. Had I not done so, she said, she might have screamed. Things are a bit different now, less fearful and panicky but more confused – particularly, sad to say, when I visit her. Sometimes when I enter her apartment or see her in one of the social rooms, she will be sitting in a daze, eyes closed, just *there*, maybe participating in an activity but more likely just being, without any – or any apparent – sense at all of her own existence. When she opens her eyes and sees me, or

---

[53] Since the time I wrote the initial version of this chapter (for the aforementioned conference), there have been some significant changes in my mother's situation. For present purposes, though, I will be referring to her situation as it was manifested at the time. It may be interesting to note here that, as I had predicted would happen, she is actually subjectively "better" now than she was then, largely because her own sense of identity has become so diminished as to leave her essentially unfazed by her situation. For details, see M. Freeman, Beyond narrative: Dementia's tragic promise, in L.-C. Hyden and J. Brockmeier (eds.) *Health, Illness, and Culture: Broken Narratives* (London: Routledge, 2008) 169–184; also, with explicit reference to the idea of identity, see M. Freeman, The stubborn myth of identity: Dementia, memory, and the narrative unconscious. *Journal of Family Life* 1 (2009). Available at www.journaloffamilylife.org/mythofidentity.

my wife or daughters, she may smile a big smile and hold out her arms for a hug hello. She has suddenly become (how shall I put it?) *mother*, mother-in-law, grandma – or something close to that. In other words, she becomes "identitied," through *us*, through our entry into her world. She may not be able to place all of us, but there will be some rudimentary recognition – of us and in turn of herself – and hence some sense of pastness, history. *That's* who I am. All is well. But generally, not for long. After a minute or two she may say something like "I don't know how my things got here" or "How did you find me?" or "Do I stay here?" At that point I might explain to her that she has been living there for a while, actually. She may then go on to ask how long, only to find out that years have passed by. This can be extremely disturbing to her, and puzzling. "Oh, my god," she will often say, staggered by her own dislocation. "Oh, my god." Then, she might utter a phrase in Yiddish, which translates roughly as, "Oh, what a person becomes" or "Oh, what becomes of a person." She simply can't believe that this is what her life has come to. But who exactly is this "she" that has been stunned into disbelief? And what is it that leads her to retain this sense, albeit damaged, of identity? Her identity is largely a *negative* one at this point, tied to what she is *not*. What are its sources? And is it possible to make sense of her situation with the "double triad" scheme put forth in this paper?

In terms of the three spheres of temporality, it seems questionable. There really are no "heterogeneous elements" of the sort Ricoeur had referred to. In fact, she has very few discrete memories at this point. There is also no explicit configurational work being done, no binding together of past experiences into some semblance of unity through reflection. There is no future – to speak of – either. That would require an element of appraisal, based largely on a sense of the past, that she is incapable of making. All there is, or at least all there appears to be, is a present. But why, then, should she be puzzled and disturbed by what she has become? She also has fairly strong defenses. When I tell her that her memory lapses have occurred before, she is either deeply saddened, completely mystified, or positively annoyed, as in, "I think I would *know* if this happened before." This bespeaks not only a sense of identity but a relatively strong one at that. Again, where does it come from? Do the three spheres of temporality apply?

On the face of it, the three spheres of otherness are questionable too. While I noted earlier that my mother often "returns to herself" when I or others from my family come to see her, the Levinasian idea of awakening her sense of responsibility seems like a stretch. Our faces awaken *something*, to be sure. But beyond this most basic dimension of awakening, it is difficult to say what else is going on. In terms of her relation to the world and to things, it is a tenuous one. She does connect to music (she's actually known for having a great memory for old tunes), and she also jumps in to play an occasional trivia or word game. But there is not much for her beyond these few objects. It might be interesting to note that, when I call her on the phone and ask what she's been doing, she will almost always say "reading" – which, at one time, was exactly what she would have been doing. However, it has been years since she has been able to read more than a couple of sentences – which, of course, will be promptly forgotten. So she is a reader who doesn't read. I suppose this is part of her identity, but only when I ask her questions about how she's spending her time. As for her relation to the Absolute, God, hypergoods, and so on, well, that doesn't seem too applicable either. And yet, "she" remains – without the same kind of narrative identity that those of us with more or less fully functioning brains have but a narrative identity – again, mainly in the form of what she is *not* – nonetheless. The implication: either narrative identity is not as bound up with the double triad as I suggested earlier, or the double triad needs to be rendered in subtler form.

I am going to opt for the latter. Consider for a moment a wish my mother had expressed a while back, not too long after she had begun to grow confused and frustrated over her existence. (Becoming aware of one's own mental demise is perhaps the most painful phase of the disease.) "I want to be a person," she said. What could she have meant by this? I can only hazard a guess. But what I think she meant was that she wanted to join the once-known world again, as the competent, self-sufficient center of moral energy that she knew, vaguely, she had once been. Notice here that she doesn't say "I want to be *myself*," which would render her lament one that concerned the specifics of her identity, but "I want to be a *person*": somehow, she has a sense, still, of what a person is, what a person does, how a person acts. That is to say, she seems to have a memory, such as it is, of how to be *a* person if not *this* person. The phrase I referred to earlier – "Oh, what a person becomes" – signals this awareness. So do her occasional complaints about being "brainless," "mindless," or "like a child." There is an image in view, still, of what kind of person she once was. But this image is less tied to the particulars of her past experience – discrete episodes – than to their culturally rooted schematic contours. Thoughtful people read; so that is what she has been doing, or so she says. One might say that she has a memory of the *form* of personal identity if not the content, the concrete substance.

This mode of memory – or, perhaps more appropriately, *remembrance*: memory, fused with mourning – seems to surface most often in the context of communicative exchange with people like me and other intimates, that is, people who *matter* to her and who, at some point in the past, had an entirely different image of who she was and what she was all about. Just recently, I confessed to being "famished" when I visited her one day. Not a good move on my part: "I wish I had something to feed you," she immediately said. As I suggested earlier, there is little doubt but that my presence can sometimes bring about this sort of lamenting, at times shame-soaked, remembrance. I sometimes wonder, in fact, whether my visits to her are a good thing or a bad thing. When she is alone or with the others who live at her place, there are few lamentations: out of sight, out of mind. Delighted though she generally is to see me, my presence disrupts this oblivion, brings back a world, albeit a strange and, at times, disturbing one. This underscores not only the relational dimension of memory but the relational dimension of identity as well: my mother is perhaps most *not-herself* – which is, in effect, her new identity – when she is with those who had once known otherwise. She can even apologize for the state of her existence. "This must be so hard for you," she has said, following one of our exchanges about how different things are now. Present and past, small stories and big ones, intermingle. A kind of future sometimes comes into being at times like these too – namely, one that is closed off, devoid of the possibility of there emerging a "new chapter" – a future *in absentia*, as it were. If there is anything she knows at this juncture in her life, it's that things aren't going to be changing for the better.

In my mother's case at least, there would seem to be no separating the three spheres of temporality from the three spheres of otherness: how she experiences time is intimately and intrinsically related to how she experiences otherness – other people, in particular. She wishes she could be the kind of mother who could whip up a meal, but as we both know, that's not going to happen. It seems significant to note in this context that, even amidst her decline, there still remains some good, compelling evidence for the continued existence of "Levinasian" energies: if there is anything that can awaken her, draw her out of her sleepy, self-enclosed state, it is the fate of others. She is still *concerned*, more concerned, in fact, about *us* than about herself. Perhaps the realm of the human Other *is* the sphere of spheres. It does appear to be the last to go.

Consider the second sphere of otherness, having to do with the various objects and activities to which she might be related. If I ask what else she's been doing besides reading, or what's been going on today, her answer is generally swift: "Nothing," she says, "absolutely nothing" – and this despite the fact that, according to the aides who work with her, she might have actually been quite busy. Along these lines, the second sphere of otherness does in fact remain applicable – precisely in terms of the felt *absence* of there existing anything in the world to which she can become truly connected. She is not especially bothered by this; even though there may be nothing to do, subjectively at any rate, that's okay at this point.

As concerns those larger goods that Buber and Taylor had spoken of, those too are palpably absent, and she seems to know this as well. It is part of her identity, fleeting as it is. In the most recent piece I wrote about her, I noted that her situation bespeaks "a kind of existential liminality, a state of being in-between presence and absence – or, put another way, a state of being wherein there is, at one and the same time, both the absence of presence, the absence of tangible memorial touchstones, and the presence of absence, the felt pressure and pain of there being something missing."[54] In this context too, she has become less troubled by this as time has passed. Indeed, she is in the process of moving beyond absence, beyond lamentation, beyond a sense of *lost* personhood. There are no more complaints about nothing to do or be. Indeed, I have no doubt that there are lengthy periods of time – when, for instance, I am out of town for a spell – when "she" herself is largely *in absentia*, just... being: waking up, eating, getting her meds, involving herself in activities every now and then. Her eyes are closed much of the time; sometimes she's dozing, sometimes just listening to what's going on around her. I am glad to see them open, and see her smile, even reach out, when I enter.

Where does all this leave us in regard to the model I have been trying to build? Judging by my mother's situation, it appears that the "double triad" of narrative identity still applies, though we may be getting close to the limit in her case, moving beyond narrative altogether. My own perspective on the issues at hand, however, suggests that the idea of narrative identity, as set forth by Ricoeur and others, needs to be rendered more subtly, and with greater attention to those aspects of it that go beyond conscious articulation, composition, emplotment, and so on. As of now, my mother has only the most minimal sense of the "episodes" of the past; most are long gone. And with very rare exceptions, she no longer engages in the kind of synoptic, reflective activity generally associated with narrative identity. (As enamored as I am with the notion of hindsight, it hardly applies to her current situation.) And yet, she still has *some* sense, albeit fleeting and obscure, of who she is – at least when I (or other remaining intimates) enter the room and "remind" her. "Who's here?" one of the aides might ask as I appear. "My son" (or, more embarrassingly, "My gorgeous son." (She often relates to me like I'm a strapping young man; occasionally, I try to correct her.)

[54] Freeman, The stubborn myth of identity.

Bearing in mind my mother's situation, I want to suggest one additional "triad" in closing, one that is tied to the idea of narrative identity itself and that is no doubt of a piece in the "normal" person, only to come undone in maladies such as dementia. I am thinking here of (1) the *particularized* narrative identity, rooted in discrete memories, events, episodes; (2) the *generalized* narrative identity, rooted in basic, culturally constituted conceptions of personhood, agency, and normality; and (3) what might simply be called *lived* narrative identity, rooted in those aspects of narrativity that exist "before" both of these, and that has its sources in foundational dimensions of temporality and otherness. For better or worse, I expect to learn more about this last aspect of the triad in the not too distant future.

Bibliography

Albright, D. Literature and psychological models of the self. In N. Neisser and R. Fivush (eds.) *The Remembering Self: Construction and Accuracy in the Self-narrative* (Cambridge University Press, 1996) 19–40.

Alexander, I. E. *Personology: Method and Content in Personality Assessment and Psychobiography* (Durham, NC: Duke University Press, 1990).

Allen, J. W. P. and Bickhard, M. H. Transcending the nativist-empiricist debate: Methodological and conceptual issues regarding infant development. *Cognitive Development* (in press).

Allport, G. W. *Personality: A Psychological Interpretation* (New York: Holt, 1937).
 The personalistic psychology of William Stern. *Character and Personality* **5** (1937) 231–246.
 William Stern: 1871–1938. *The American Journal of Psychology* **51** (1938) 770–773.

Allport, G. W. and Odbert, H. S. Trait names: A psychological study. *Psychological Monographs* **47** (1936).

Anderson, L. *Autobiography* (London: Routledge, 2001).

Anscombe, G. E. M. *Intention* (Oxford: Blackwell, 1957).

Appiah, K. A. *Experiments in Ethics* (Harvard University Press, 2008).

Aquinas, T. *Summa Theologica* (New York: Benzinger Bros., 1947).

Atkinson, R. The life story interview as a bridge in narrative inquiry. In J. D. Clandinin (ed.) *Handbook of Narrative Inquiry* (Thousand Oaks, CA: Sage, 2007) 224–245.

Augustinus, A. *On the Holy Trinity* (Grand Rapids, MI: Eerdmans, 1956).
 Confessions, H. Chadwick (trans.) (Oxford University Press, 1991).

Austin, J. L. A plea for excuses. *Proceedings of the Aristotelian Society* **57** (1957) 1–30.

Avramides, A. *Other Minds* (London: Routledge, 2001).

Axelrod, R. and Hamilton, W. D. The evolution of cooperation. *Science* **211** (1981) 1,390–1,396.

Baddeley, J. D. and Singer, J. A. Charting the life story's path: Narrative identity across the life span. In J. D. Clandinin (ed.) *Handbook of Narrative Inquiry* (Thousand Oaks, CA: Sage, 2007) 177–202.

Bakan, D. *The Duality of Human Existence: Isolation and Communion in Western Man* (Boston: Beacon Press, 1966).

Bakhtin, M. M. *The Dialogic Imagination* (Austin: University of Texas Press, 1975).

Toward a Philosophy of the Act, V. Liapunov and M. Holquist (eds.) (Austin: University of Texas Press, 1993).

Bamberg, M. Positioning between structure and performance. *Journal of Narrative and Life History* 7 (1997) 335–342.

Stories: big or small – why do we care? *Narrative Inquiry* 16 (2006) 139–147.

Narration and its contribution to self and identity. *Theory and Psychology* 21 (2011) 3–24.

Barenbaum, N. B. and Winter, D. G. History of modern personality theory and research. In O. P. John, R. W. Robins, and L. A. Pervin (eds.) *Handbook of Personality Theory and Research* (New York: Guilford Press, 2008) 3–26.

Barney, R. Aristotle's argument for a human function. *Oxford Studies in Ancient Philosophy* 34 (2008) 293–322.

Barresi, J. Extending self-consciousness into the future. In C. Moore and K. Lemmon (eds.) *The Self in Time: Developmental Perspectives* (Hillsdale, NJ: Erlbaum, 2001) 141–161.

Some boundary conditions on embodied agents sharing a common world. In I. Wachsmuth, M. Lenzen, and G. Knoblich (eds.) *Embodied Communication in Humans and Machines* (Oxford University Press, 2008) 29–52.

On seeing our selves and others as persons. *New Ideas in Psychology* 30 (2012) 120–130.

Barresi, J. and Moore, C. Intentional relations and social understanding. *Behavioral and Brain Sciences* 19 (1996) 107–122.

The neuroscience of social understanding. In J. Zlatev, T. Racine, C. Sinha, and E. Itkonen (eds.) *The Shared Mind: Perspectives on Intersubjectivity* (Amsterdam: John Benjamins, 2008) 39–66.

Bateson, M. C. *Composing a Life* (New York: Plume, 1990).

Beck, U., Giddens, A., and Lash, S. *Reflexive Modernization: Politics, Tradition and Aesthetics in the Modern Social Order* (Cambridge, UK: Polity Press, 1994).

Behar, R. *Translated Woman: Crossing the Border with Esperanza's Story* (Boston: Beacon Press, 1993).

Behrens, H. and Deutsch, W. Die Tagebücher von Clara und William Stern [The diaries of Clara and William Stern]. In W. Deutsch (ed.) *Über die Verborgene Aktualität von William Stern* (Frankfurt am Main: Peter Lang Verlag, 1991) 19–36.

Bem, D. J. and Allen, S. On predicting some of the people some of the time: The search for cross-situational consistencies in behavior. *Psychological Review* 81 (1974) 506–520.

Benjamin, L. T. Jr. *A Brief History of Modern Psychology* (Malden, MA: Blackwell, 2007).

Bennett, M. R. and Hacker, P. M. S. *Philosophical Foundations of Neuroscience* (Oxford: Blackwell, 2003).

Berger, P. L. and Luckmann, T. *The Social Construction of Reality* (New York: Doubleday, 1966).

Bermúdez, J. L. *The Paradox of Self-consciousness* (Cambridge, MA: MIT Press, 1998).

Bickhard, M. H. *Cognition, Convention, and Communication* (New York: Praeger Publishers, 1980).

A model of developmental and psychological processes. PhD dissertation, University of Chicago (1973). Published as Bickhard, M. H. A model of developmental and psychological processes. *Genetic Psychology Monographs* **102** (1980) 61–116.

Commentary on the age 4 transition. *Human Development* **35** (1992) 182–192.

Representational content in humans and machines. *Journal of Experimental and Theoretical Artificial Intelligence* **5** (1993) 285–333.

Emergence. In P. B. Andersen, C. Emmeche, N. O. Finnemann, and P. V. Christiansen (eds.) *Downward Causation* (Aarhus, Denmark: University of Aarhus Press, 2000) 322–348.

The social ontology of persons. In J. I. M. Carpendale and U. Müller (eds.) *Social Interaction and the Development of Knowledge* (Mahwah, NJ: Erlbaum, 2004) 111–132.

Developmental normativity and normative development. In L. Smith and J. Voneche (eds.) *Norms in Human Development* (Cambridge University Press, 2006) 57–76.

Language as an interaction system. *New Ideas in Psychology* **25** (2) (2007) 171–187.

Are you social? The ontological and developmental emergence of the person. In U. Müller, J. I. M. Carpendale, N. Budwig, and B. Sokol (eds.) *Social Life and Social Knowledge* (New York: Taylor and Francis, 2008) 17–42.

Social ontology as convention. *Topoi* **27** (1–2) (2008) 139–149.

The interactivist model. *Synthese* **166** (3) (2009) 547–591.

Interactivism. In J. Symons and P. Calvo (eds.) *The Routledge Companion to Philosophy of Psychology* (London: Routledge, 2009) 346–359.

Some consequences (and enablings) of process metaphysics. *Axiomathes* **21** (2011) 3–32.

A process ontology for persons and their development. *New Ideas in Psychology* **30** (2012) 107–119.

The Whole Person: Toward a Naturalism of Persons – Contributions to an Ontological Psychology (in preparation).

Bickhard, M. H. and Richie, D. M. *On the Nature of Representation: A Case Study of James Gibson's Theory of Perception* (New York: Praeger Publishers, 1983).

Bonatti, L., Frot, E., Zangl, R., and Mehler, M. The human first hypothesis: Identification of conspecifics and individuation of objects in the young infant. *Cognitive Psychology* **44** (2002) 388–426.

Bourne, E. The state of research on ego identity: A review and appraisal. *Journal of Youth and Adolescence* **7** (1978) 223–251.

Brockmeier, J. Autobiographical time. *Narrative Inquiry* **10** (2000) 51–73.

From the end to the beginning: Retrospective teleology in autobiography. In J. Brockmeier and D. Carbaugh (eds.) *Narrative and Identity: Studies in Autobiography, Self and Culture* (Amsterdam: John Benjamins Publishing Company, 2001) 247–280.

Brockmeier, J. and Carbaugh, D. (eds.) *Narrative and Identity: Studies in Autobiography, Self and Culture* (Amsterdam: John Benjamins Publishing Company, 2001).

Bruner, J. *Actual Minds, Possible Worlds* (Cambridge, MA: Harvard University Press, 1986).
Acts of Meaning (Cambridge, MA: Harvard University Press, 1990).
The narrative construction of reality. *Critical Inquiry* **18** (1) (1991) 1–21.
Making Stories: Law, Literature, Life (New York: Farrar, Straus and Giroux, 2002).
Buber, M. *Between Man and Man* (New York: Charles Scribner's and Sons, 1965).
I and Thou (New York: Charles Scribner's and Sons, 1970).
Bühring, G. *William Stern oder Streben nach Einheit* (Frankfurt am Main: Peter Lang Verlag, 1996).
Burke, K. *A Grammar of Motives* (New York: Prentice-Hall, 1945).
Burkitt, I. Psychology in the field of being: Merleau-Ponty, ontology, and social constructionism. *Theory and Psychology* **13** (2003) 319–338.
Byrne, R. and Whiten, A. (eds.) *Machiavellian Intelligence: Social Expertise and the Evolution of Intellect in Monkeys, Apes, and Humans* (Oxford University Press, 1989).
Call, J. and Tomasello, M. Does the chimpanzee have a theory of mind? 30 years later. *Trends in Cognitive Science* **12** (2008) 187–192.
Calvin, W. H. *A Brief History of the Mind* (New York: Oxford University Press, 2004).
Campbell, D. T. Evolutionary epistemology. In P. A. Schilpp (ed.) *The Philosophy of Karl Popper* (LaSalle, IL: Open Court, 1974) 413–463.
Levels of organization, downward causation, and the selection-theory approach to evolutionary epistemology. In G. Greenberg and E. Tobach (eds.) *Theories of the Evolution of Knowing* (Hillsdale, NJ: Lawrence Erlbaum Associates, 1990) 1–17.
Campbell, R. J. A process-based model for an interactive ontology. *Synthese* **166** (3) (2009) 453–477.
Campbell, R. L. and Bickhard, M. H. Types of constraints on development: An interactivist approach. *Developmental Review* **12** (3) (1992) 311–338.
Carr, D. *Time, Narrative, and History* (Bloomington, IN: Indiana University Press, 1986).
Carrithers, M. An alternative social history of the self. In M. Carrithers, S. Collins, and S. Lukes (eds.) *The Category of the Person: Anthropology, Philosophy, History* (Cambridge University Press, 1985) 234–256.
The Book of Memory: A Study of Memory in Medieval Culture (Cambridge University Press, 1990).
Cicero, M. T. *On Obligations* (Stanford, CA: Stanford University Press, 2000) part I.
Clandinin, J. D. (ed.) *Handbook of Narrative Inquiry* (Thousand Oaks, CA: Sage, 2007).
Cohler, B. J. and Hammack, P. L. Making a gay identity: Story and the construction of a coherent self. In D. P. McAdams, R. Josselson, and A. Lieblich (eds.) *Identity and Story: Creating Self in Narrative* (Washington, DC: American Psychological Association, 2006) 151–172.
Cohn, J. *Wertwissenschaft* (Stuttgart: Frommans, 1932).

Cole, M. *Cultural Psychology: A Once and Future Discipline* (Cambridge, MA: Harvard University Press, 1996).

Cooter, R. *The Cultural Meaning of Popular Science: Phrenology and the Organization of Consent in Nineteenth-century Britain* (Cambridge University Press, 1984).

Costa, R. E. and Shimp, C. P. Methods courses and texts in psychology: "Textbook science" and "tourist brochures." *Journal of Theoretical and Philosophical Psychology* **31** (2011) 25–43.

Cromby, J. Between constructionism and neuroscience: The societal co-constitution of embodied subjectivity. *Theory and Psychology* **14** (2004) 797–821.

Currie, M. *Postmodern Narrative Theory* (New York: St. Martin's Press, 1998).

Daiute, C. and Lightfoot, C. (eds.) *Narrative Analysis: Studying the Development of Individuals in Society* (Thousand Oaks, CA: Sage, 2004).

Danziger, K. *Constructing the Subject: Historical Origins of Psychological Research* (Cambridge University Press, 1990).

Naming the Mind: How Psychology Found its Language (London: Sage, 1997).

The historical formation of selves. In R. D. Ashmore and L. Jussim (eds.) *Self and Identity: Fundamental Issues* (New York: Oxford University Press, 1997) 137–159.

Making social psychology experimental: A conceptual history, 1920–1970. *Journal of the History of the Behavioral Sciences* **36** (2000) 329–347.

Darwall, S. *Virtue Ethics* (Oxford: Blackwell, 2003).

de Saussure, F. *Course in General Linguistics* (New York: Philosophical Library, 1959).

de Waal, F. B. M. Putting the altruism back into altruism: The evolution of empathy. *Annual Review of Psychology* **59** (2008) 279–300.

Descartes, R. *A Discourse on the Method of Correctly Conducting One's Reason and Seeking Truth in the Sciences*, I. Maclean (trans.) (Oxford University Press, 2006, orig. 1637).

Deutsch, W. (ed.), *Über die Verborgene Aktualität von William Stern* (Frankfurt am Main: Peter Lang Verlag, 1991).

Dilthey, W. Ideen über eine beschreibende und zergliedernde Psychologie [Toward a descriptive and analytical psychology]. *Sitzungsberichte der Akademie der Wissenschaften zu Berlin, zweiter Halbband* (1894) 1309–1407.

Donald, M. *Origins of the Modern Mind: Three Stages of the Evolution of Culture and Cognition* (Cambridge, MA: Harvard University Press, 1991).

A Mind so Rare: The Evolution of Human Consciousness (New York: Norton, 2001).

Dow, J. On the joint engagement of persons: Self-consciousness, the symmetry thesis and person perception. *Philosophical Psychology* (in press).

Dreyfus, H. L. *Being-in-the-World: A Commentary on Heidegger's "Being and time,"* *Division I* (Cambridge, MA: The MIT Press, 1991).

Dreyfus, H. L. and Hall, H. (eds.) *Heidegger: A Critical Reader* (Oxford: Blackwell, 1992).

Dumont, F. *A History of Personality Psychology: Theory, Science and Research from Hellenism to the Twenty-first Century* (New York: Cambridge University Press, 2010).

Eakin, P. J. *Living Autobiographically: How We Create Identity in Narrative* (Ithaca, NY: Cornell University Press, 2008).

Ebbinghaus, H. Über erklärende und beschreibende Psychologie [On explanatory and descriptive psychology]. *Zeitschrift für Psychologie* **9** (1896) 161–205.

Psychology: An Elementary Textbook, Max Meyer (trans.) (Boston, NY: D.C. Heath and Co. Publishers, 1908).

Elsbree, L. *The Rituals of Life: Patterns in Narrative* (Port Washington, NY: Kennikat Press, 1982).

Epstein, S. The stability of behavior: I. On predicting most of the people much of the Time. *Journal of Personality and Social Psychology* **37** (1979) 1,097–1,126.

Erikson, E. H. *Childhood and Society*, second edn (New York: Norton, 1963).

Identity, Youth and Crisis (New York: Norton, 1968).

Gandhi's Truth: On the Origins of Militant Nonviolence (New York: W. W. Norton and Company, 1993).

Young Man Luther: A Study in Psychoanalysis and History (New York: W. W. Norton and Company, 1993).

Erneling, C. E. *Understanding Language Acquisition: The Framework of Learning* (Albany, NY: State University of New York Press, 1993).

Fivush, R. and Haden, C. A. (eds.) *Autobiographical Memory and the Construction of a Narrative Self* (Mahwah, NJ: Erlbaum, 2003).

Foucault, M. *The History of Sexuality I: An Introduction* (New York: Random House, 1978).

What is Enlightenment? in P. Rabinow (ed.) *The Foucault Reader* (London: Penguin, 1984) 32–50.

Technologies of the self. In L. H. Martin, H. Gutman, and P. H. Hutton (eds.) *Technologies of the Self: A Seminar with Michel Foucault* (Amherst, MA: University of Massachusetts Press, 1988) 16–49.

The Birth of Biopolitics: Lectures at the Collège de France 1978–1979 (Basingstoke: Palgrave Macmillan, 2008).

Frank, A. W. *The Wounded Storyteller: Body, Illness and Ethics* (University of Chicago Press, 1995).

Franz, C. and Stewart, A. (eds.) *Women Creating Lives: Identities, Resilience and Resistance* (Boulder, CO: Westview Press, 1994).

Freeman, M. History, narrative, and life-span developmental knowledge. *Human Development* **27** (1984) 1–19.

Rewriting the Self: History, Memory, Narrative (London: Routledge, 1993).

Why narrative? Hermeneutics, historical understanding, and the significance of stories. *Journal of Narrative and Life History* **7** (1997) 169–176.

From substance to story: Narrative identity and the reconstruction of the self. In J. Brockmeier and D. Carbaugh (eds.) *Narrative and Identity: Studies in Autobiography, Self and Culture* (Amsterdam: John Benjamins Publishing Company, 2001) 283–298.

Life "on holiday"? *Narrative Inquiry* **16** (2006) 131–138.

Narrative and relation: The place of the Other in the story of the Self. In R. Josselson, A. Lieblich, and D. McAdams (eds.) *The Meaning of Others: Narrative Studies of Relationships* (Washington, DC: APA Books, 2007) 11–19.

Beyond narrative: Dementia's tragic promise. In L.-C. Hyden and J. Brockmeier (eds.) *Health, Illness, and Culture: Broken Narratives* (London: Routledge, 2008) 169–184.

The stubborn myth of identity: Dementia, memory, and the narrative unconscious. *Journal of Family Life* 1 (2009). Available at www.journaloffamilylife. org/mythofidentity.

Hindsight: The Promise and Peril of Looking Backward (New York: Oxford University Press, 2010).

Stories, big and small: Toward a synthesis. *Theory and Psychology* 21 (2011) 114–121.

Freeman, M. and Brockmeier, J. Narrative integrity: Autobiographical identity and the meaning of the "good life." In J. Brockmeier and D. Carbaugh (eds.) *Narrative and Identity: Studies in Autobiography, Self and Culture* (Amsterdam: John Benjamins Publishing Company, 2001) 75–99.

Freeman, M. and Robinson, R. The development within: An alternative approach to the study of lives. *New Ideas in Psychology* 8 (1990) 53–72.

Freeman, W. J. *How Brains Make Up their Minds* (London: Phoenix, 2000).

Freud, S. *Introductory Lectures on Psycho-analysis* (London: Allen and Unwin, 1922).

Frye, N. *Anatomy of Criticism* (Princeton University Press, 1957).

Fukuyama, F. The end of history. *The National Interest* 16 (Summer 1989).

Gadamer, H.-G. *Truth and Method* (New York: Crossroad, 1982).

Gallup, G. G. Jr. Chimpanzees: Self recognition. *Science* 167 (1970) 86–87.

Gallup, G. G. Jr., Anderson, J. R., and Platek, S. M. Self-recognition. In S. Gallagher (ed.) *The Oxford Handbook of Self* (Oxford University Press, 2010) 80–110.

Gazzaniga, M. S. *The Mind's Past* (Berkeley, CA: University of California Press, 1998).

Georgakopoulou, A. Thinking big with small stories in narrative and identity analysis. *Narrative Inquiry* 16 (2006) 129–137.

Gergen, K. J. *The Saturated Self: Dilemmas of Identity in Contemporary Life* (New York: Basic Books, 1991).

Gilbert, M. *On Social Facts* (Princeton University Press, 1989).

Gill, C. *The Structured Self in Hellenistic and Roman Thought* (Oxford University Press, 2006).

The ancient self: Issues and approaches. In P. Remes and J. Sihvola (eds.) *Ancient Philosophy of the Self* (New York: Springer, 2008) 35–56.

Gillespie, A. G. H. Mead: Theorist of the social act. *Journal for the Theory of Social Behaviour* 35 (2005) 19–39.

Games and the development of perspective taking. *Human Development* 49 (2006) 87–92.

Position exchange: The social development of agency. *New Ideas in Psychology* 30 (2012) 32–46.

Gillespie, A. and Cornish, F. What can be said? Identity as a constraint on knowledge production. *Papers on Social Representations* **19** (5) (2010) 1–13.

Gillespie, A. and Richardson, B. Exchanging social positions: Enhancing perspective taking within a cooperative problem solving task. *European Journal of Social Psychology* **40** (2011) 1–9.

Gintis, H., Bowles, S., Boyd, R., and Fehr, E. Explaining altruistic behavior in humans. *Evolution and Human Behavior* **24** (2003) 153–172.

Goldman, A. *Simulating Minds: The Philosophy, Psychology and Neuroscience of Mindreading* (Oxford University Press, 2006).

Goldstein, J. *Console and Classify: The French Psychiatric Profession in the Nineteenth Century* (Cambridge University Press, 1987).

Gordon, N. Foucault's subject: An ontological reading. *Polity* **31** (1995) 395–414.

Green, C. D., Shore, M. and Teo, T. *The Transformation of Psychology: Influences of 19th-Century Philosophy, Technology, and Natural Science* (Washington, DC: American Psychological Association, 2004).

Greenberg, J. R., Hamann, K., Warneken, F., and Tomasello, M. Chimpanzee helping in collaborative and noncollaborative contexts. *Animal Behaviour* **80** (2010) 873–880.

Greer, S. Is there a "self" in self research? Or, how measuring the self made it disappear. *Social Practice/Psychological Theorizing* **1** (2007) 51–68.

Gregg, G. S. The raw and the bland: A structural model of narrative identity. In D. P. McAdams, R. Josselson, and A. Lieblich (eds.) *Identity and Story: Creating Self in Narrative* (Washington, DC: American Psychological Association, 2006) 63–88.

Guignon, C., History and commitment in the early Heidegger. In H. L. Dreyfus and H. Hall (eds.) *Heidegger: A Critical Reader* (Oxford: Blackwell, 1992).

Heidegger's concept of freedom, 1927–1930. In D. Dahlstrom (ed.) *Interpreting Heidegger: Critical Essays* (Cambridge University Press, 2011) 79–105.

Gurevich, A. *The Origins of European Individualism* (Oxford: Blackwell, 1995).

Habermas, T. and Bluck, S. Getting a life: The emergence of the life story in adolescence. *Psychological Bulletin* **126** (2000) 748–769.

Hacker, P. M. S. *Wittgenstein: Mind and Will, Vol. 4 of an Analytical Commentary on the Philosophical Investigations* (Oxford: Blackwell, 1996).

Human Nature: The Categorial Framework (Oxford: Blackwell, 2007).

Hacking, I. *Rewriting the Soul: Multiple Personality and the Sciences of Memory* (Princeton University Press, 1995).

The looping effect of human kinds. In D. Sperber, D. Premack, and A. J. Premack (eds.) *Causal Cognition: A Multidisciplinary Debate* (Oxford: Clarendon, 1995) 351–383.

Mad Travellers: Reflections on the Reality of Transient Mental Illness (Charlottesville, VA: University of Virginia Press, 1998).

Historical Ontology (Cambridge, MA: Harvard University Press, 2002).

Between Michel Foucault and Erving Goffman: Between discourse in the abstract and face-to-face interaction. *Economy and Society* **33** (2004) 277–302.

Kinds of People: Moving Targets. The Tenth British Academy Lecture (London, 2006, April 11).

Natural Kinds: Rosy Dawn, Scholastic Twilight. Paper presented to the Royal Institute of Philosophy (London, 2006, February 17).

Hadot, P. *Philosophy as a Way of Life* (Oxford: Blackwell, 1995).

Hankiss, A. On the mythological rearranging of one's life history. In D. Bertaux (ed.) *Biography and Society: The Life History Approach in the Social Sciences* (Beverly Hills, CA: Sage, 1981) 203–209.

Hansen, W. Review of William Stern's *Psychologie der Frühen Kindheit*, zweite Auflage [Review of William Stern's *Psychology of Early Childhood*, second edition]. *Virteljahresschrift für wissenschaftliche Pädagogik* 8 (1922) 121–122.

Hare, B. From hominoid to hominid mind: What changed and why? *Annual Review of Anthropology* 40 (2011) 293–309.

Harré, R. *Personal Being: A Theory for Individual Psychology* (Cambridge, MA: Harvard University Press, 1984).

Cognitive Science: A Philosophical Introduction (London: Sage, 2002).

Discursive psychology and the boundaries of sense. *Organization Studies* 25 (2004) 1,435–1,453.

Harré, R. and Gillett, G. *The Discursive Mind* (Thousand Oaks, CA: Sage Publications, 1994).

Harré, R. and Tissaw, M. A. *Wittgenstein and Psychology: A Practical Guide* (Aldershot: Ashgate, 2005).

Harré, R. and Van Langenhove, L. Varieties of positioning. *Journal for the Theory of Social Behavior* 21 (1991) 393–407.

(eds.) *Positioning Theory: Moral Contexts of Intentional Actions* (Oxford: Blackwell, 1999).

Harré, R., Moghaddam, F. M., Cairnie, T. P., Rothbart, D., and Sabat, S. R. Recent advances in positioning theory. *Theory and Psychology* 19 (2009) 5–31.

Heidegger, M. *Being and Time*, J. Macquarrie and E. Robinson (trans.) (New York: Harper and Row, 1962, orig. 1927).

The Concept of Time, W. McNeill (trans.) of a 1924 lecture (Oxford: Blackwell, 1992, orig. 1989).

Martin Heidegger: Basic writings, D. F. Krell (ed.) (San Francisco: Harper, 1993).

Basic Concepts of Ancient Philosophy, R. Rojcewicz (trans.) (Bloomington: Indiana University Press, 2008, orig. 1993).

The Essence of Human Freedom: An Introduction to Philosophy, T. Sadler (trans.) (London: Continuum, 2005, orig. 1982).

Heilbrun, G. C. *Writing a Woman's Life* (New York: Norton, 1988).

Held, L. I., Jr. *Quirks of Human Anatomy: An Evo-devo Look at the Human Body* (Cambridge University Press, 2009).

Hermans, H. J. M. Voicing the self: From information processing to dialogical interchange. *Psychological Bulletin* 119 (1) (1996) 31–50.

The dialogical self: Toward a theory of personal and cultural positioning. *Culture and Psychology* 7 (3) (2001) 243–281.

Hermans, H. J. M. and Dimaggio, G. Self, identity, and globalization in times of uncertainty: A dialogical analysis. *Review of General Psychology* 11 (2007) 31–61.

Hermans, H. J. M. and Hermans-Konopka, A. *Dialogical Self Theory: Positioning and Counter-positioning in a Globalizing Society* (Cambridge University Press, 2010).

Hobbes, T. *Leviathan* (Oxford: Clarendon Press, 2006, orig. 1651).

Hofstee, W. K. B. *Unbehagen* in individual differences – a review. *Journal of Individual Differences* 28 (2007) 252–253.

Holiday, A. *Moral Powers: Normative Necessity in Language and History* (London: Routledge, 1988).

Hollis, M. Of masks and men. In M. Carrithers, S. Collins, and S. Lukes (eds.) *The Category of the Person: Anthropology, Philosophy, History* (Cambridge University Press, 1985) 217–233.

Hooker, C. A. Interaction and bio-cognitive order. *Synthese* 166 (3) (2009) 513–546.

Humphrey, N. K. The social function of intellect. In P. P. G. Bateson and R. A. Hinde (eds.) *Growing Points in Ethology* (London: Cambridge University Press, 1976) 303–317.

Hundert, E. J. The European Enlightenment and the history of the self. In R. Porter (ed.) *Rewriting the Self: Histories from the Renaissance to the Present* (London: Routledge, 1997) 72–83.

Ilyenkov, E. V. *The Dialectics of the Abstract and the Concrete in Marx's Capital* (Moscow: Progress, 1982).

Jablonka, E. and Lamb, M. J. *Evolution in Four Dimensions* (Cambridge, MA: MIT Press, 2005).

James, W. *Psychology* (Greenwich, CT: Fawcett, 1892/1963).

Janet, P. *L'Automatisme Psychologique: Essai de Psychologie Expérimentale sur les Formes Inférieures de l'Activité Humaine* (Paris: Alcan, 1889).

Jensen, K., Hare, B., Call, J., and Tomasello, M. What's in it for me? Self-regard precludes altruism and spite in chimpanzees. *Proceedings of the Royal Society: B* 273 (2006) 1,013–1,021.

John, O. P., Angleitner, A., and Ostendorf, F. The lexical approach to personality: A historical review of trait taxonomic research. *European Journal of Personality* 2 (1988), 171–203.

Josselson, R. *Finding herself: Pathways to Identity Development in Women* (San Francisco: Jossey-Bass, 1987).

The Space Between Us: Exploring the Dimensions of Human Relationships (San Francisco: Jossey-Bass, 1992).

(ed.) *Ethics and Process in the Narrative Study of Lives. The Narrative Study of Lives, Vol. 4* (Thousand Oaks, CA: Sage, 1996).

Revising herself: The Story of Women's Identity from College to Midlife (New York: Oxford University Press, 1996).

Josselson, R. and Lieblich, A. (eds.) *The Narrative Study of Lives, Vol. 1* (Thousand Oaks, CA: Sage, 1993).

(eds.) *Interpreting Experience: The Narrative Study of Lives, Vol. 3* (Thousand Oaks, CA: Sage, 1995).

(eds.) *Making Meaning of Narratives. The Narrative Study of Lives, Vol. 6* (Thousand Oaks, CA: Sage, 1999).

Josselson, R., Lieblich, A., and McAdams, D. P. (eds.) *Up Close and Personal: The Teaching and Learning of Narrative Research* (Washington, DC: American Psychological Association, 2003).

(eds.) *The Meaning of Others: Narrative Studies of Relationships* (Washington, DC: American Psychological Association, 2007).

Kelley, D. R. *The Human Measure: Social Thought in the Western Legal Traditions* (Cambridge, MA: Harvard University Press, 1990).

Kerby, A. P. *Narrative and the Self* (Bloomington, IN: Indiana University Press, 1991).

Kirschner, S. R. and Martin, J. (eds.) *The Sociocultural Turn in Psychology: the Contextual Emergence of Mind and Self* (New York: Columbia University Press, 2010).

Kraus, W. The narrative negotiation of identity and belonging. *Narrative Inquiry* **16** (1) (2006) 103–111.

Labov, W. Speech actions and reactions in personal narratives. In D. Tannen (ed.) *Analyzing Discourse: Text and Talk* (Washington, DC: Georgetown University Press, 1982) 219–247.

Labov, W. and Waletzky, J. Narrative analysis: Oral versions of personal experience. In J. Helm (ed.) *Essays on the Verbal and Visual Arts* (Seattle, WA: American Ethnological Society, 1967) 12–44.

Lamiell, J. T. William Stern: More than "the I.Q. Guy." In G. A. Kimble, C. Alan Boneau, and M. Wertheimer (eds.) *Portraits of Pioneers in Psychology, Vol. 2* (Washington, DC, and Mahwah, NJ: American Psychological Association Books and Lawrence Erlbaum Associates, 1996).

Individuals and the differences between them. In R. Hogan, J. Johnson, and S. Briggs (eds.) *Handbook of Personality Psychology* (New York: Academic Press, 1997) 117–141.

Beyond Individual and Group Differences: Human Individuality, Scientific Psychology, and William Stern's Critical Personalism (London: Sage, 2003).

William Stern (1871–1938) und der "Ursprungsmythos" der differentiellen Psychologie. *Journal für Psychologie* **14** (2006) 253–273.

On sustaining critical discourse with mainstream personality investigators: Problems and prospects. *Theory and Psychology* **17** (2007) 169–185.

Psychology and personalism. *New Ideas in Psychology* **28** (2010) 110–134.

William Stern (1871–1938): A Brief Introduction to His Life and Works (Lengerich, Germany: Pabst Science Publishers, 2010).

Statisticism in personality psychologists' use of trait constructs: What is it? How was it contracted? Is there a cure? *New Ideas in Psychology*, in press.

Lamiell, J. T. and Deutsch, W. (eds.) Psychology and critical personalism: A special issue. *Theory and Psychology* **10** (2000) 715–876.

Lamiell, J. T. and Laux, L. (eds.) Personalistic thinking: A special issue. *New Ideas in Psychology* **28** (2010) 105–262.

Leesen, T. G. *Gaius meets Cicero: Law and Rhetoric in the School Controversies* (Leiden: Nijhoff, 2010).

Leontiev, A. N. *Problems of the Development of Mind* (Moscow: Progress Publishers, 1981).

Levinas, E. *Ethics and Infinity* (Pittsburgh, PA: Duquesne University Press, 1985).
Outside the Subject (Palo Alto, CA: Stanford University Press, 1994).
Substitution. In A. T. Peperzak, S. Critchley, and R. Bernasconi (eds.) *Emmanuel Levinas: Basic Philosophical Writings* (Bloomington, IN: Indiana University Press, 1996) 80–95.
Alterity and Transcendence (New York: Columbia University Press, 1999).

Lévi-Strauss, C. (ed.) *L'Identité* (Paris: Presses Universitaires de France, 1977) 9–12.

Lewis, D. K. *Convention* (Cambridge, MA: Harvard University Press, 1969).

Lewis, M. D. The dialogical brain: Contributions of emotional neurobiology to understanding the dialogical self. *Theory and Psychology* **12** (2002) 175–190.

Lieblich, A. and Josselson, R. (eds.) *Exploring Identity and Gender. The Narrative Study of Lives, Vol. 2* (Thousand Oaks, CA: Sage, 1994).
(eds.) *The Narrative Study of Lives, Vol. 5* (Thousand Oaks, CA: Sage, 1997).

Lieblich, A., McAdams, D. P., and Josselson, R. (eds.) *Healing Plots: The Narrative Basis of Psychotherapy* (Washington, DC: American Psychological Association, 2004).

Lieblich, A., Tuval-Mashiach, R., and Zilber, T. *Narrative Research: Reading, Analysis and Interpretation* (Thousand Oaks, CA: Sage, 1998).

Linde, C. *Life Stories: The Creation of Coherence* (New York: Oxford University Press, 1993).

Locke, J. *An Essay Concerning Human Understanding* (New York: Dover, 1959), Book II.

Loftus, E. *Memory* (New York: Addison-Wesley, 1980).

Lombardo, G. P. and Foschi, R. The concept of personality in 19th-century French and 20th-century American psychology. *History of Psychology*, **6** (2003) 123–142.

Lück, H. E. and Löwisch, D.-J. (eds.) *Der Briefwechsel Zwischen William Stern und Jonas Cohn: Dokumente einer Freundschaft Zwischen Zwei Wissenschaftlern* (Frankfurt am Main: Peter Lang Verlag, 1994).

Luhmann, N. The individuality of the individual: Historical meanings and contemporary problems. In T. C. Heller, M. Sosna, and D. E. Wellbery (eds.) *Reconstructing Individualism: Autonomy, Individuality and the Self in Western Thought* (Stanford, CA: Stanford University Press, 1986) 313–325.

MacIntyre, A. *After Virtue: A Study in Moral Theory* (Notre Dame, IN: Indiana University Press, 1981).

Marcia, J. E. Development and validation of ego-identity status. *Journal of Personality and Social Psychology* **3** (5) (1966) 551–558.

Marino, L., Connor, R. C., Fordyce, R. E., Herman, L. M., Hof, P. R. *et al.* Cetaceans have complex brains for complex cognition. *PLOS Biology* **5** (2007) 966–972.

Martin, J. Positions, perspectives, and persons. *Human Development* **49** (2006) 93–95.
Reinterpreting internalization and agency through G. H. Mead's perspectival realism. *Human Development* **49** (2006) 65–86.

Martin, J. and Gillespie, A. A neo-Meadian approach to human agency: Relating the social and the psychological in the ontogenesis of perspective-coordinating persons. *Integrative Psychological and Behavioral Science* **44** (2010) 252–272.

Martin, J. and Sugarman, J. *The Psychology of Human Possibility and Constraint* (Albany: State University of New York Press, 1999).

A theory of personhood for psychology. In D. B. Hill and M. J. Kral (eds.) *About Psychology: Essays at the Crossroads of History, Theory and Philosophy* (Albany, NY: State University of New York Press, 2003) 73–87.

Martin, J., Sokol, B., and Elfers, T. Taking and coordinating perspectives: From pre-reflective interactivity, through reflective intersubjectivity, to meta-reflective sociality. *Human Development* **51** (2008) 294–317.

Martin, J., Sugarman, J., and Thompson, J. *Psychology and the Question of Agency* (Albany, NY: State University of New York Press, 2003).

Marx, K. Theses on Feuerbach. In R. C. Tucker (ed.) *The Marx–Engels Reader*, second edn (New York: W. W. Norton, 1978) 143–146.

Marx, K. and Engels, F. The German ideology. In R. C. Tucker (ed.) *The Marx–Engels Reader*, second edn (New York: W. W. Norton, 1978) 146–200.

Mascuch, M. *Origins of the Individualist Self: Autobiography and Self-identity in England, 1571–1791* (Stanford, CA: Stanford University Press, 1996).

McAdams, D. P. *Power, Intimacy and the Life Story: Personological Inquiries into Identity* (New York: The Guilford Press, 1985).

Biography, narrative, and lives: An introduction. *Journal of Personality* **56** (1) (1988) 1–18.

The Stories We Live By: Personal Myths and the Making of the Self (New York: William Morrow, 1993).

A conceptual history of personality psychology. In R. Hogan, J. Johnson, and S. Briggs (eds.) *Handbook of Personality Psychology* (San Diego: Academic Press, 1997) 3–39.

The case for unity in the (post)modern self: A modest proposal. In R. Ashmore and L. Jussim (eds.) *Self and Identity: Fundamental Issues* (New York: Oxford University Press, 1997) 46–78.

The Person: An Integrated Introduction to Personality Psychology, third edn (Fort Worth: Harcourt College Publishers, 2001).

McAdams, D. P. and Bowman, P. J. Narrating life's turning points: Redemption and contamination. In D. P. McAdams, R. Josselson, and A. Lieblich (eds.) *Turns in the Road: Narrative Studies of Lives in Transition* (Washington, DC: American Psychological Association, 2001) 3–34.

McAdams, D. P. and Logan, R. L. Creative work, love and the dialectic in selected life stories of academics. In D. P. McAdams, R. Josselson, and A. Lieblich (eds.) *Identity and Story: Creating Self in Narrative* (Washington, DC: American Psychological Association, 2006) 89–108.

McAdams, D. P. and Pals, J. L. A new big five: Fundamental principles for an integrative science of personality. *American Psychologist* **61** (2006) 204–217.

McAdams, D. P., Josselson R., and Lieblich A. (eds.) *Turns in the Road: Narrative Studies of Lives in Transition* (Washington, DC: American Psychological Association, 2001) 3–34.

(eds.) *Identity and Story: Creating Self in Narrative* (Washington, DC: American Psychological Association, 2006).

McCarthy, T. The critique of impure reason: Foucault and the Frankfurt School. *Political Theory* **18** (1990) 437–469.

McCrae, R. R. and Costa, P. T. Jr. Trait explanations in personality psychology. *European Journal of Personality* **9** (1997) 231–252.

Mead, G. H. *The Philosophy of the Present*, A. E. Murphy (ed.) (University of Chicago Press, 1932).

Mind, Self, and Society from the Standpoint of a Social Behaviorist, C. W. Morris (ed.) (University of Chicago Press, 1934).

The Philosophy of the Act, C. W. Morris *et al.* (eds.) (University of Chicago Press, 1938).

Miller, P. and Rose, N. *Governing the Present: Administering Economic, Social and Personal Life* (Cambridge: Polity, 2008).

Misch, G. *A History of Autobiography in Antiquity* (London: Routledge, 1950).

Mischel, W. *Personality and Assessment* (New York: Wiley, 1968).

Mishler, E. G. *Storylines: Craftartists' Narratives of Identity* (Cambridge, MA: Harvard University Press, 1999).

Moghaddam, F. M., Harré, R., and Lee, N. (eds.) *Global Conflict Resolution Through Positioning Analysis* (New York: Springer, 2008).

Momigliano, A. Marcel Mauss and the quest for the person in Greek biography and autobiography. In M. Carrithers, S. Collins, and S. Lukes (eds.) *The Category of the Person: Anthropology, Philosophy, History* (Cambridge University Press, 1985) 83–92.

Moore, C. Representing intentional relations and acting intentionally in infancy: Current insights and open questions. In G. Knoblich, I. Thornton, M. Grosjean, and M. Shiffrar (eds.) *Human Body Perception from the Inside Out* (New York: Oxford University Press, 2006) 427–442.

Moore, C. and Barresi, J. The construction of commonsense psychology in infancy. In P. Zelazo, M. Chandler, and E. Crone (eds.) *Developmental Social Cognitive Neuroscience* (New York: Psychology Press, 2009) 43–62.

Moore, C. and Lemmon, K. (eds.) *The Self in Time: Developmental Perspectives* (Hillsdale, NJ: Erlbaum, 2001).

Moore, C., Barresi, J., and Thompson, C. The cognitive basis of future-oriented prosocial behavior. *Social Development* **7** (1998) 198–218.

Mulhall, S. Hacker on human nature. *The Philosophical Quarterly* **60** (2009) 406–412.

Münsterberg, H. *Grundzüge der Psychologie [Foundations of Psychology]* (Leipzig: Barth, 1900).

Psychology and Industrial Efficiency (Boston and New York: Houghton-Mifflin, 1913).

Murdoch, I. *The Sovereignty of Good* (London: Routledge, 1970).

Metaphysics as a Guide to Morals (London: Penguin, 1993).

Myerhoff, B. C. *Number our Days* (New York: Simon and Schuster, 1978).

Newen, A. and Schlicht, T. Understanding other minds: A criticism of Goldman's simulation theory and an outline of the person model theory. *Grazer Philosophische Studien* **79** (2009) 209–242.

Nicholson, I. A. M. *Inventing Personality: Gordon Allport and the Science of Selfhood* (Washington, DC: American Psychological Association, 2003).

Nielsen, M. The imitative behaviour of children and chimpanzees: A window on the transmission of cultural traditions. *Primatologie* (in press).

Nowak, M. A. Five rules for the evolution of cooperation. *Science* **314** (2006) 1,560–1,563.

Olney, J. *Memory and Narrative: The Weave of Life Writing* (Chicago University Press, 1998).

Osborne, T. and Rose, N. Do the social sciences create phenomena? The example of public opinion research. *British Journal of Sociology* **50** (1999) 367–396.

Pack, A. and Herman, L. M. Dolphin social cognition and joint attention: Our current understanding. *Aquatic Mammals* **32** (2006) 443–460.

Pals, J. L. Constructing the "springboard effect": Causal connections, self-making and growth within the life story. In D. P. McAdams, R. Josselson, and A. Lieblich (eds.) *Identity and Story: Creating Self in Narrative* (Washington, DC: American Psychological Association, 2006) 175–200.

Narrative identity processing of difficult life experiences: Pathways of personality development and possible self-transformation in adulthood. *Journal of Personality* **74** (2006) 1,079–1,110.

Pepper, S. *World Hypotheses* (Berkeley: University of California Press, 1942).

Plutarch, *Greek Lives: A Selection of Nine Greek Lives*, R. Waterfield (trans.) (New York: Oxford University Press, 1998).

Roman Lives: A Selection of Eight Roman Lives, R. Waterfield (trans.) (New York: Oxford University Press, 1999).

Polkinghorne, D. *Narrative Knowing and the Human Sciences* (New York: State University of New York Press, 1988).

Narrative configuration in qualitative analysis. *International Journal of Qualitative Studies in Education* **8** (1995) 5–23.

Porter, T. M. *The Rise of Statistical Thinking: 1820–1900* (Princeton University Press, 1986).

Poulet, G. *Studies in Human Time* (New York: Harper, 1959).

Premack, D. and Woodruff, G. Does the chimpanzee have a theory of mind? *Behavioral and Brain Sciences* **1** (1978) 515–525.

Prilleltensky, I. Values, assumptions, and practices. Assessing the moral implications of psychological discourse and action. *American Psychologist* **52** (1997) 517–535.

Reiss, T. J. *Mirages of the Selfe: Patterns of Personhood in Ancient and Early Modern Europe* (Stanford, CA: Stanford University Press, 2003).

Reissman, C. K. Narrative analysis. In M. S. Lewis-Beck, A. Bryman, and T. Futing Liao (eds.) *The SAGE Encyclopedia of Social Science Research Methods* (Thousand Oaks, CA: Sage, 2004) 705–709.

Reissman, C. K. and Speedy, J. Narrative inquiry in the psychotherapy professions: A critical review. In J. D. Clandinin (ed.) *Handbook of Narrative Inquiry: Mapping a Methodology* (Thousand Oaks, CA: Sage, 2007) 426–456.

Ribot, T. *Les Maladies de la Personnalité* [*Diseases of the Personality*] (Paris: Alcan, 1885).

Richardson, F. C., Fowers, B. J., and Guignon, C. B. *Re-envisioning Psychology: Moral Dimensions of Theory and Practice* (San Francisco: Jossey-Bass, 1999).

Ricoeur, P. *Freud and Philosophy: An Essay on Interpretation* (New Haven, CT: Yale University Press, 1970).

The Conflict of Interpretations (Evanston, IL: Northwestern University Press, 1974).

Hermeneutics and the Human Sciences (Cambridge University Press, 1981).

Narrative time. In W. J. T. Mitchell (ed.) *On Narrative* (University of Chicago Press, 1981) 165–186.

Life in quest of narrative. In D. Wood (ed.) *On Paul Ricoeur: Narrative and Interpretation* (London: Routledge, 1991) 20–33.

Oneself as Another (University of Chicago Press, 1992).

Rimmon-Kenan, S. The story of "I": Illness and narrative identity. *Narrative* **10** (1) (2002) 9–27.

Rogers, A. G. The unsayable, Lacanian psychoanalysis, and the art of narrative interviewing. In J. D. Clandinin (ed.) *Handbook of Narrative Inquiry* (Thousand Oaks, CA: Sage, 2007) 99–119.

Rose, N. Power and subjectivity: Critical history and psychology. In C. F. Graumann and K. Gergen (eds.) *Historical Dimensions of Psychological Discourse* (Cambridge University Press, 1996) 103–124.

Assembling the modern self. In R. Porter (ed.) *Rewriting the Self: Histories from the Renaissance to the Present* (New York: Routledge, 1997) 224–248.

Inventing Ourselves: Psychology, Power, and Personhood (Cambridge University Press, 1998).

Governing the Soul: The Shaping of the Private Self, 2nd edn (London: Free Association Books, 1999).

Rosenwald, G. C. and Ochberg, R. L. (eds.) *Storied Lives: The Cultural Politics of Self-understanding* (New Haven, CT: Yale University Press, 1992).

Rousseau, J.-J. *The Confessions of Jean-Jacques Rousseau*, J. M. Cohen (trans.) (Harmondsworth: Penguin, 1953).

Rychlak, J. F. *A Philosophy of Science for Personality Theory*, second edn (Malabar, FL: Krieger, 1981).

The Psychology of Rigorous Humanism, second edn (New York University Press, 1988).

Sarbin, T. R. (ed.) *Narrative Psychology: The Storied Nature of Human Conduct* (New York: Praeger, 1986).

Sartre, J.-P. *Essays in Existentialism* (Secaucus, NJ: The Citadel Press, 1964).

Sawchuk, P. and Stetsenko, A. Sociology for a non-canonical activity theory: Exploring intersections and complementarities. *Mind, Culture and Activity* **15** (2008) 339–360.

Sawicki, J. *Disciplining Foucault: Feminism, Power, and the Body* (London: Routledge, 1991).

Schacter, D. L. *The Seven Sins of Memory (How the Mind Forgets and Remembers)* (Boston, MA: Houghton Mifflin, 2001).

Scheibe, K. E. Self narratives and adventure. In T. R. Sarbin (ed.) *Narrative Psychology: The Storied Nature of Human Conduct* (New York: Praeger, 1986) 129–151.

Schelling, T. C. *The Strategy of Conflict* (New York: Oxford University Press, 1963).

Schore, A. N. *Affect Regulation and the Origin of the Self: The Neurobiology of Emotional Development* (Hillsdale, NJ: Erlbaum, 1994).

Early organization of the nonlinear right brain and development of a predisposition to psychiatric disorders. *Development and Psychopathology* **9** (1997) 595–631.

Seemann, A. Person perception. *Philosophical Explorations* **11** (2008) 245–262.

Sellars, W. *Science, Perception, and Reality* (Atascadero, CA: Ridgeview Press, 1963).

Sheringham, M. *French Autobiography Devices and Desires: Rousseau to Perec* (Oxford: Clarendon Press, 1993).

Shostak, M. *Nisa: The Life and Words of a !Kung Woman* (Cambridge, MA: Harvard University Press, 1981).

Shotter, J. and Gergen, K. J. (eds.) *Texts of identity* (London: Sage, 1989).

Singer, J. A. Narrative identity and meaning making across the adult lifespan: An introduction. *Journal of Personality* **72** (3) (2004) 437–460.

Spence, D. P. *Narrative Truth and Historical Truth* (New York: W. W. Norton, 1982).

Spencer, J. P., Blumberg, M. S., McMurray, B., Robinson, S. R., Samuelson, L. K., and Tomblin, J. B. Short arms and talking eggs: Why we abide the nativist-empiricist debate. *Child Development Perspectives* **2** (2009) 79–87.

Stam, H. J. The dispersal of subjectivity and the problem of persons in psychology. In W. E. Smythe (ed.) *Toward a Psychology of Persons* (Mahwah, NJ: Erlbaum, 1998) 221–244.

Stern, W. *Über Psychologie der Individuellen Differenzen (Ideen zu einer "Differentiellen Psychologie")* [*On the Psychology of Individual Differences (Toward a "Differential Psychology")*] (Leipzig: Barth, 1900).

Person und Sache: System der Philosophischen Weltanschauung. Erster Band: Ableitung und Grundlehre [*Person and Thing: A Systematic Philosophical Worldview. Vol. 1: Rationale and Basic Tenets*] (Leipzig: Barth, 1906).

Die Differentielle Psychologie in ihren Methodischen Grundlagen [*Methodological Foundations of Differential Psychology*] (Leipzig: Barth, 1911).

Psychologie [Psychology]. In D. Sarason (ed.) *Das Jahr 1913: Ein Gesamtbild der Kulturentwicklung* (Leipzig/Berlin: Teubner, 1914) 414–421.

Vorgedanken zur Weltanschauung [*Preliminary Ideas Toward a Worldview*] (Leipzig: Barth, 1915).

Die Psychologie und der Personalismus [*Psychology and Personalism*] (Leipzig: Barth, 1917).

Person und Sache: System der Philosophischen Weltanschauung. Zweiter Band: Die Menschliche Persönlichkeit [*Person and Thing: A Systematic Philosophical Worldview. Vol. 2: The Human Personality*] (Leipzig: Barth, 1918).

Psychologie der Frühen Kindheit bis zum Sechsten Lebensjahre, zweite Auflage [*Psychology of Early Childhood up to the Sixth Year of Life*, 2nd edn.] (Leipzig: Quelle and Meyer, 1921).

Person und Sache: System des Kritischen Personalismus. Dritter Band: Wertphiloso-phie [Person and Thing: The System of Critical Personalism. Vol. 3: Philosophy of Value] (Leipzig: Barth, 1924).

Selbstdarstellung [Self-portrayal]. In R. Schmidt (ed.) *Philosophie der Gegenwart in Selbstdarstellung, Vol. 6* (Leipzig: Barth, 1927) 128–184.

Personalistische Psychologie [Personalistic psychology]. In E. Saupe (ed.) *Einführung in die Neuere Psychologie* (Osterwieck am Harz: A. W. Zickfeldt Verlag, 1927).

Studien zur Personwissenschaft, Erster Teil: Personalistik als Wissenschaft [Studies in the Science of Persons, Part One: Personalistics as Science] (Leipzig: Barth, 1930).

William Stern, S. Langer (trans.). In C. Murchison (ed.) *A History of Psychology in Autobiography, Vol. 1* (Worcester, MA: Clark University Press, 1930) 335–388.

General Psychology from the Personalistic Standpoint, H. D. Spoerl (trans.) (New York: The Macmillan Company, 1938).

Allgemeine Psychologie auf Personalistischer Grundlage (Den Haag: Nijhoff, 1950).

Psychology and personalism, J. T. Lamiell (trans.) *New Ideas in Psychology* 28 (2010) 110–134.

Stetsenko, A. Introduction to "tool and sign" by Lev Vygotsky. In R. Rieber and D. Robbinson (eds.) *Essential Vygotsky* (New York: Kluwer Academic/Plenum, 2004) 499–510.

Activity as object-related: Resolving the dichotomy of individual and collective planes of activity. *Mind, Culture, and Activity* 12 (2005) 70–88.

Being-through-doing: Bakhtin and Vygotsky in dialogue. *Cultural Studies of Science Education* 2 (2007) 25–37.

From relational ontology to transformative activist stance on development and learning: Expanding Vygotsky's (CHAT) project. *Cultural Studies of Science Education* 3 (2008) 471–491.

Vygotsky and the conceptual revolution in developmental sciences: Towards a unified (non-additive) account of human development. In M. Fleer, M. Hedegaard, J. Tudge, and A. Prout (eds.) *World Year Book of Education. Constructing Childhood: Global–Local Policies and Practices* (London: Routledge, 2009) 125–142.

Standing on the shoulders of giants: A balancing act of dialectically theorizing conceptual understanding on the grounds of Vygotsky's project. In W.-M. Roth and K. Tobin (eds.) *Re/structuring Science Education: ReUniting Psychological and Sociological Perspectives* (New York: Springer, 2010) 53–72.

Teaching-learning and development as activist projects of historical Becoming: Expanding Vygotsky's approach to pedagogy. *Pedagogies: An International Journal* 5 (2010) 6–16.

Personhood: An activist project of historical becoming through collaborative pursuits of social transformation. *New Ideas in Psychology* 30 (2012) 144–153.

Stetsenko, A. and Arievitch, I. M. The self in cultural-historical activity theory: Reclaiming the unity of social and individual dimensions of human development. *Theory and Psychology* **14** (2004) 475–503.

Vygotskian collaborative project of social transformation: History, politics, and practice in knowledge construction. *The International Journal of Critical Psychology* **12** (2004) 58–80.

Cultural-historical activity theory: Foundational worldview and major principles. In J. Martin and S. Kirschner (eds.) *Sociocultural Perspectives in Psychology: The Contextual Emergence of Mind and Self* (New York: Columbia University Press, 2010) 231–253.

Stevens, J. R. and Hauser, M. D. Why be nice? Psychological constraints on the evolution of cooperation. *Trends in Cognitive Sciences* **8** (2004) 60–65.

Strawson, P. F. *Individuals: An Essay in Descriptive Metaphysics* (London: Methuen, 1959).

Suddendorf, T. and Corballis, M. C. The evolution of foresight: What is mental time travel, and is it unique to humans? *Behavioral and Brain Sciences* **30** (2007) 299–351.

Sugarman, J. Persons and moral agency. *Theory and Psychology* **15** (2005) 793–811.

Historical ontology and psychological description. *Journal of Theoretical and Philosophical Psychology* **29** (2009) 5–15.

Practical rationality and the questionable promise of positive psychology. *Journal of Humanistic Psychology* **47** (2007) 175–197.

Sulloway, F. J. *Freud: Biologist of the Mind* (New York: Basic Books, 1979).

Tanner, L. N. *Dewey's Laboratory School* (New York: Teachers College Press, 1997).

Taylor, C. *Human Agency and Language: Philosophical Papers 1* (Cambridge University Press, 1985).

Language and human nature. In C. Taylor, *Human Agency and Language: Philosophical Papers I* (Cambridge University Press, 1985) 215–247.

Sources of the Self: The Making of the Modern Identity (Cambridge, MA: Harvard University Press, 1989).

The Ethics of Authenticity (Cambridge, MA: Harvard University Press, 1991).

Philosophical Arguments (Cambridge, MA: Harvard University Press, 1995).

Taylor, S. *Positive Illusions: Creative Self-deception and the Healthy Mind* (New York: Basic Books, 1991).

Thompson, C., Barresi, J., and Moore, C. The development of future-oriented prudence and altruism in preschool children. *Cognitive Development* **12** (1997) 199–212.

Thorndike, E. L. *Individuality* (New York: Houghton-Mifflin, 1911).

Thorne, A. Personal memory telling and personality development. *Personality and Social Psychology Review* **4** (2000) 45–56.

Tissaw, M. A. Psychological symbiosis: Personalistic and constructionist considerations. *Theory and Psychology* **10** (2000) 847–876.

Making sense of neonatal imitation. *Theory and Psychology* **17** (2007) 217–242.

A critical look at critical (neo)personalism: *Unitas multiplex* and the "person" concept. *New Ideas in Psychology* **28** (2010) 159–167.

Tomasello, M. and Moll, H. The gap is social: Human shared intentionality and culture. In P. M. Kappeler and J. B. Silk (eds.) *Mind the Gap* (Berlin/Heidelberg: Springer Verlag, 2010) 331–349.

Tomasello, M., Carpenter, M., Call, J., Behne, T., and Moll, H. Understanding and sharing intentions: The origins of cultural cognition. *Behavioral and Brain Sciences* 28 (2005) 675–735.

Toulmin, S. and Leary, D. E. The cult of empiricism in psychology, and beyond. In S. Koch and D. E. Leary (eds.) *A Century of Psychology as Science* (New York: McGraw-Hill, 1985) 594–617.

Trivers, R. L. The evolution of reciprocal altruism. *Quarterly Review of Biology* 46 (1971) 35–57.

Social Evolution (Menlo Park: Benjamin/Cummings Publishing Company, 1985).

Natural Selection and Social Theory: Selected Papers of Robert L. Trivers (Evolution and Cognition Series) (Oxford University Press, 2002).

Reciprocal altruism 30 years later. In P. M. Kappeler and C. P. van Schaik (eds.) *Cooperation in Primates and Humans: Mechanisms and Evolution* (Berlin: Springer-Verlag, 2006) 67–83.

Tschechne, M. *William Stern* (Hamburg: Ellert and Richter Verlag, 2010).

Tuval-Mashiach, R. "Where is the story going?" Narrative forms and identity construction in the life stories of Israeli men and women. In D. P. McAdams, R. Josselson, and A. Lieblich (eds.) *Identity and Story: Creating Self in Narrative* (Washington, DC: American Psychological Association, 2006) 249–268.

Valsiner, J. Toward a new science of the person. *Theory and Psychology* 15 (2005) 401–406.

Valsiner, J. and van der Veer, R. *The Social Mind: Construction of the Idea* (Cambridge University Press, 2000).

Verwey, G. *Psychiatry in an Anthropological and Biomedical Context* (Dordrecht: Reidel, 1985).

Vygotsky, L. S. *Thought and Language*, M. i Rech' (trans.) and A. Kozulin (ed.) (Cambridge, MA: The MIT Press, 1986).

The history of the development of higher mental functions. In R. W. Rieber (ed.) *The Collected Works of L. S. Vygotsky: The History of the Development of Higher Mental Functions, Vol. 4* (New York and London: Plenum Press, 1997) 1–251.

Wagner, P. *A Sociology of Modernity: Liberty and Discipline* (London: Routledge, 1994).

Walsh, P. G. Introduction. In M. T. Cicero, *On Obligations* (Stanford, CA: Stanford University Press, 2000) ix–xlvii.

Watson, A. *The Evolution of Western Private Law* (Baltimore: Johns Hopkins University Press, 2001).

Watson, J. B. *The Ways of Behaviorism* (New York: Harper and Brothers, 1928).

Weintraub, K. J. *The Value of the Individual: Self and Circumstance in Autobiography* (University of Chicago Press, 1978).

Werner, H. and Kaplan, B. The developmental approach to cognition: Its relevance to the psychological interpretation of anthropological and ethnolinguistic data. *American Anthropologist* 58 (1956) 866–880.

Williams, G. C. *Evolution through Group Selection* (Oxford: Blackwell, 1986).
Williams, R. N., and Beyers, M. S. Personalism, social constructionism and the foundation of the ethical. *Theory and Psychology* 11 (2001) 119–134.
Wilson, D. S. and Sober, E. Reintroducing group selection to the human behavioral sciences. *Behavioral and Brain Sciences* 17 (1994) 585–654.
Wittgenstein, L. *Philosophical Investigations*, G. E. M. Anscombe (trans.) (Oxford: Blackwell, 1953).
   On Certainty, G. E. M. Anscombe and G. H. Von Wright (eds.) D. Paul and G. E. M. Anscombe (trans.) (New York: Harper and Row, 1972).
   Remarks on the Philosophy of Psychology, Vol. 2, C. G. Luckhardt and M. A. E. Aue (trans.) (Oxford: Blackwell, 1980).
Wolin, R. (ed.) *The Heidegger Controversy: A Critical Reader* (Cambridge, MA: The MIT Press, 1993).
Wright, J. *The Moral Animal* (New York: Basic Books, 1994).
Wundt, W. *Die Psychologie im Kampf ums Dasein*, zweite Auflage [*Psychology's Struggle for Existence*, second edn] (Leipzig: Kröner, 1913).
Wylie, R.C. *The Self Concept* (Lincoln: University of Nebraska, 1974).

Index

abilities, 2, 19, 28, 29, 30–3, 36, 37, 115, 149, 150, 156, 163, 174, 175, 176
actions under descriptions, 84
activism, 98, 184, 186, 187, 188, 194
activist deeds, 193, 198
Adler, A., 9
agency, 2, 12, 25, 33, 44–6, 48, 49, 96, 97, 98, 150, 158, 163, 165, 166, 168, 171, 182–4, 185, 188, 189, 193, 198, 207, 216, 218, 220, 241
agents, 10, 11, 14, 15, 36, 41, 46, 47, 48, 55, 56, 96, 97, 100, 133, 134, 135, 136, 137, 140, 141, 143, 144, 153, 165–71, 174, 177, 179, 184, 185, 187, 195, 198, 213
Allport, G., 9, 60, 78, 79, 110, 120, 222
analytical philosophy, 20, 24, 26
animal, 2, 28, 29, 30, 38, 62, 137, 153, 190
apperceive, 167–9, 175
apperception, 167, 168, 225
Appiah, K. A., 164
Aristotle, 30, 44–6, 48, 54, 55, 178, 212
asymmetry principle, 27, 31
attunement, 47
authentic, 40, 41, 48–50, 52, 53, 56, 98, 228
authentic historicity, 52–4
authenticity, 41, 50, 89, 235

Bakhtin, M. M., 147, 195, 222
Baldwin, J. M., 3, 9
Barresi, J., 13, 14, 127
behaviors, 1, 5, 8, 22, 29, 37, 86, 107
Being and Time, 40, 46, 48, 52, 54, 56
Being-in-the-world, 47, 48
Being-towards-death, 51
Bickhard, M., 1, 14
biophysical, 1, 2, 8, 16, 97, 148, 153, 163
bracketing, 42

branching indications, 167
Bruner, J., 206, 211–14, 216

Calkins, M., 3
care, 46, 49, 233
Cartesian-empiricist tradition, 25
causal chain, 166
causal explanation, 111
character, 2, 6, 46, 53, 60, 65, 99, 178, 215, 230
chimpanzee, 139–41
co-constitute, 169, 170, 179
cognitive psychology, 6, 7
collaborative transformative practice, 185, 190–2, 195, 196, 197
commitment, 9, 54, 184, 187, 196, 197, 210
communication, 154, 155, 217, 232
community, 1, 11, 46, 48, 52, 68, 98, 107, 153, 213
competitive, 69, 139, 141, 144
comportment, 45
computation, 7
computational models, 7
computations, 165
conditionalized indications, 167
conduct, 2, 64, 65, 67, 89, 91, 99, 100, 182, 183
consciousness, 5, 30, 47, 69, 70, 74, 87, 107, 108, 114, 137, 154, 161, 225, 234
constructs, 23, 207, 213
consumerism, 93
contribution, 15, 194, 196, 198, 199, 213, 215
convention, 169, 170, 171, 174, 176
cooperative, 131, 139–44, 153, 155, 157
coordinated interactivity, 153–6, 158
coordinated perspective taking, 149
coordination, 149, 150, 153, 155, 156, 157, 159, 160, 161, 163

CPSIA information can be obtained at www.ICGtesting.com
Printed in the USA
LVOW10s0350091214

417851LV00013B/241/P